# CRAZY LIKE A FOX

# CRAZY
## LIKE A
# FOX

## One Principal's
## Triumph in
## the Inner City

Dr. Ben Chavis with Carey Blakely

NEW AMERICAN LIBRARY

New American Library
Published by New American Library, a division of
Penguin Group (USA) Inc., 375 Hudson Street,
New York, New York 10014, USA
Penguin Group (Canada), 90 Eglinton Avenue East, Suite 700, Toronto,
Ontario M4P 2Y3, Canada (a division of Pearson Penguin Canada Inc.)
Penguin Books Ltd., 80 Strand, London WC2R 0RL, England
Penguin Ireland, 25 St. Stephen's Green, Dublin 2,
Ireland (a division of Penguin Books Ltd.)
Penguin Group (Australia), 250 Camberwell Road, Camberwell, Victoria 3124,
Australia (a division of Pearson Australia Group Pty. Ltd.)
Penguin Books India Pvt. Ltd., 11 Community Centre, Panchsheel Park,
New Delhi - 110 017, India
Penguin Group (NZ), 67 Apollo Drive, Rosedale, North Shore 0632,
New Zealand (a division of Pearson New Zealand Ltd.)
Penguin Books (South Africa) (Pty.) Ltd., 24 Sturdee Avenue,
Rosebank, Johannesburg 2196, South Africa

Penguin Books Ltd., Registered Offices:
80 Strand, London WC2R 0RL, England

First published by New American Library,
a division of Penguin Group (USA) Inc.

First Printing, September 2009
10   9   8   7   6   5   4   3   2   1

 REGISTERED TRADEMARK—MARCA REGISTRADA

LIBRARY OF CONGRESS CATALOGING-IN-PUBLICATION DATA:

Chavis, Ben.
Crazy like a fox: one principal's triumph in the inner city/Dr. Ben Chavis with Carey Blakely.
p.   cm.
ISBN 978-0-451-22818-5
1. Chavis, Ben.   2. School principals—United States.   3. Education, Urban—United States.
4. Educational change—United States.   5. School improvement programs—United States.
6. School management and organizations—United States.   I. Blakely, Carey.   II. Title.
LA2317.C4814A3  2009
373.12'01092—dc22          2009015574
[B]

Set in Sabon
Designed by Patrice Sheridan

Printed in the United States of America

PUBLISHER'S NOTE
This publication is designed to provide accurate and authoritative information in regard to the subject matter covered. It is sold with the understanding that the publisher is not engaged in rendering legal, accounting or other professional services. If you require legal advice or other expert assistance, you should seek the services of a competent professional.

Further, publisher does not have any control over and does not assume any responsibility for author or third-party Web sites or their content.

This book is dedicated to my family and friends. To educators committed to preparing students with the skills to participate in free market capitalism! A special dedication to President George W. Bush, Senator Ted Kennedy, and bipartisan politicians who supported the No Child Left Behind Act of 2002—the greatest public school legislation ever passed for our children. And finally, I dedicate this book to the memory of Sgt. Mark Dunakin, Officer John Hege, Sgt. Ervin Romans, and Sgt. Daniel Sakai, members of the Oakland police force who tragically gave their lives on March 21, 2009, while protecting our community.

—*Ben Chavis*

I dedicate this book to Mom, Dad, Matt, Nana, Grandpa, Grandma Mary, and Pop Pop (Thomas Hugh Blakely, Sr., 1912–2003); to the AIPCS/ AIPHS family past, present, and future; to my friends; to Joe; and to those educators who work hard to enrich the lives of their students.

—*Carey Blakely*

# Acknowledgments

Ben Chavis and Carey Blakely would like to acknowledge several people who were instrumental in getting this book published: Anne Bohner, former editor at NAL/Penguin, who believed in this project and stepped forward to push for, sign, and set it on its way; Mark Chait, senior editor at NAL/Penguin, who picked up where Anne left off, effectively guiding us through the second half of the process with enthusiasm and an eye toward the big picture; Ellis B. Levine, attorney for Cowan DeBaets Abrahams & Sheppard LLP, who performed the legal read of the manuscript with much appreciated humor and advice; Zach Cordner, photographer, and his team who captured and created a bold cover image; Bill Harris, the copy editor, for his thorough and consistent work; Kara Welsh, the publisher, for signing this book and backing it; thank you, Kara!; and all the other staff members at NAL/Penguin who made their contributions to this book through design, layout, editing, and marketing.

Thanks as well to Rae Belisle and Bill Lucia, President and Policy Director, respectively, of EdVoice, for advocating for quality public schools; Debra Calington and John Stossel of ABC for profiling our school on *20/20* to an international audience; and the Lake Merritt Breakfast Club members for support of AIPCS and Oakland.

Carey Blakely additionally would like to acknowledge:

My family for standing by me with love and support every step of the writing/editing/publishing way; Nana (Hazel Jones), you often seemed like my biggest fan during the process, and I appreciate all the conversations we had about the book; my friends for the fun times, laughter, and encouragement—some days you made all the difference!; Barbara Swovelin, an excellent high school English teacher, for inspiring me to think and write at an early age; Margaret Dodson for the much needed insight and the priceless lesson of being true to oneself; Joe Raffetto for being such a sweetheart and buoying up my spirits with your positive attitude and adventurous approach to life; the interviewees for sharing your voices and perspectives; former AIPCS and AIPHS staff members for your dedication and assistance; the students at AIPCS and AIPHS whom I had the pleasure and benefit to work with and for.

# Note to the Reader

While teaching at American Indian Public Charter School (AIPCS), I sought and received Dr. Ben Chavis's permission to write a book about the school and his life.

After trying different styles and approaches to the material, I decided to write the book in the first-person from Dr. Chavis's point of view, because I wanted to capture the direct, intimate feel of a memoir in his voice. We collaborated to get the manuscript in its current form.

I consider Dr. Chavis a great friend and mentor. I worked for him for four years as a teacher and administrator and was moved by the story that is his life. I feel fortunate to have received the opportunity to write the world through his eyes; it was a unique, illuminating, often humorous, and sometimes startling perspective.

As he is one to bluntly state his opinions, this book provides a frank, subjective account of his experiences as principal of AIPCS. *Crazy Like a Fox* is by no means neutral, and some identities in the text have been changed to protect privacy.

—Carey Blakely

# Contents

|  | *Introduction* | 1 |
| Chapter 1: | The Zoo | 7 |
| Chapter 2: | The Oakland Raider | 16 |
| Chapter 3: | A Second Chance | 28 |
| Chapter 4: | A New Beginning | 35 |
| Chapter 5: | Creating a Family with the Self-Contained Classroom | 47 |
| Chapter 6: | Looping and the Extended Family | 57 |
| Chapter 7: | Family Involvement | 63 |
| Chapter 8: | Meet the Escobars | 72 |
| Chapter 9: | High Expectations and an Academic Focus | 84 |
| Chapter 10: | The Quest for Improvement | 96 |
| Chapter 11: | The Emperor Who Wore No Clothes and the Boy Who Called Him Out | 101 |
| Chapter 12: | You Are Judged by Your Race Whether You Like It or Not | 116 |
| Chapter 13: | Poor? If You Say So | 124 |
| Chapter 14: | Sacrifice | 132 |
| Chapter 15: | Free Market Capitalism in the Classroom | 139 |
| Chapter 16: | Schools Have Enough Money | 147 |
| Chapter 17: | Sign on the Dotted Line | 157 |

Chapter 18:   Guided by a Firm Hand                        167
Chapter 19:   Nate                                        173
Chapter 20:   Taming Wild Horses                          181
Chapter 21:   A Method to the Madness                     190
Chapter 22:   Ben Fumbles His Way Through
              Elementary School                           198
Chapter 23:   Out from Under the Hype of Violence         205
Chapter 24:   Up from the Bottoms: Bootlegging and
              Preaching: How I Learned the Gift of Gab
              and a Love of Free Market Capitalism        215
Chapter 25:   Cleanliness: A Chore and a Mentality        228
Chapter 26:   Mental Work or Physical Labor:
              You Make the Choice                         236
Chapter 27:   Big Bad Bossman                             246
Chapter 28:   Sophath: One Among Us                       257
Conclusion:   Creating Educational Excellence
              Through Replication                         264
              *Appendix*                                  277

# CRAZY LIKE A FOX

# Introduction

I look around here at the students in their khaki pants and white collared shirts standing proudly and smiling before me in a clean, newly painted gymnasium in Oakland, California, patiently waiting to receive their hard-earned perfect attendance money. Some of the eighth-graders have not missed a single day of school since they enrolled in American Indian Public Charter School in sixth grade. Soon they'll be walking down the aisle with 150 one-dollar bills in hand. Many of the graduating eighth-graders will board a flight to Washington, D.C., on an all-expenses-paid trip as a reward for their dedication and hard work. I hope that as that plane takes off they will look in each other's faces and find greatness and all they have striven toward and accomplished.

The students before me are poor American Indians, Asians, blacks, Hispanics, and whites. They have outperformed students their own age in Oakland, in California, and in the United States. They are an elite class in a high-achieving school that in 2000 was on the brink of closure because of lousy attendance rates, lousy test scores, and incompetent leadership. In 2008, American Indian Public Charter School had the highest test scores of any public school in Oakland; it was the fifth-highest-ranking middle school in California out of approximately 1,300 middle schools in the state; it was a past recipient of the National Blue Ribbon Award, an honor bestowed upon the top 250 public or private schools in the nation by the United States Department of Education.

By contrast, in 2000, American Indian Public Charter School was the worst middle school in Oakland. It had an attendance rate of about 65 percent and a student body who could not read, write, do math or any other academic tasks at grade level. In this very gymnasium that was once carpeted and covered in mud and trash, students would sneak onto the stage and behind the stairwell to have sex or smoke pot. The school was a failed social experiment in multiculturalism and touchy-feely educational practices. The kids ran wild because there was no structure, no expectations, and no academic framework set in place.

When I stepped onto the scene in 2000, a hardheaded American Indian raised by sharecroppers in rural North Carolina, I was embarrassed to see such a failing institution represented in name by American Indians. When the board offered me the job as principal in the hope that I could prevent American Indian Public Charter School from being shut down, I told them I'd only take it if they let me go my own way and do what I thought was best. They agreed, and soon I had the opportunity of a lifetime to take a school from the scrap heap and weld it back together using the educational methods I believed in.

This book recounts the story of how all that went down in this city we call Oakland.

Katy Murphy of the *Oakland Tribune* wrote an article in 2007 about me and the school titled "Madman, Genius or Both? Charter School Principal's 'Tough Love' Controversial." Some critics say my use of public shaming and politically incorrect terms such as "darkies" cross the line of acceptable educational practice. I prepare students for the realities of social stereotyping by getting them to see the pride and humor in being darkies, whities, half-breeds, or mixed breeds.

I hardly think of myself as a madman or a genius, and I don't think it's "tough love," just common sense. But, as I share some stories about my life and American Indian Public Charter School, you can decide for yourself.

I will tell you up front my four main education beliefs.

1.  I do not believe we are all equal. We all have "equal opportunity" to get a public education in the United States, and it takes hard work and discipline. Many left-wing educators see minorities as victims and promote social justice and cultural diversity as the method to educate them. Minority and poor students need academic justice in order to excel in school and

life, which requires educators to focus on a rigorous English, mathematics, science, and social-science curriculum.

2. I believe it is easier for a school to succeed with economically disadvantaged students than with the middle class or rich. These poor students come from families without good educations and are easier to motivate. As a principal, how would I motivate Bill Gates's children, who have everything? What would they gain from me?

3. Public schools have enough money. Taxpayers have been conned for years—by public school administrators, teachers unions, and school boards who beg for more money—into thinking the problem with schools is that they need more funding. This is the biggest lie in public education in this country. Did you know that more money is given to public schools that are failing and destroying kids than to schools that are educating students? The financial incentive in America is to be a failing school.

4. I implemented a golden rule at American Indian Public Charter School for staff, students, and families that reflects my belief: If you act like a winner, you'll be treated like a winner. If you act like a fool, you'll be treated like a fool. Many adults involved in schools who act like fools need to be thrown off the boat because they are causing it to sink.

Before sharing my story, let's go over some terms that will be repeated throughout the book.

**Charter School:** American Indian Public Charter School (AIPCS) is a charter school. A charter school is a public school that is tax-supported but operates independently of its local school district. It has a written agreement (called a charter) with the district, county, or the state that authorized and approved it. If a charter school does not live up to its goals and agreements as specified in the written agreement, its charter can be revoked or not renewed. All charter schools must take part in statewide standardized testing. In general, charter schools receive less money per pupil than regular public schools.

The charter school movement is a reaction to the poorly performing and inefficient public school system, particularly at the middle and high school level. Charter schools cut through some of the red tape that bogs down traditional public schools. They also compete with traditional public schools and private schools, which, in theory, should benefit students. This is not always the case in practice. Since inner-city public schools are particularly troubled, the charter movement has really taken hold in many urban areas like Oakland. Opponents to charter schools say charters are destroying the public schools by taking students and, therefore, funding away from public schools. If public schools fail to serve the needs of their students, shouldn't families have the right to seek better educational opportunities for their children? There are about three thousand five hundred charter schools in the United States, which is less than 4 percent of the total number of public schools in the country.

**Secondary Schools:** Secondary schools are middle schools, junior high schools, and high schools. In general, elementary schools are doing a great job in this country and are competitive at the international level. Once students enroll in secondary schools, however, their academic performance plummets.

**The American Indian Model of Education:** At American Indian Public Charter School, we use an educational framework that I've named the American Indian Model of Education, also referred to in the book as AIM to Educate or AIM-Ed. The model has four main components: (1) family culture, (2) accountability/structure, (3) high expectations, and (4) free market capitalism. As with any system, AIM to Educate has changed over time, but its general purpose and essence at American Indian Public Charter School have remained intact since I became principal in July of 2000.

The model consists of self-contained classrooms (no class rotation except for P.E.); looping (teachers spend three years with their students from sixth through eighth grade); a standards-based textbook curriculum focused on rigorous academics, with particular emphasis and time placed on language arts and math; an extended year calendar; financial rewards to promote perfect attendance and a free market capitalistic mind-set in our students and staff; and a culture of hard work and "no nonsense," as I like to call it.

**Sister Schools:** Our sister schools are the charter schools in Oakland using the American Indian Model of Education. By the time this book was being written, we had launched two new schools in Oakland with the intention of opening more in the future. The two schools are American Indian Public High School (AIPHS) and American Indian Public Charter School II (AIPCS II), a middle school. My colleague Jorge Lopez implemented AIM-Ed at Oakland Charter Academy (OCA), an existing middle school, and at a new charter high school called Oakland Charter High School (OCHS).

Our small middle school serves about two hundred American Indians, Asians, blacks, Hispanics, and whites in East Oakland, the vast majority of whom are poor. In the inner city, where homicide and home-less rates are high while expectations for academic achievement are low, American Indian Public Charter School is a diamond in the rough indeed and an academic triumph.

# chapter one

# The Zoo

"The road to hell is paved with good intentions."

—*An idiom possibly originating from St. Bernard of Clairvaux,*
*a French monk (1090–1153)*

Before I became its principal, people called American Indian Public Charter School the zoo. The neighbors hated it. They saw the school as a noisy, trashy nuisance—a blight on the community. They couldn't stand the behavior of the students, who, with little supervision or control, wreaked havoc in the area. It was like a zoo with no zookeeper.

The students smoked cigarettes, fought, drank, and broke beer and liquor bottles on Magee Avenue, the road lining the school. There were old, dingy mattresses nearby where they had sex. A staff member allegedly sold drugs to the students, some of whom snuck into a toolshed on campus to smoke pot. Students threw water balloons off the roof and computers out the class windows.

People say the road to hell is paved with good intentions. American Indian Public Charter School was a clear case of that.

The school was founded in 1996 with the goal of promoting American Indian culture while improving the academic performance of American Indians in Oakland, who, as a whole, were doing terribly in school. Of all the ethnic groups, American Indians had the highest dropout rate, the lowest attendance rate, and the lowest graduation rate in the Oakland Unified School District (OUSD). In other words, they were the worst players on an already bad team in Oakland. The American Indian Public Charter School was open to non-Indians, but the majority of the forty to fifty students who enrolled in the school in its first four years of operation were Indian.

Many people are surprised to know that Oakland has a significant American Indian population. Indians moved from reservations to cities like Oakland, Chicago, and Salt Lake City when the Bureau of Indian Affairs ran a relocation program from 1948 to 1979. The relocation program was a way for younger folks, typically between eighteen and thirty-five years of age, to acquire jobs skills, employment, and a new start in places like Oakland. As with most things concerning Indians, the program was controversial. Some thought it gave Indians an opportunity to get out of poverty, receive an education, and have solid employment. Others thought it forced Indians off reservations without improving the quality of their jobs or living conditions. To me the program was about choice.

American Indian Public Charter School was supposed to provide choice for Indians and others seeking an alternative to the larger public middle schools in Oakland. Unfortunately, the students who decided to attend the school did not receive the academics and structure they so direly needed. The American Indian Public Charter School was in many ways a failure, a joke, a sham.

The school was doomed before it even started. When I heard the potential founders of American Indian Public Charter School decided to focus on bead making, drumming, and self-esteem classes, I wanted nothing to do with it. Because I was involved in the California school choice movement, I was informed about the school's plans. It wasn't a personal fit. I have no tolerance for fools who play around attempting to be ethnic when they're supposed to educate students. As a Lumbee Indian raised in a sharecropper's shack during my early childhood in rural North Carolina, the philosophy behind the planning and implementation of American Indian Public Charter School was shameful to me and an embarrassment to the name and image of American Indians.

When it opened, classes at American Indian Public Charter School started later than the other district public schools because it was believed American Indians couldn't get up early in the morning. Do you see how racist we can be against our own people? They called it "Indian time." At 9:00 a.m. each day, instead of starting the school day with an academic course, students and staff gathered in a large circle to discuss their feelings and concerns. The adults would talk about their personal problems in front of the youth.

During my upbringing in Robeson County, North Carolina, Lumbee adults and children did not sit around together in a circle at school discussing feelings. I have also lived with Apaches, Navajos, Yaqui, and Pima Indians, and I assure you none of them sat in circles airing their personal problems to children at home. Most of the staff at American Indian Public Charter School had no clue about American Indian or any other culture.

What was going on at American Indian Public Charter School was a bunch of urban, wannabe Indian nonsense. The staff were pseudo-Indians, and they were screwing up kids. They had this fantasy of "We're gonna sit around and we're gonna play the drum and we're gonna pass the sage." To me, there wasn't one real Indian staff member in that place. They were born in the city, had major identity problems, and didn't know much about Indians. I grew up in a small Indian community, so I don't need to go around wearing my identity on my shirt. I don't need no feathers. I don't need no beads hanging in my car. I have Indian relatives, and that is enough for me and my family when it comes to knowing who we are.

One of the principals (there were several) who worked at American Indian Public Charter School, Chief Bad Example, often worked as an emcee at powwows. Chief Bad Example would run off to the powwows and miss school. What kind of model is set for students when the principal skips work to play Indian?

The so-called American Indian image of the school was based on lies and fantasy: fake Indian names and fantasy Indian culture in the form of therapy circles. Martin Waukazoo, then the executive director of the Native American Health Center in Oakland, helped establish the school, but he got cold feet and withdrew from the planning when he disagreed with the direction it was headed in. Waukazoo was quoted in Emily Wilson's *East Bay Express* article "Beating a New Kind of Drum" as saying: "They were doing too many fuzzy, warm things like bead-making classes and drum classes. Those are good hobbies, but our kids need to learn to read and write. I felt it was doing more harm than good."

The misunderstanding and parading of Indian culture at American Indian Public Charter School was minor compared to the lack of learning and discipline going on at the school. Truancy was a serious problem. Students would either not come to school at all or they would leave during the school day. There was no mechanism in place to control student movement into and out of the building. Students could enter and exit from both the front and the back stairwell. Because the offices were located by the front entrance, it was easy for students to slip out the back. Some would leave and go drink 40s (cheap bottles of malt liquor) in front of an apartment building across the street or in the toolshed. They'd go back to class drunk. Some students would sneak off to have sex in one of the many divey places at hand: under the stairwell, in the abandoned house next door, on the stage in the gym, in the bathrooms, or under the 580 freeway bridge.

You're probably wondering how I became involved with American Indian Public Charter School after initially wanting nothing to do with it. After spending many years working in elementary, secondary, and college education, I decided to leave my positions as an administrative specialist in public education and an adjunct faculty member in the Department of Education at the University of Arizona in December 1999. A few months later, in March 2000, my friend Evelyn Lamenti, a Navajo woman and the director of the Office of Indian Education for Oakland Unified School District, called me. Ms. Lamenti said American Indian Public Charter School was in trouble, and she believed I of all people could turn it around. Though flattered, I wasn't really interested in working there. Based on what I already knew, I figured the school's board would never let me operate in the manner needed to be successful.

Ms. Lamenti asked me to visit American Indian Public Charter School. I sent a resume thinking an interview would offer me the opportunity to see what was going on at the school, which at that point had been in operation for four years.

From the school's founding in 1996 to the time I was contacted in 2000, the school plunged into a downward spiral because of all the problems mentioned above. After sending in the resume, I received no response from anyone involved with American Indian Public Charter School for two months. Then, in late May 2000, Nicole Edgar, a school board member, called for an interview regarding the position of principal. The current principal was serving a short interim term to provide oversight while the board sought a longer-term replacement. She asked me to book a flight and said she'd reimburse my expenses.

What the board didn't tell me was that the school's academic and financial standing had hit such a low point that the Oakland Unified

School District was threatening to shut it down. I learned later after arriving in Oakland that district officials had scheduled a meeting to discuss revoking the school's charter. They thought American Indian Public Charter School was a school beyond hope of saving.

During the trip to Oakland in June, I wanted to see the school for myself without anyone putting a pretty spin on it. I made an unofficial and unaccompanied visit to American Indian Public Charter School before my interview with the school's board.

I parked my car on Magee Avenue and took a look around. On the sidewalk in front of the school were cigarette butts, broken glass from beer bottles, and trash of all sorts: gum, food wrappers, and soda cans. An old mattress propped up in the weeds sat in front of the school. A Dumpster overflowed with trash and food scraps, and maggots and flies crawled all over it. I found out later that the students were receiving free meals at the school through the Free and Reduced-Price Lunch Program, but they didn't like the food, so their waste piled up, and the June heat brought maggots and flies. Discarded desks and trash lined the walkway to the school.

To the right was an abandoned old house that looked like it should be condemned. It was the type of place you picture crackheads, bums, and prostitutes crawling into for a quick fix. Apparently that was indeed the case, as it was said to be a love nest for the students and others. A poorly constructed wooden fence, which clearly would never hold back any rainwater or prevent a mudslide, sagged into the walkway between the school and the abandoned old house. Looking down into the gym from the walkway, I could see a carpeted floor cluttered with trash.

I walked up a set of stairs into the school. I assumed there would be a sign for the office. This is the case at most schools, but I didn't see an office, a principal, or a secretary. Confused and nosy, I kept walking straight ahead and then turned left down the hallway, where wannabe gangsters in baggy pants hung out, some talking, some play fighting, some bumping and grinding against each other with music blaring in the background.

A young, heavyset guy in a Hawaiian shirt, pale green shorts, and flip-flops walked in my direction. I couldn't tell if he was a student or a teacher, so I asked him. He said he was James Lookout, a teacher at the school. I said, "What's going on today?" The kids seemed so wild and it was the beginning of June, so maybe there was some kind of celebration. Mr. Lookout said, "School. This is a school day." I asked him where the principal was, and he said he didn't know. Mr. Lookout didn't instruct me to sign in anywhere or check in at the office. In fact, no one asked me anything the whole time I was on campus. That's a major safety concern. Would you want your child in a school where any random person off the street could wander in at will? Staff should say to anyone who walks into the school, "May I help you?" and have that person sign in. If President Theodore Roosevelt and his Rough Riders came through that door, I'd make sure they checked in at the office.

Since no one asked any questions, I just walked into the classrooms observing. One has to poke about and be uninhibited to be a good, hands-on researcher among chaos. Like Mr. Lookout in his flip-flops, the teachers were dressed casually, to say the least. There were more kids in the hallway than in any one classroom, and neither location maintained any sense of control. Broken windows, holes in the walls, computers stacked in corners—the place was an eyesore. I could see why they called this school the zoo.

I talked to some students who were lounging out in the hall to see what they had to say. When I asked if they were planning on coming back next year, every student I spoke with said "no" or "hell, no." They said the place was a joke. I asked a student named Leroy, who came across as a tough guy, where the principal was. He said, "We don't have no principal. I run this place." The students' attitude of wannabe gangsters did not surprise me. They were wannabe gangsters, while many staff members were wannabe Indians. I walked around the grounds of the campus and saw a toolshed surrounded by trees that hid pot-smoking students from view. The toolshed was in a dirt playground area that stretched out to Thirty-fifth Avenue. Like the rest of the school's grounds, it was covered in trash and weeds and unsupervised, with gang graffiti painted on the fence and the walls. This was a place where students could get away with anything they wanted.

My overall impression from the visit to American Indian Public Charter School was, "What a fucking mess." It was a nasty, filthy, chaotic school of low expectations, high truancy, and poor academic achievement. Most people would have been turned off. They would have walked out of the school and thought, "Good luck. Find someone else for this job."

But I thought it was the ideal job situation! I'm the guy who cleans up. It was an opportunity to take a school from scratch, a toss-away, and put my own ideas and practices into it. That way, I could have total responsibility for the structure and educational philosophy of the school. If I could take American Indian Public Charter School after it had hit rock bottom and make it a success, this would demonstrate that my educational methods with poor minority students worked.

After taking a self-guided tour, I found the interim principal, an elderly Navajo Indian man named Mr. Thomas Yazzie, in his office. Mr. Yazzie was soft-spoken and had been raised on the Navajo reservation. He had worked in Sanders, Arizona, and we knew some of the same people. He said Oakland Unified had sent a letter asking American Indian Public Charter School to address a number of issues and to come before a district subcommittee board to discuss the school's plans for rectifying those issues. He was confused and didn't know where to begin, because much of what was requested by the district had to do with paperwork and issues dating back to well before Mr. Yazzie was appointed interim principal. He handed me the district's letter, which was dated sometime in April. While reading it over, I saw the meeting was to be held that very same day! I thought, "These guys are going to lose this school. The meeting is today, they're unprepared, and they haven't addressed any of these issues." It was exciting, too, because I love a good drama and wanted to see what would happen. I said to Mr. Yazzie, "Well, sir, you've got your work cut out for you." He agreed and smiled warily.

When I met with the AIPCS board later that afternoon, they mentioned the school hearing. I acknowledged being aware of it and said I would like to attend. Intrigued by what I might see or experience, I arrived at the meeting and observed what went down with the first charter school on the cutting block. The half-Mexican, half-Jewish principal representing that school, Mr. Jose Rosenbaum, conveyed to me through his actions that he had learned nothing about how to effectively run a school or how to accept blame for its shortcomings. He made matters worse by going on the defensive, refusing to admit any of the school's faults, and accusing the district of being out to get him. Apparently Mr. Jose Rosenbaum had worked for Oakland Unified previously and felt it was a witch hunt. Regardless, his hearing went terribly and I could tell the district curriculum committee had had it up to their eyeballs with him. They voted unanimously to close the Hispanic charter school down. The Hispanic families headed south down the hallway with heads bent down and a rejected look, as though they were being deported to Mexico. Most of the kids were smiling because the principal had said there would be no more school.

I realized American Indian Public Charter School needed at least one person on that district curriculum committee to support us. We needed a different strategy from Mr. Rosenbaum's. The key was to get this subcommittee to give the school a chance and some time to address the district's complaints. Otherwise, the decision to close AIPCS would move on to the final authority of the Oakland Unified School District Board, and it would be the end of American Indian Public Charter School.

I told the AIPCS board members that they couldn't blame the district like Mr. Rosenbaum had done. We needed to admit AIPCS's faults and disarm the district curriculum committee. How can you make a mess of a school and then blame the school board? You need to acknowledge your mistakes and have a plan to prevent them in the future.

No sooner did I explain what the strategy should be than Mike Little Feather, a young AIPCS board member and a college student in his early twenties, started to argue combatively with the curriculum committee members. I asked him to take a deep breath, quiet down, and talk less. We informed the district curriculum committee that mistakes had been made at American Indian Public Charter School, but we had a plan to prevent such problems in the future. We were going to hire a new principal, employ new staff, clean up the school, and provide a sound, structured, academic education for students. I said the earlier school board had failed, but there was a new board and we wanted another chance. We would work hard to turn the school around.

When we finished, Mr. Dan Siegel, a member of the district curriculum committee, said American Indians had been oppressed for five hundred years and he refused to continue the oppression. This was the chance we needed. With Mr. Siegel's dissenting voice rising to the forefront of the discussion, you could tell the tide was shifting for us. The district curriculum committee agreed to give American Indian Public Charter School sixty days to make some improvements before coming before them again. I learned afterward that Mr. Dan Siegel had been president of the student body at UC Berkeley in 1969. It fascinated me that thirty years later he was still fighting for the same types of causes he had in his younger years, because I find that most people aren't as consistent in their beliefs over time.

The superintendent, Mr. Dennis Chaconas, did not agree with the district curriculum committee's decision. Three years later he was in the same position; however, this time it was the state taking over Oakland Unified School District with a $100 million bailout loan. Mr. Chaconas didn't fare as well with the California State Department of Education as we did with the curriculum committee.

We had bought some precious time before the next district meeting. The school was alive for now.

# chapter two

# The Oakland Raider

---

"Every new beginning comes from some other beginning's end."

—*Seneca,*
*Roman rhetorician and writer (c. 60 BC–c. AD 37)*

---

There was no doubt we could remake American Indian Public Charter School into a great school by changing its image and implementing a new structured educational model. The zoo wasn't going to become Harvard overnight, but when the right mechanisms were put in place and constant improvements sought, I believed wholeheartedly AIPCS would transform into a model school.

After the district curriculum committee meeting, I waited several weeks to hear back from the AIPCS board. It was around the end of June 2000 when Nicole Edgar called and offered me the job as principal.

Though excited, I had to first make sure my intentions and methods were clear. I wouldn't take the position unless the AIPCS board let me go in my own direction. It was time to stop beating drums, to stop playing Indian. I wanted to get rid of "Indian time" and all the other nonsense and teach our children language arts and mathematics. The board didn't necessarily share my opinions, but they did agree the school needed a new path.

Raiding was the part of Indian culture I embraced at American Indian Public Charter School. What did the Lumbee Indian people do in the past? Raid. We'd go on raiding parties, steal goods from other tribes and white people, bring back the goods in order to take care of our families, and take over other lands and people. It was a way of life to ensure our survival as a Lumbee Indian people. Becoming principal of American Indian Public Charter School was like a corporate raid, a hostile takeover. We had to fight to keep the school open. AIPCS needed a fresh start and a new culture, so I planned to hire a team who could take us in a better direction and work toward a vision of academic success and structured learning.

The fight to keep the school open was not over. Oakland Unified School District hadn't made a final decision, but I needed to proceed on the assumption that American Indian Public Charter School would continue to operate. There was no time to sit around and hope and wait. It was June. If school was to resume in September, there was a whole lot of hiring/firing, cleaning up, goal setting, and image remaking to do. Furthermore, Oakland Unified would partly base their decision on progress they could see at the school. If they didn't see a change for the better when we met with the curriculum committee again in August, they would surely close AIPCS down.

As a raider, and not like the losing Oakland Raiders of 2008–2009, I quickly and unflinchingly assumed control. Over the course of a couple of months, I fired the entire staff except for a smart, white female named Jill Rogers, who had graduated from Cornell and ran an academic program after school called MESA that focused on math, engineering, and science. To ensure the Indian playtime and masquerade would stop, I had to get rid of the staff who were more interested in culture than academics and replace them with smart, dependable teachers capable of providing a structured environment. It didn't matter to me what race or social class the teachers were as long as they could teach academics. I sought people who had intelligence and drive.

All the board members wanted me to hire American Indian teachers for that upcoming school year. To be honest, I have never believed you need Indians to teach Indian students. You need smart people to teach Indian students. If you want to do a child a favor, hire a great teacher to educate him. The whole political agenda in education of "We need more Indians, we need more black teachers" is racist, ridiculous, and often provides inept educators with a way of getting on the payroll. Just because someone's Indian doesn't mean he's a better role model for an Indian child than someone who's not Indian. Smart, reliable, and hardworking people who care about all children being educated are good role models regardless of their race, and that's whom I intended to hire.

First I employed Carmelita. She was part black and part Mexican and smart. Carmelita had a roommate named Shelley Jones, a black woman, who had a strong background in science, mathematics, and common sense. Both had just graduated from UC Berkeley and needed jobs. Then I hired Mina Assefa as an administrative assistant to complete our full-time staffing needs. Mina was a recent graduate of Mills College whose father was Ethiopian and whose mother was Iowa Indian. Carmelita, Shelley, and Mina were three intelligent women who had no idea what they were about to get into at AIPCS.

Previously, a middle school and high school had coexisted within American Indian Public Charter School, which required many teachers and resulted in an ineffective class rotation system that put seventh-graders in the same classrooms with eleventh-graders. AIPCS had added a new grade level each year, so the student body ranged from sixth to eleventh grade. One concession I made to the district curriculum committee who granted us sixty days to make improvements was to get rid of the high school—the high school students were absorbed by other schools in Oakland Unified—and focus on building a better middle school.

It wasn't really a concession, though, because it's what I wanted. The best way to make a difference in children's educations is to reach them when they're young. By the time a student is in ninth grade and he's had a lousy education his whole life, it's almost impossible to bring him up to grade level with his peers. Sure, you can make some improvements, but you're not going to graduate him at a twelfth-grade academic level when he starts ninth grade with the skills and knowledge of a fourth-grader. The best way to create a school culture is to start from scratch and to build grade by grade at either an elementary or middle school. Since I couldn't do that in this case, I could at least cut out the high school part of American Indian Public Charter School in order to focus exclusively on the younger students and build a new middle school culture with them.

Once that strong academic culture was established at the middle school, we opened a high school, American Indian Public High School (AIPHS), six years later, in 2006. American Indian Public High School provides American Indian Public Charter School students (and other students from the district) with the opportunity to continue receiving a rigorous education in grades nine through twelve. Later, once AIPCS and AIPHS were on firm ground and operating smoothly, we opened a second middle school called American Indian Public Charter School II in order to provide our academic model (AIM-Ed) to more of Oakland's children. We hope to continue replicating the model throughout the city. But all that came later. Again, the point was to focus on the first school—in this case American Indian Public Charter School—to ensure it functioned extremely well before moving ahead with other plans, such as replication.

Sixth-, seventh-, and eighth-graders (around forty to fifty of them) were expected to attend American Indian Public Charter School in September 2000 if the school remained open. I planned to divide the student body into two self-contained classes. "Self-contained" means that one teacher teaches all subjects to a group of students. That is the arrangement found in elementary schools. I chose to get rid of class rotation at AIPCS and replace it with the more controlled and personal environment of the self-contained classroom. Carmelita would teach all subjects to sixth-graders and the lower-achieving seventh-graders. Shelley would be responsible for the higher-achieving seventh-graders and all the eighth-graders.

The board had previously tried to micromanage teachers, a situation I decided to prevent moving forward. Schools need a separation of powers just like governments do. There are roles for board members, principals, teachers, and other staff members. The lines of authority need to be clear if the school is to function well. I informed the board they would approve the hires, budget plans, policy, and governance, but they weren't going to tell teachers or other employees how to do their jobs.

When it became clear to the board that I also wasn't going to keep any of the cultural classes that the school had in the past, such as drumming, many of them became disinterested and left when their terms were up. The board member Mike Little Feather, who had previously taught bead making, quickly lost interest in AIPCS when the class was dropped. Without the pay and perks of playing Indian, he and others moved on to something else that suited their social-justice interests.

Given the circumstances, my transition with the board went fairly smoothly, but it wasn't without its conflicts. I had a confrontation with one board member over getting rid of the janitor, who was an American Indian woman named Betty Messy Maker, whom the board had hired before I became principal. She showed up two weeks late and made things dirtier than they were before she started. Her children threw trash on the floor, and she set her baby's nasty diapers on the teacher's desk, which smelled up the classroom. Betty Messy Maker's work was lousy, and I was pissed from that point on with her. Ain't nothing I hate more than a filthy person. While Ms. Messy Maker was in a classroom taking her sweet ole time, I walked into the office to tell Ms. Mary Strongheart, a board member, that I was going to get rid of the lady imitating a janitor. Ms. Strongheart said, "You can't do that. She's an important figure in the Indian community."

First of all, these board members were so out of touch with what a real community is, never mind who is important in one. There was no community behind American Indian Public Charter School. That was all part of the fantasy tribal image of the school. No one wanted to support the school because it was an embarrassment. A community is a group of people who work together, support each other's efforts, look after each other's children, and strive to improve their circum-stances together as a whole. That didn't exist at the school. Many American Indian and non-Indian families whose children attended AIPCS didn't like the school and didn't want their children going there in the future.

Second, you can't run an effective organization when people are too afraid to fire those who are worthless as tits on a bull. I told Ms. Strong-heart she could take my job if she wasn't going to let me do my job as principal. I wasn't going to put up with the board's micromanagement. Ms. Strongheart said, "Wait a minute. Okay, I see what you're saying, but you realize people will be mad." I thought that was funny. People will be mad? No shit. Of course they will be. Do you think I care whether people will be upset with me when I'm hiring employees who can make a school great for students?

Over time, the AIPCS board became a really helpful and supportive force that allowed us to turn the school around. Between 2001 and 2003, I had an excellent board consisting of the following members: Nicole Edgar, a businessperson from the original AIPCS board; Dirk Tillotson, a lawyer; Rupert Lupe, a White Mountain Apache tribal member; Bobby Farlis, a staff member at San Francisco State Univer-sity; Sylvia Thomas, a local educator; Dr. Robert Cooter and Dr. Laura Armstrong, advisors to the board; and Rose Lee (board president), the parent of the first two Chinese students to attend AIPCS, one of whom (Kevin) came to us with Ds and Fs and had to be retained. Paul Cobb,

Alice Spearman, and other OUSD board members were great to work with as well.

When school board members like those named above get beyond their own personal agendas and work for student interests, their decision making leads to a productive school system. Often you find the opposite on school boards: people who look to hire their friends and relatives and/or to promote their own brand of politics. The focus becomes on the adults, not the students. I think a better system would be to have one public school board for the whole state of California. This would resemble the University of California (UC) school system. The UC system has one board of twenty-six people called the Regents that oversee the governance and organization of all the UC schools across the state. If there were one governing board for all California K–12 public schools, there would be less nepotism and local politics bogging down the school systems. In Oakland Unified School District, school board elections are usually scheduled at separate times from the election of the governor, Congress members, or the president. Could it be this election system is designed to ensure low turnout among the general population and give teachers unions a leg up?

My dealings with some of the board members, like Ms. Strongheart, whose terms were active when I first became principal, weren't as fluid, but I still managed to get things done. After getting rid of the janitor, the former teachers, and the secretary, and hiring two new teachers and an administrative assistant, the personnel part of the raid was complete; however, there were plenty more obstacles to overcome.

As part of the image makeover, I considered getting rid of the name American Indian Public Charter School because I thought the school was an embarrassment to American Indians. Schools and streets named after minorities are usually bad. For example, most schools named Martin Luther King, Jr., Thurgood Marshall, or Malcolm X are low-performing. The roads we have to honor Dr. King are the nastiest roads in almost every city. When I talked about this with my friend Dr. Laura Head, who was a black studies professor at San Francisco State, she asked me if it was the name that was making the school bad or if it was the way they had been doing things. I said it was the way they had been doing things. She said, "Well, why don't you make it into a good school and leave the name American Indian Public Charter School?" That was great advice, and I'm glad she woke me up out of a dumbness haze that day, because it's important to kick the trend of naming poorly run organizations after minorities. I set out with the new intention of running a successful school represented in name by American Indians.

After keeping the school name and hiring new staff, teachers who were young, smart, and motivated, I had to tackle a daunting problem: the school was in serious debt. AIPCS was a quarter of a million dollars in the red in rent, textbooks, supplies, building repairs, and other costs. I've always believed a school is a business and needs to be run like one. I have no tolerance for principals and boards who can't manage their money. It would take three years to get the school out of debt and become financially stable. In the first year, my business lent money to the school to pay the bills. With AIPCS board approval, I loaned money for rent and other costs at 0 percent interest. When I was informed it was illegal to make 0 percent interest loans, I charged 1 percent interest the second year.

The school's fiscal disarray was caused by the previous leaders' irresponsibility. I firmly believe, and this is something I'll talk more about later, that public schools have enough money to operate effectively and efficiently. What schools often lack is good money management. Mismanagement and incompetence were the reasons American Indian Public Charter School went into debt.

The first key to wise financial management is not spending money you don't have. American Indian Public Charter School went outside their budgetary means. A glaring example of their foolish spending was the installation of a computer network with a start-up cost of about $90,000. The students couldn't read or write, so what were they going to do with computers? Furthermore, the kids used to break them, so they didn't have to do their assignments, and they would steal parts, like the mouse. Computers are expensive to purchase, install, and maintain. Why spend a significant amount on technology when the students haven't mastered the mental skills necessary for using it?

I dismantled the network and got rid of most of the computers. I gave each teacher a computer and put two in the office. To this day, I haven't purchased student computers at American Indian Public Charter School, because our students need to focus on core academics, and textbooks provide the best method for achieving this goal. The fact I am so indifferent to technology when so many educators drool over it comes as a shock to some people. Go visit an inner-city high school with low academic achievement and you'll most likely find nice computer labs with expensive technology but no textbooks in the classrooms. Where is the logic in this herd thinking?

Some former AIPCS board members gained financially from their affiliation with the school when they got paid for teaching their fantasy culture courses or worked as paid "consultants" for the school. I always say there's a reason why the words "consultant" and "construction" start with the prefix "con-," and my reason has nothing to do with grammar. What exactly they were "consulting" on remains a mystery, because no wise thoughts had gone into the curriculum or financial management.

Another way in which American Indian Public Charter School wasted money was by sending employees to expensive conferences. If there is a Conference Heaven or a Conference Hell out there, I am sure American Indians and educators are overrepresented. Many Indian educators enjoy getting away, visiting relatives, shopping, and taking a self-directed workshop on the joys of sex. Conferences provide those opportunities. People can do whatever they like with their own money, but when schools or local governments send employees to faraway conferences with all expenses paid, it is usually little more than a party on the taxpayer dollar.

Another problem with the previous AIPCS board was that the principal served on it. School boards should reserve the power to fire or check the authority of the principal, but when the principal serves on the board, how can they be objective?

There was a large discrepancy in the funding the school should have had and what it actually had left. Ms. Sue Dumberman, a so-called medicine woman who was hired as principal even though she didn't have a degree, was terminated because of poor financial management. Chief Bad Example started the job with a beat-up car and left it with a new four-wheel-drive pickup. The legal cost involved in proving wrongdoing was not worth the money or time apparently, because not much was ever done to follow up on the fiscal disarray of American Indian Public Charter School. This also seems to be the case in many public schools throughout the United States.

Additionally, AIPCS's financial papers were a mess. The record keeping was so bad that the 2000 audit couldn't be completed. The auditor said there weren't enough files or documentation for him to complete an accurate report. No matter how you cut it, money had been grossly mismanaged, leaving American Indian Public Charter School with sizeable debts to pay.

The debt didn't scare me, nor did the deplorable state of the campus. In fact, my initial attraction to the school and repair of it resemble my real estate tendencies. I have had a real estate business for three decades and often buy dilapidated property that many people would not invest in because of the extent of the repairs required. Once restored, the no-longer-run-down buildings and houses turn a profit. I enjoy the process of transforming an eyesore into a nice building and take pride in the turnaround. Due to my years of experience in real estate and construction, I can renovate property in a quick, cost-efficient manner. I expect construction workers will try to con me, so I take precautions by overseeing the construction process and visiting the work sites daily. Many schools get grossly overcharged because they don't question whether a contractor's price is legitimate for the job at hand.

One major goal I had for that summer of 2000 was to physically fix up the school. Because I didn't know if we would stay open, I wasn't about to pour lots of money into construction, but I knew it was important to do a thorough cleaning and give the rented school a cost-effective face-lift.

It seemed like a good idea to talk to some of the school's neighbors to introduce myself and let them know of my plans to clean up and to hear their concerns. The neighbors hated the school and wanted it closed. They had complained to Jean Quan, the OUSD board member who represented the family members in the area. It wasn't fair that a low-performing school with no student control or discipline had diminished the quality of these community members' lives. It was time to set matters straight.

I knocked on Shirley's door. She lives next to our school, and at the time hers was the only Chinese family on the block. Shirley eyed me suspiciously and wouldn't even come out of the house. She talked to me through the screen door. I told her I would be the new principal of American Indian Public Charter School and that positive changes would be coming soon. Shirley looked straight at me and said, "They nasty kids." I agreed with her. After I talked to her for a while, Shirley was more receptive. She shared how the students used to fight and smoke dope and throw their trash in front of her home. Shirley was tired of the mess and the noise. Who could blame her?

Another neighbor, Daniel, a tall black man who lived in an apartment across the street from the school, also revealed his displeasure. He told me the students used to drink 40s in front of his place and cause a ruckus. He was a big, formidable-looking guy, yet those fools had held him hostage. I told him, "We're going to clean this place up." He looked at me and laughed. "We?" he said. "They're going to beat your ass." Later, when he saw the positive direction the school had taken, he introduced me to his friend Rocky, a black cowboy, and said, "This is a principal here. He's a damn miracle worker." We became friends and would sit on the tailgate of his green pickup truck and talk. When he found out I liked boiled chicken feet, he brought some by the office. We chowed down as the rest of the staff gagged. Shirley also brought me a cake. Poor minorities may not have much money, so the ultimate compliment is when they give you food. Shirley still lives next door and is much happier with the way the students behave now. Daniel got cancer a couple years later and got smaller and smaller before he passed. He was a good man. It's not much of a consolation at all, but at least I know he spent the rest of his years in peace instead of being harassed on a daily basis by students acting like fools. I miss him to this day.

Based on the feedback from Shirley, Daniel, and other neighbors, I decided to make the students enter and exit from Thirty-fifth Avenue instead of Magee Avenue, where the neighbors lived. Unlike Magee Avenue, which is a small residential street, Thirty-fifth Avenue is a large thoroughfare with fewer homes. It was important to build relationships with the neighbors who hated the school and wanted to see it closed down. Moving the comings and goings of the students away from their homes was an easy way to prevent the smoking, drinking, and fighting that had plagued them before. We also barred students from going out the back gate of the school onto Magee Avenue.

Part of the cleaning process that summer involved picking up trash on the sidewalks and on Magee Avenue daily. The neighborhood had become such an undesirable place because of the school's negative influence, and people treated it like one. Luckily I had great help in cleaning up from a few people who were driven to see American Indian Public Charter School transform.

One of those people was Tommy Seaton, a Navajo Indian with long black hair worn in a ponytail, who came to Oakland in 1963 during the Indian relocation program. Tommy had a granddaughter at American Indian Public Charter School, so he wanted to contribute his painting skills in order to help improve the image of the school. Tommy and his Hopi friend filled in the large holes in the walls and painted the interior of the building. Though the board paid him $500 for his labor, he donated the money back because he knew AIPCS was deep in debt. From that point on, Tommy became my close friend and my go-to man when I need painting done. He paints American Indian Public Charter School every year, as well as our new schools, American Indian Public High School and American Indian Public Charter School II, and other buildings I own, and he's paid very well for his excellent work.

Tommy, his wife, Donna, their two goddaughters, a student named Daniel Harjo, Shelley, Carmelita, Mina, and I worked hard cleaning up the school that summer. We tore down the toolshed in the playground area, where students used to sneak off to smoke pot, drink, and have sexual encounters. We repaired the toilets and replaced broken windows. We moved a lot of junk out of the building. One reason I tell the current staff to never accept donations to the school is because people dump their crap off on them. Prior to 2000, the staff at American Indian Public Charter School had been taking anything people wanted to give: broken tables, crummy books, old computers, lead paint. The building became a dumping ground for people's unwanted junk. It's expensive to pay for trash disposal in urban areas, so it's cheaper to donate it to organizations like schools. I'm not saying all people who donate to schools give junk; that is definitely not the case, but schools need to be selective about what they accept so they don't turn into eyesores and firetraps like AIPCS was in those days. Because trash disposal was so expensive, we stacked the clutter in a somewhat hidden alley on school property and covered it with tarps until it could be moved affordably.

Daniel Harjo, the Creek Indian student I hired to help clean that summer, had the worst reputation of any student at American Indian Public Charter School. He had thrown a computer out the window earlier in the year. He was fifteen and was going to repeat eighth grade. I brought him into the office and asked him if it was true that he threw a computer out the window. He said it was. I asked, "Do you realize what a badass Indian you are? Do you know how many people dream of throwing a computer out the window? But you actually did it." He looked surprised and laughed; he didn't expect a principal to talk to him this way. He told me how much of a joke the school had been the previous year. My strategy was to take Daniel, the student who was considered the worst-behaved kid in the school, and bring him over to my side and turn him into my enforcer. The other students were intimidated by Daniel, so he had influence that I wanted to use to the school's advantage and to his, because I wanted to teach the boy valuable lessons and make him a leader.

I knew Daniel lived in total poverty and slept many cold nights in his garage. Since I paid him to help clean the school, Daniel got a little money, something he needed and wanted. He also learned responsibility: being on time, working hard, following directions. Daniel was street smart and quick at math, but he had been cheated out of a good education and was academically remedial. As you'll see later, Daniel became my main scout and part of the raiding party among the student body at American Indian Public Charter School.

After just two weeks of thorough cleaning with Daniel and the others, the school looked much better. We were on our way, and community members could see a physical change in the school. We had started to create a pleasant, safe environment for our students at AIPCS.

The question remained: Would Oakland Unified School District agree to give American Indian Public Charter School a second chance?

# chapter three

# A Second Chance

"Ben Chavis, I remember my husband saying that if any charter school would succeed, it would be yours."

—Rose Friedman, the wife and colleague of Milton Friedman, the 1976 Nobel Prize–winning economist, in her handwritten letter to me dated July 9, 2007

"I endured the difficult times at AIPCS because I knew I was a part of greatness. How many times in your life can you say that?"

—Jerry Mishkin, former AIPCS teacher and administrator from 2002 to 2006

We were scheduled to meet with the district curriculum committee again in August. In addition to Dan Siegel, the board member who said he wouldn't oppress American Indians, we needed one more vote in our favor or a nonvote. Three votes from the district curriculum committee to shut us down would most likely seal our doom. As it stood, if Mr. Siegel were our only supporter on the district curriculum board, our case would be sent to the district school board, which had final authority and would most likely revoke our charter. The key, then, was to gain the favor of one other board member on the district curriculum committee, because if two of the four members did not vote to close the school down (by either a "yes" in our favor or a nonvote), American Indian Public Charter School would remain open.

I invited the district curriculum committee to visit the school to show them what we had accomplished and discuss our plans for the upcoming year. Only one person from the committee showed up, a black female attorney with dreadlocks named Wilda White. Wilda had been appointed to the OUSD board by Mayor Jerry Brown. He had gotten the voters to approve a measure that would allow him to appoint three school board members. It did not quite work out as he had planned because they usually voted against his position. After their term was up, Mayor Brown stopped the practice. I guess that's what you call another failed attempt to fix the political public education system. He had more success as mayor in improving our city of Oakland.

Ms. Wilda White rode in on a skateboard to the school that day. She was neither friendly nor unfriendly, but kind of calm and reserved. I walked Ms. White through the school pointing out the classrooms and the textbooks we planned to use, exuding as much charisma during the tour as I possibly could. She commented that the school looked clean and said she heard it had been filthy before. I'm not sure if she had ever visited AIPCS prior to that time, but I do know it's common for Oakland Unified to send letters and memos and to hold meetings before they even see a school with their own eyes.

Walking down the hall, we came across Carmelita and Shelley, who were ready to roll their sleeves up and take on the task of teaching. It must have helped that the two teachers were female and smart, like the board member, because she seemed to instantly warm up to them. All was going well, so I started to relax. Then Ms. White asked the teachers if they had teaching credentials, which they did not. Quickly I said, "They are enrolled in a credential program." She seemed to ponder that and then indicated she needed to get going. As we walked through the front door, down the stairs, and out to Thirty-fifth Avenue together, Ms. White turned to me and said, "I'm not going to vote to keep you open." My heart sped up. She continued, "But I'm also not going to vote to close you down." Before I could say God is a woman and she loves some Ben Chavis, Ms. White gave me a smile and darted off down Thirty-fifth Avenue on her skateboard. I was so relieved and knew we'd be set for a while.

She must have changed her mind before the board meeting because she did vote for us. American Indian Public Charter School remained open because we had two votes of support: one from Mr. Dan Siegel and one from Ms. Wilda White, the dreadlocked lawyer who was one hell of a skateboarder.

I attended the next district board meeting to state my appreciation that Oakland Unified had given AIPCS a second chance because I knew the superintendent wasn't happy about the curriculum committee's decision. I wanted to get off on a good foot with the district. During the meeting, I stood up before the superintendent, Mr. Dennis Chaconas, and other members of the Oakland Unified Board of Education and thanked them for giving the school an opportunity to set things right. As principal I promised to create positive change at the school with the help of a new staff. I vowed that if the students' test scores and attendance rates did not improve by the end of the year, I would give half of my salary back to the school and donate the other half to my favorite charity.

That statement made an impression on the board, I could tell. They might have been thinking I was some crazy Indian making crazy promises, but at least they had an out. I respect people who state their intentions with conviction and put consequences on the line, because it demonstrates their willingness to make something happen while also expressing that they don't plan on making excuses or requesting endless chances. I wanted to convey to the Oakland Unified board that I didn't have an interest in taking over American Indian Public Charter School because of the need for money or the need for a job. I wanted to make something positive happen in the students' lives, and if I didn't, I wasn't going to stick around and muck things up even more.

Promises and speeches aside, I knew we were going to have our work cut out for us. When the California standardized test results from the previous year (before I became principal) arrived, I saw how tough a row we had to hoe.

When I opened up the packages containing the reports, the first thing I wanted to know was the school's Academic Performance Index score. The Academic Performance Index (API) is California's school ranking system. It rates schools according to their standardized test results. Based on each student's performance on each test, an overall school score is derived called the Academic Performance Index. That score falls between 200 and 1,000 points, with 200 being the absolute lowest and 1,000 being the absolute highest. The California Department of Education considers an API of 800 the benchmark of excellence and the goal to which all California schools should strive.

American Indian Public Charter School did not qualify for an API score for the 1999–2000 year because not enough students were tested who were supposed to be, a violation of California education code. It didn't appear that the staff at American Indian Public Charter School cheated by intentionally withholding students from testing. From what I gathered, they were unorganized, didn't follow protocol, didn't fill out the paperwork correctly, and didn't send back all the test materials they were supposed to. Even when a school does not qualify for an Academic Performance Index score, the individual tests submitted to the state get scored and analyzed. The results for American Indian Public Charter School painted a bleak picture.

None of the sixth-, seventh-, or eighth-graders at AIPCS tested at or above the fiftieth percentile on the state or the national exams in math. Not one. In addition, none of the seventh-graders tested at or above the fiftieth percentile in reading. Eight percent of sixth-graders and 17 percent of eighth-graders tested at or above the fiftieth percentile in reading.

Of all the students whose test scores were processed for the 1999–2000 academic year, only one student tested proficient in all her subject tests. Being "proficient" means at grade level. Since she was the only proficient student, that meant all the other students at American Indian Public Charter School were below grade level or remedial.

The ultimate goal for all students in California is to be "proficient" or "advanced" on their end-of-the-year standardized tests (the STAR tests, which stands for "Standardized Testing and Reporting"). The STAR tests measure if students have mastered the standards, or grade-level skills and objectives. If a student tests "basic" in math, let's say, that means he is below grade level but close to getting there. If he is "below basic" or "far below basic," then he is farther and very far, respectively, from being at grade level. Each state has its own terms, but the basic goal of the No Child Left Behind Act is for every student to perform at academic grade level.

Based on the individual STAR results, I estimated that if American Indian Public Charter School had qualified for an Academic Performance Index score for the 1999–2000 school year, it would have been in the low to mid-300s. Of the sixteen middle schools in Oakland with valid APIs that year, only one, Havenscourt Middle School, had an API low enough to put them in the 300s. Their API was 370. If you concede that AIPCS would have had a lower API than Havenscourt Middle School, that would make American Indian Public Charter School the lowest-performing middle school in Oakland Unified School District in the 1999–2000 school year.

These students were academically remedial to the point of being pathetic, but it wasn't their fault. Do you really think all of them could have been dumb or incapable of learning? The students weren't being taught or guided. That's an important point. Too often blame is placed on students and families for lousy standards-based test scores. Some educators will say these minorities are poor, they don't know English, their parents are uneducated, so how can we possibly achieve with them? Instead of attempting to give all students a rigorous academic education of high expectations, politicians and school administrators in the inner city often play the victim card. They treat students as victims of circumstance and poverty who can't do the academic work of their middle-class peers. In the place of academic rigor, low-performing public schools provide culture classes and fun activities, so the kids just whittle the days away in silliness. School becomes a joke and the students know it. The joke ends up being on them, and then it's no longer funny during adulthood when they are not qualified for a job or to enroll in college.

It was the same thing with playing Indian at AIPCS. The drumming and other cultural activities took up too much time in the school day. More time needed to be spent on academics. Extracurricular activities are great for enhancing the learning experience of students performing well academically. When students can barely read, write, or do basic math, like those at AIPCS, educators cannot afford to take time out of the school day to play around with passing the sage and beating drums.

The cultural activities offered in the morning were not attended by most students. AIPCS students were given a choice about what they wanted to participate in. That sounds great in theory, but let me tell you something about ghetto students: If you give them choices and say they can do this or that and you don't hold them responsible for what they choose, they just won't do anything. The kids skipped the morning activities. I believe the bead making, tribal dancing, and other culture courses should have been offered after school. The playing of Indian seemed to appeal more to the staff than to the students. Most of the teachers had poor mathematics and language arts skills, so how could they teach those subjects?

The students skipped school so often that I estimate the attendance rate for the 1999–2000 school year was 65 percent. Having a low attendance rate causes two major problems: First, when students are not in school, they can't learn. Second, schools only get paid in California when students are present. Every absence causes a cut in state funding.

My goal for the 2000–2001 school year was to improve the image of the school, set it on the right track, and raise it up from its place as the worst middle school in Oakland. You must have goals; the goals need to be achievable; and the students and staff must know the goals that have been set for them. In many failing public schools, the students and staff cannot tell you what academic performance level they have reached. We wanted to increase the attendance rate significantly, build academic skills, and introduce structure and discipline.

There was a concern the school wouldn't have enough students for the 2000–2001 school year. We knew some students would return just because it's easier to attend the school you know. Some call it a herd mentality that families have when it comes to choosing schools. They go where they've been guided and where people they know attend school. That summer I did a lot of on-the-fly public relations. Everywhere I went I talked about the school and the changes we'd been making. I met Carol Wahpepah, who worked with the Native American Resource Center, and started coordinating activities with them. In order to get all the necessary paperwork done on top of cleaning up the school and building relationships with community members, I'd stay at the school sometimes until three a.m. Most days that summer my schedule went from seven a.m. to ten p.m. This allowed enough time to cover all aspects of the job. This may seem like long hours; however, it was not work to me. It was a competition, just like sports, to prove I had a good team at AIPCS. The students and teachers needed a good head coach to give them direction and leadership.

It is important to be clear about what you want to accomplish. Because of that, we set objectives by which to measure student progress before starting the 2000–2001 school year. The following measurements were used: (1) Student attendance would be at least 95 percent each year; (2) the suspension and expulsion rate would be under 1 percent; and (3) the school would make yearly improvements by scoring at least 5 percent above the previous year's STAR results.

We also drafted a mission statement as a way of expressing what American Indian Public Charter School planned to achieve with its students. The mission statement has changed slightly over time, but the general gist remains the same. The mission of the school was and still is to prepare students to be competitive members in a free market capitalist society. I say "free market" because that is the purest form of capitalism that allows anybody—no matter what the person's race or gender is—to do business with anybody else. Other forms of capitalism can discriminate. For example, I grew up in America's capitalist society in the 1950s and '60s, but I wasn't free to eat in any restaurant I wanted to because I was an Indian. That would have been different in a free market. The 2008 mission statement reads:

> The American Indian Public Charter School serves two hundred inner-city students in sixth through eighth grade. The focus of AIPCS is excellent student attendance (99%), which helps to ensure that the academic needs of American Indian students and others interested in attending our school are met. We will provide students with an education to enhance their academic skills in reading, writing, spelling, mathematics, science, social science, business, and humanities in order to compete and be productive members in a free market capitalist society. This will be a collaborative effort between school, family, and community.

We stick to the mission in order to accomplish the mission. That sounds like common sense, right? Well, you'd be amazed how many schools stray from their mission, re-create it, forget about it, or halfheartedly adhere to it. I make sure that each student memorizes the mission statement and reviews our goals throughout the year. I'm stubborn as a mule when it comes to following AIPCS's mission because it keeps us on the right educational track.

# chapter four

# A New Beginning

"My first year at AIPCS was to say the least shameful. . . . An average day of class included drawing while the teacher read and maybe if we had time, a few math problems—no science; my teacher hated it. And as for history and social science, I have no idea why we never did it. There was no P.E. and we had nowhere to eat lunch. This was a school for students that had been kicked out of every other school in Oakland and had nowhere else to go. Violence, drugs, and sexual acts were more commonly witnessed than students in class studying. The teachers were lazy and had little optimism for the future of their students. The school was in desperate need of a cleansing."

—*Edward Moreno,*
*a former AIPCS student who now attends Dartmouth College*

On the first day of the 2000–2001 academic year, about thirty students showed up, including Edward Moreno (above), a Mexican–Yaqui Indian who was in the seventh grade. (Later that year, the enrollment increased to about sixty students.) I stood at the front door to greet the students and point them toward their classrooms. Once they were situated, I walked into each classroom and spoke about my vision for the school.

During lunch on the first day I addressed all the students at once. I said, "This ain't going to be the way it was before. You're not going to be coming to school late, skipping school, or beating up students. You're going to come to school and learn." I paused to see their reaction. There wasn't much of one, so I continued. "We need to get things straight. I am the head coach and run this school. You half-breeds who think you can beat my ass, come line up on the left side of the gym. We need to settle this now." That got their attention. Then an eighth-grade student called out, "Dr. Chavis is crazee, and he means business!" I told them they would come to school. Those who came every day would get a free trip to Disneyland. Those late sleepers and street runners who didn't come to school would be retained.

I summoned Daniel Harjo, the eighth-grade student who helped clean during the summer and who was going to be my student representative. We stood together and I said, "We're going to have a boxing club at AIPCS. Anyone who gets into a fight is going to have to box Daniel, our champion. Do you understand?" The students looked at us in disbelief, and a big rain of laughter broke out. Daniel was considered the toughest kid at the school who got in the most trouble. Plus, he was big for his age, so none of them wanted to mess with him. When I dismissed the students from lunch, Daniel said to me with a smile, "Dr. Chavis, you're too tight on us." I just laughed and told him he had after-school detention for complaining. He said, "Don't I get a break?" I said, "Nope, you get a detention." Daniel enjoyed his newfound power, and it gave him a purpose for attending school. He paid attention and behaved so that he could work with the students who didn't behave or follow directions, but like them, he also had his own fair share of detentions to serve.

Students at AIPCS receive one hour of after-school detention if they are late to school, miss homework, break school rules, or misbehave. Detentions provide consequences for student behavior, which in turn provides structure. If you do your work, come to school on time, and pay attention in class, you'll have the freedom to leave at the end of the day. If you don't do your work, are tardy, or talk in class, you'll be spending another hour of quiet time in a classroom doing schoolwork and sometimes chores. It is now a rule at AIPCS that if you get two detentions in a week, you'll have to attend Saturday school, which is held from 8:30 a.m. to 1:00 p.m. on certain Saturdays. Saturday school is like a longer, weekend version of detention. Saturday school, like after-school detention, provides students with consequences and structure.

The first day of school passed without incident, which is typical in my opinion. Students are generally quiet and observant on the first day or two of school because they're trying to figure out what their teachers and principals are like and who's going to be in their class. Once they get comfortable, they start to act out.

I made sure to set a precedent with them that I was different and wasn't going to take their antics. When they saw me run kids from other schools off campus with a broom in my hand, they laughed and started to get the picture. When they heard me have it out with a crazy parent or a trespassing thug on campus, they knew I didn't play. Their teachers didn't play, either. We also had Daniel on our side, which encouraged other students to become part of our team.

The students started to come around to the fact that the goofing off was over and they were going to a real school now. Like typical students, they would challenge the staff to see what they could get away with. We used whatever tactic worked to maintain control and to discipline and educate them.

For example, some students in Ms. Shelley Jones's seventh- and eighth-grade class were taking liberty with the word "nigger." Shelley was black and could talk smack for a sister who had Spanish-speaking maids from birth until college. She put an end to the students saying "nigger" in class real quick. But Ana, a sixth-grade Mexican-Indian girl in the other class, constantly used the "n" word. I decided to teach her a lesson, so I talked to some black girls and said, "You know, your classmate is calling you girls niggers. You should not put up with that behavior and you should have a talk with her." Sure enough they did. They got in her face and gave her a piece of their mind. She came to me crying and said the girls were mean to her. I said, "That's what happens when you go around running your mouth and calling people niggers." She brought her mama in the next day, and her mom was all riled up, demanding to know what happened. When I told her that her daughter had been calling blacks niggers and they got pissed, the mom turned to her and said, "I told you not to say that and that they were going to get you sooner or later." Ana didn't call anyone else a "nigger" at AIPCS after that.

As a staff, we were determined to improve the attendance rate, which had been about 65 percent the year before. When students didn't show up for school and wouldn't answer the phone when the secretary or I called to see where they were, I'd show up at their house and bring them to school.

I'd walk around to the back door because families don't expect a principal to show up there. It catches them off guard. I'd knock and usually the student's mom would answer the door. I'd say, "Is sleepy-head here?"

The mom would say, "Who are you?"

"I'm the principal at American Indian Public Charter School. Your son hasn't come to school for three days now. No one has called us to explain where he is. We've been calling you. Did you get our messages?"

At that point the mom usually got embarrassed or defensive. If she got embarrassed, she'd allow me to bring him to school without protest. I'd walk in the student's room, where he was sleeping soundly. You can imagine how surprised he'd be to wake up with the principal's face staring down at him. I'd say, "Boy, are you ready for school?" His mom would look at me nervously and I'd say, "This boy's just lazy. Aren't you, boy?" He'd look mortified. I'd tell him it was his responsibility, not his mama's, to get to school and learn. He'd pull his pants, shirt, socks, and shoes on faster than you could say, "Get ready." Then he'd have to listen to me talk the whole drive back to school.

Once at AIPCS, I'd take the student up in front of his classmates and teacher and then ask them to guess where I had just been. I'd say, "Yep, that's right. At sleepyhead's house. It was ten o'clock in the morning and he was lying in bed sleeping like a baby, snoring, his hair sticking up every which way." The kids would laugh. I'm big on embarrassment because it works well with my American Indian, Asian, black, and Hispanic students. I'd rather have a student get embarrassed by me and learn a lesson than to be an embarrassment to himself, his family, or his race by committing a major crime that placed him in prison for life.

When I'd show up at their door, some family members would say, "This is harassment. You can't just come to our house." I'd reply that they couldn't keep their kids out of school. By law, children need to be in school. When families didn't cooperate and instead let their child miss school or run the streets, I had another method to fall back on.

I would call their home, change my voice, and pretend to be with Child Protective Services. I'd say it had come to my attention that their child had repeatedly missed school, which concerned us about the quality of parenting and could result in their welfare check being held up. We wanted to ensure the child received an education. That method worked 100 percent of the time. Why should children be held hostage by the losers they are raised by when we can make sure they get an education and stop the cycle of stupidity? I take my commitment to educating young people seriously.

Negligent parents who allowed their children to miss school could sometimes be found at the local Indian watering hole called the Hilltop Bar. It's closed now, but it served some deadbeats and winners for five decades. In fact, the Hilltop Bar was the oldest American Indian institution in Oakland, established by Indians from the relocation program. How pathetic is that? The oldest American Indian establishment in Oakland was a bar. This was their way of contributing to the community. It pissed me off how they painted pictures of Geronimo and Sitting Bull by the front entrance so that everyone driving down Macarthur Avenue near AIPCS could see Indian heroes desecrated by a bunch of drunks. It was rumored that some students at American Indian Public Charter School were so mad about the display of Geronimo and Sitting Bull's pictures on the front of a bar that they snuck down one night and painted over their portraits. I could not prove this was true.

I used to go down to the Hilltop Bar to embarrass the parents of AIPCS students who were missing school. One time Ms. Betty Night Owl didn't show up for a meeting with me about her daughter, who was frequently absent. I went by the Hilltop Bar to see if Ms. Night Owl was there. Sure enough, she was perched at the bar. I approached her and said, "Ms. Night Owl, you can't come to a school meeting, but your ass can get drunk at a bar." Some drunk asked, "Who in the hell is that man running his mouth in our place?" I looked at him and said, "I'm Ben Chavis, the principal of her daughter's school. Do you have a fucking problem with me?" The drunk was surprised that I did not back down to him inside the bar surrounded by other red lovers of the liquid spirits. I walked closer to him and he said with the speech of someone who had had too many drinks, "I agree with you her kid should be in school." The people in the bar broke out laughing. One guy said, "Set up a round of drinks for the principal," and everyone started laughing except Ms. Night Owl.

She said, "I don't appreciate you talking to me like this in public." I said, "Well, I don't appreciate you standing me up and wasting my time and cheating your daughter out of an education." Many of the local American Indian and non-Indian community members considered me crazy for having confrontations like that one with people. I chose to be crazy when dealing with some of the drunks and adult fools because it worked and it benefited my students' education. From that point on, her daughter was in school and did very well.

Not all of the truancy problems had to do with students staying home. Some students would pretend they had left for school, but they'd hang out on the streets instead of going to class. We had another tactic for addressing that problem. I got to know the gangbangers who gambled and dealt dope on the corner of Thirty-fifth and Macarthur, one block from AIPCS. I'd throw the bones (dice) with them and shoot the breeze because there was a method to my madness. While the sun glinted off the gold grills on their front teeth, I told them I was the principal at the nearby middle school and that I'd pay them five dollars a head for any of the students they caught skipping school and brought back to AIPCS. Drug dealers are intent on making easy money; that's their business. I teamed up with them to make sure my students got an education. Everybody loves to talk about working together as a community, but if you really want a community in the ghetto, you'd better have the drug dealers behind you, because they get people to act when money is involved. It's unfortunate, but it is undeniable that drug dealers influence many young people in a negative way. I tried to turn that influence in a more positive direction.

The drug dealers joined me one day at the school during lunch. In front of the whole student body I said, "I've hired Mr. Grill and his boys to bring you back to school. If they see any of you skipping class, they're going to drag you back here and get paid for it." I told Mr. Grill and his gang to take a good look around so they could recognize the students if they saw them on the street. The kids were shocked. One of the drug dealers said, "I'll beat your asses, too." I jokingly replied they could do that on their own time. I just wanted the students back on campus as quickly as possible and in good physical condition to do their work.

That meeting caused a buzz around campus as the students said in awe, "Dr. Chavis knows the drug dealers! He's crazy." The rumor was going around that I used to be a gangbanger in Oakland and knew everybody in the city. I went along with the myth that I ran the streets back in the day. Little did they know I grew up a sharecropper as a youngster working my butt off in the corn and tobacco fields of North Carolina.

I didn't "run the streets" in the gangbanging sense of the term, but I did literally run the streets, especially my first year as principal. I had been a cross-country and track runner in high school and college, and running was something I continued to do until hurting my knee in 2004. Running allowed me to be visible. The students and families would see me in East Oakland, West Oakland, South Oakland, and North Oakland. I covered a lot of distance and ran varied routes. Running provided me with PR opportunities. I'd stop and talk to people and check out different neighborhoods. It was a way of getting my face and name out there and telling people about the school. I'd meet church leaders, for instance, who would ask me to come talk to their congregations about my plans for American Indian Public Charter School. It was great because I enjoy going to church and working with the preachers to improve education.

During my first year as principal we achieved the benchmark of a 95 percent daily attendance rate. That was a fantastic accomplishment compared with the 65 percent attendance rate from the previous year.

The teachers worked hard in the self-contained classrooms to build basic academic skills and bring the students closer to grade level. We used up-to-date, standards-based textbooks to cover the curriculum. We implemented more structure and discipline, such as the after-school detention program, that made students accountable for their actions. This was the beginning of the American Indian Model of Education.

As mentioned in the introduction and demonstrated in more depth in the appendix, the American Indian Model of Education is our school's educational framework. Its four main components are family culture, high expectations, free market capitalism, and accountability/structure. The four directions are an important symbol to me personally and to my tribe, the Lumbees, so the four strands have symbolic significance. Though AIM-Ed has changed and will continue to change over time, the essence of its purpose and framework has remained the same since I became principal in 2000.

The teachers were strict, and I was "crazy," as some people refer to me. Crazy like a fox is the way I look at it. I behave aggressively, demand success, and keep the fools at bay, as it says in Proverbs in the Bible.

I also look out for my own, like a fox would do. I do what I can to bring attention to the students and staff when it is beneficial, but I also make sure to divert attention onto me when I'm trying to protect them. When an angry mother storms through the door demanding to speak immediately with a teacher, I shift her focus onto me so the teacher and students can go about their business in the classroom. If I can be the voice of reason with the mother, I'll be the voice of reason. If that's not the language she's willing to understand at the moment, I can play the fool instead.

This diversion tactic reminds me of two foxes that used to live inside a hole in the chinaberry tree in front of our sharecropper's shack in North Carolina. I was a little boy when my mom ran them out, and I was in tears. I really liked those two foxes. The next fall during hunting season, I watched as a neighbor, Mr. Buddy, pursued them through the fields with his gun. The male fox ran in a separate direction from the female so as to divert the hunter's attention. As he ran toward the swamp, the farmer shot and killed him, and the female fox got away. The next spring when they were burning the fields to fertilize the soil, the hunter once again started to chase the female fox. I watched dumbfounded as she ran right through the fire. Her little red body with a white-tipped tail ran straight into the flames! Seems crazy, right? Well, we discovered later that she had run in the opposite direction of her four cubs in order to protect them. The cubs lay safely in a foxhole along the canal at the edge of a field, thanks to the mother who spared them. She ended up with a slightly burnt tail thanks to those heroics, so I started calling her Little Smoky.

At AIPCS from the beginning we worked together as a family, always keeping the kids' best interests in mind. If we had to take some heat, we took some heat, as long as in the end we stayed true to our purpose. We implemented AIM-Ed and stuck to it. The academic focus and structured environment of self-contained classrooms led to yearly improvements. Many schools try one system one year and another one a different year, so that the curriculum becomes a hodgepodge of different approaches. I had a vision of what would work with poor minorities. When the increase in attendance rates and test scores proved that the ideas and practices worked, we stuck with them and built upon them. It wasn't magic. It was a sound education model, hard work, and persistence.

When children have to work hard and smart in class and are not afforded the opportunity to goof off, they will learn. Everyone put their noses to the grindstone and pushed American Indian Public Charter School onto a new track. The students improved and began to embrace AIM-Ed with its high expectations, academic learning, good behavior, and consistent attendance.

We had become a family. In a family you have disagreements, and that was the case at AIPCS. As the leader of the family, I made sure we stayed focused on our mission, and those who attempted to go in another direction were put back on track. I have noticed that some people will say of me, "I don't agree with his method of embarrassing students, staff, or families." It's easy to disagree with my method of education. If people have a better method that has proven to work in educating students in Oakland, I would be the first to implement it. To date, not one person has presented a better education model than AIM-Ed that is supported by student achievement results. So, I move forward, continuing to educate our students with AIM to Educate because it works.

At the end of the 2000–2001 school year, AIPCS scored a 436 on the Academic Performance Index (API). While 436 was certainly not a great score and was only about halfway to the benchmark of excellence (800), it was a major improvement over the prior year's performance. American Indian Public Charter School improved by merely obtaining official results (unlike the year before) and thereby becoming a legitimate school. With the API score of 436 we beat four other Oakland middle schools, placing us at number twelve out of sixteen.

In the following tables, you will find the percentages of students scoring at or above the fiftieth percentile at American Indian Public Charter School and Oakland Unified School District between the years of 2000 and 2001. The 2000 results for AIPCS were before I was principal. The 2001 results show the improvements made once the AIM-Ed model was implemented and a school culture based on academic achievement and responsible behavior was established. You can observe from the data how much AIPCS students improved over one year compared to the performance of students in Oakland Unified that year.

### American Indian Public Charter School Students Who Scored At or Above the Fiftieth Percentile, 2000–2001*

|           | Reading | | Mathematics | |
|-----------|---------|---------|---------|---------|
|           | 2000 | 2001 | 2000 | 2001 |
| Grade 6   | 8%   | 33.6% | 0%  | 29.5% |
| Grade 7   | 0%   | 43.4% | 0%  | 31.8% |
| Grade 8   | 17%  | 46.4% | 0%  | 29.5% |

*Note: This data is based on STAR 9 standardized tests. All eighth-graders at AIPCS take the algebra test, while most eighth-graders in the Oakland Unified School District take general math.

Oakland Unified School District Students Who Scored
At or Above the Fiftieth Percentile, 2000–2001*

|          | Reading |       | Mathematics |       |
|----------|---------|-------|-------------|-------|
|          | 2000    | 2001  | 2000        | 2001  |
| Grade 6  | 22%     | 22%   | 29%         | 30%   |
| Grade 7  | 24%     | 24%   | 28%         | 30%   |
| Grade 8  | 26%     | 26%   | 26%         | 25%   |

*Note: This data is based on STAR 9 standardized tests. All eighth-graders at AIPCS take the algebra test, while most eighth-graders in the Oakland Unified School District take general math.

We reached our goals at American Indian Public Charter School for the 2000–2001 school year by improving the image of the school, setting it on the right track, and raising it up from its place as the worst middle school in Oakland. We also increased the attendance rate significantly, built academic skills, and introduced structure and discipline to the student body.

After setting the AIM-Ed in place, I looked forward to the positive results. A good educational model, like many systems, will lead to significant academic performance increases by the second year. Look at sports for an analogy. A new college football coach who takes over a failing program cannot be expected to take his team to the national championship the first year. The coach has to work hard and improve the talent he has on his team. His ability to recruit is going to be stifled by the team's bad reputation, but he strives to bring out the best in his players, who practice their skills. The players have to adjust to his new offensive and defensive strategies. The fans watch and realize the athletes are more disciplined, in better physical shape, and they work together as a team.

After his first year, the coach is able to attract new athletes who believe in his methods and program. People want to be part of a successful, dynamic organization. After a couple of years of continual development, the coach creates a winning team that people respect. This process mirrors what happened at American Indian Public Charter School.

Looking back on it, that first year at the school was survival mode. We got kids to show up, work harder, and learn more than they had the previous year. We introduced structure and got the school moving in the right direction, which proved us worthy of the second chance given by Oakland Unified School District. The first year laid the basic groundwork for the subsequent years, when more structure, discipline, and rules developed. With those additions came more student academic accomplishments.

I knew American Indian Public Charter School would thrive, because as the story goes in my family, I'm blessed, and great things happen to me. Why am I blessed?

The day I was born there was a flood. It had rained hard on Lumberton, North Carolina, for four days and four nights. From her bed at home, my sixteen-year-old mother struggled to give birth to me, her first child.

When she lost consciousness, my relatives carried her out to the end of the dirt road through the floodwaters of the Lumber River. They flagged down a car and took her into the American Indian wing of the segregated Lumberton hospital. Malnourished and young, my mom barely survived her first birth. Bearing the name of Benford, given to me by my grandma, Lela, I emerged into the world with all signs indicating I would be blessed.

See, the number four is sacred to the Lumbee Indians. Since I was born after four days and four nights of rain on the fourteenth of January, my Lumbee family members say I am special.

The Lumbee Indians from my neck of the woods also believed my maternal grandmother Lela could see into the future because she was born with a veil over her eyes. Witnessing the portentous flooding and the symbolism and struggle surrounding my birth, Grandma Lela announced that I was to be the "blessed" one in the family, the child to whom only good things would happen.

I go through the world thinking I'll eventually come out on top of any situation, and I'm always going to win. Is that some self-esteem or what? I smile and laugh all the time, like a person who has pulled something over on the world.

I won't be held back by complaining or bad situations. When the cards don't fall as I had hoped or life takes a turn for the worst, I know I'm gonna bounce back sooner or later. Sometimes I take the notion of being blessed very seriously; other times I joke about it. One of my favorite lines to say is, "God is a woman, and she loves some Ben Chavis." That always gets me laughing and puts me in a good mood.

I am the "illegitimate" spawn of two teenaged Lumbee Indians who raised me in a sharecropper's shack with no electricity in the rural South. I grew up among my extended family (none of whom had an education) and survived poverty, an abusive father, and various other setbacks, but I had many wonderful family members and extremely fond memories of childhood. I am the blessed bastard child with a strong lust for life and a determination to succeed.

Charter schools are bastards, too. They're treated like the illegitimate offspring of the public school system. Charter schools get less money than the regular public schools; they're expected to fail, and the legitimacy of their very existence is questioned. What are these schools, and who said they could be here? Kind of like me: Who is this crazy Indian, and what does he think he's doing? Well, sometimes it may take a bastard to know one.

But that's no excuse to be a failure. Illegitimate, legitimate, minority, white, rich, poor, private, public, and charter school students all need a structured learning environment. Students who enter middle school especially need structure. Psychologists, social workers, sociologists, and educators are constantly stating that middle school students' bodies are changing; they're undergoing puberty, unsure about their identity, and facing numerous other issues. How do American schools typically prepare these students for their difficult transition through the middle school years? They enroll them in six to eight classes with different teachers. Because this is a time when students need stability and a sound family relationship with adults, I created self-contained classrooms at American Indian Public Charter School.

chapter five

# Creating a Family with the Self-Contained Classroom

"I got the role of seeing who my father really was. To me it was like an open opportunity to see what men are like who don't have any respect for the family. I grew up believing that you should always take care of your family and you should always do what's best for them and that no matter what, families come first. I was raised that way . . . I kind of got the impression that somehow the family was going to be broken up, but Mom was always going to keep it together, and that's what she did. We grew up [mom, brother, grandparents], lived together, and supported each other."

—*Kevin Lee, an eleventh-grader at AIPHS in 2007–2008; he attended AIPCS starting seventh grade as a retained (held-back) student, and went from Ds and Fs at Bret Harte Middle School to a 3.42 GPA the next year; his mom, Rose Lee, was once the AIPCS board president*

"My mom always told us that when we were in school we needed to show how smart we were because you can do well even though you have a single parent who is supporting the family. You don't need a dad or both parents around to be successful."

—*Chris Lee (Kevin's brother, Rose's son), a tenth-grader at AIPHS in 2007–2008 and graduate of AIPCS; he went from average grades to honor roll*

We create a family at AIPCS. At the core of American Indian Public Charter School's AIM-Ed are the self-contained classroom and a process called "looping," in which teachers follow their students from one grade level to the next. The self-contained classroom, where students remain with the same teacher every day for all subjects except P.E., provides children with stability. Teachers stay with their students for the duration of the day and follow them from one grade level to the next (termed "looping" by educators who like to assign names to things). Ideally one teacher works with the same group of students from sixth through eighth grade at American Indian Public Charter School.

Self-contained classrooms and looping create strong, family-like relationships and reliability. Children who are accustomed to the dynamics of an extended family thrive under structure, rules, and strong personal relationships, yet in most middle schools, students are rotated between six to eight teachers like auto parts on Ford's assembly line.

Many American Indian Public Charter School students and others in Oakland have messed-up home lives. Because of the challenging and unpredictable circumstances they often face, they feel more secure immersed in a controlled learning environment. We can't be in charge of what happens to students at home or in the streets, but we can create stability for them in school so they'll know what is expected of them. We are there to support them and to ensure they are successful.

In order to provide structure and a family environment, my first year as principal we implemented the self-contained classroom right away. The classroom teachers taught their students all subjects, including physical education. The school was so debt-ridden that we didn't have enough money to hire a separate staff person for P.E., so I covered their P.E. classes one day a week to give them a break. The next year we hired a physical education teacher, so when students had P.E. class, their teacher had a prep period. Currently, the only class rotation at American Indian Public Charter School occurs for physical education and for Mandarin, which is only taken by the eighth-graders. Classroom teachers teach their students all the other subjects: language arts, mathematics, science, and history.

The physical education and Mandarin (Chinese language) classes last about forty minutes each, so that is the length of each teacher's prep period on Monday through Thursday. During that time, teachers prepare for upcoming classes, use the copy machine, grade, meet with students' families, and so on. Friday has always been an early-release day. Students come to school at 8:30 a.m., as usual, but instead of leaving school at 3:00 p.m., they get out at 12:40 p.m. On Fridays, there is no lunch and no P.E. For four hours and ten minutes, the students are in their classrooms with their teacher, learning. The early-release day gives students and teachers the opportunity to take care of doctors' appointments, class work, or other personal matters. Below is a sample Monday-to-Thursday sixth-grade class schedule:

| | |
|---|---|
| 8:30–10:00 | Language Arts |
| 10:00–11:30 | Math |
| 11:30–12:00 | Science |
| 12:00–12:20 | Lunch |
| 12:20–12:40 | Science (continued) |
| 12:40–1:30 | History |
| 1:30–2:10 | P.E. |
| 2:10–3:00 | Elective |

American Indian Public Charter School's use of the self-contained classroom is an anomaly in secondary education. Elementary schools in America generally use self-contained classrooms through fourth or fifth grade, but most middle schools and high schools follow a class rotation system in which students move rooms and change teachers for each academic subject.

My experience in elementary schools as a teacher and administrator prior to becoming principal at AIPCS convinced me that the elementary school education model is more efficient than the secondary school model. Students perform better academically in elementary schools than in secondary schools. American students are competitive with other countries up until about fifth grade, but by the time they enroll in secondary school they're not even a distant threat.

Look at the Academic Performance Index scores for elementary, middle, and high schools in California from the 2006–2007 academic year:

Overall API score for California second- through sixth-graders:       761
Overall API score for California seventh- and eighth-graders:       720
Overall API score for California ninth- through eleventh-graders:       689

Keep in mind that the California Department of Education's benchmark of excellence is 800. That means, as a whole, California's public schools are underperforming at all age levels; however, the elementary schools are the closest to reaching the bar.

The Academic Performance Index scores drop off as students progress from elementary to middle school and then drop again as middle school students continue on to high school. For all subgroups, this general decline holds true. For example, the API scores for California's socioeconomically disadvantaged students in 2006–2007 went as follows: 697 (second through sixth grade), 647 (seventh and eighth grade), 616 (ninth through eleventh grade).

For disabled students, the scores were 582, 504, 464.

For white students, the scores were: 840, 807, 765.

This means California's students fare worse in school as they move up in the public education system even after many of the low performers drop out in secondary school. This trend is not unique to California. Generally speaking, student performance decreases overall as students advance onward in the American education system. Could it be that the impersonal class rotation system fails to bring about structure or academic success in America's secondary schools?

Since I was a cross-country and track athlete and coach, I often view situations in terms of running. To me, the American public education system can be seen as a relay team. There are four runners, each of whom is responsible for one leg of the mile relay: (1) The first leg consists of kindergarten through fifth grade (elementary school); this is one of our best runners, who can compete with anybody else in the world; (2) running the second leg, the sixth through eighth grades (middle school), is a below-average athlete who starts to drop behind in the race; (3) by the time he passes the baton to the third athlete, the ninth through twelfth grades (high school), several other runners have moved ahead and a major gap is created; the third relay runner falls even farther behind and may even pull up and drop out of the race; (4) if he's able to hand the baton to the fourth and final runner, the college and university system, he'll see the fourth runner moving faster and more powerfully than any other runner on the track. Our American higher education system is the best in the world. Our elementary schools are strong. The other two legs of the relay, middle school and high school, are the weakest parts of the relay and need more work.

Elementary school students have fewer discipline problems than middle and high school students. To me, the problem is not the kids. The problem is the system. The lack of structure in secondary schools accounts for many of the academic and behavioral issues found in middle and high schools. The decline in academic performance as students move up through the secondary system reinforces my belief.

From personal experience, I've found that women tend to run elementary schools, while men tend to be secondary school principals. I think women are better school administrators than men and do a more effective and efficient job of managing schools in general than men do as a whole. That is just my opinion.

I'm impressed with America's elementary schools, which are designed to meet the needs of their children. Elementary students are more likely to do their homework, establish productive working relationships with their teachers, classmates, and principal, and enjoy school. By using self-contained classrooms, elementary students build relationships with their teachers. Being with the same adult every day all day naturally creates stability. Middle and high schools lose the stability fostered in elementary schools when they place students in six different classes with six different teachers every day. When students enter secondary school, they are placed on the assembly line, and the system quickly falls apart. What I refer to as the assembly line is class rotation. You take science; I'll take history; he'll teach English; she'll teach math. Secondary schools fragment a student's life into parts. Ideally each part joins the others to create a whole education, but in reality anyone who's been through high school knows there are good teachers and bad teachers, teachers who care and those who don't. That can be true in elementary schools, too, of course, but when one teacher is in charge of one group of students for all subjects and for an entire year, more teacher accountability/structure tends to enter the picture.

Henry Ford's assembly-line method worked great with cars, but it sure screwed millions of students. There aren't many original ideas in education. We look elsewhere for inspiration but don't always consider whether it will apply well to our field. It was, like, Ford's doing it with cars, let's try it with kids. We set up this impersonal system in secondary schools that fails on many levels. I always say you couldn't create a better system to destroy kids than what we call public education in grades six through twelve, especially for kids who are fragile, troubled, or from poverty. Children need stability. Every sociological statistic tells us they need stability, so why do we use methods that create inconstancy in their lives?

I implemented the self-contained classroom at American Indian Public Charter School because it produces accountability, structure, and stability. Students don't slip through the cracks when they are with the same teacher for most of the day; they build strong relationships with their teachers and become people who are known, recognized, and acknowledged. There is no chance for an American Indian Public Charter School student to feel like just another number when he is with the same instructor and same peers day after day for three years. In a self-contained classroom, the teacher takes more responsibility for each student's education, whereas when a student rotates classes, several teachers split responsibility for his learning and performance. That means no single person is held completely accountable or responsible for any one child in a school.

In a school using rotation, a quiet, lazy student who sits in the back of the class, like myself in junior high school, can easily slide through the system. Each teacher only saw me for about forty-five minutes a day, so many overlooked the thought of challenging me when I wasn't disruptive because they had other responsibilities to attend to in class. Some students' entire middle and high school experience could be characterized as being unnoticed, getting by with the least amount of effort and learning possible, and lacking motivation and stimulation. No single individual is to blame for the child's education or lack of it; the fault lies with the system we have designed for public secondary schools.

Rotating through six to eight classes requires students to have strong *internal* motivation in order to get the most out of their education, yet the majority of students need *external* motivation. They need consequences for ditching class, for being late, for not completing homework. They need to be pushed and held accountable. That's especially true for many adolescent boys of all races.

I wasn't internally motivated when it came to academics until my twenties. As a teen, I was lazy and uninterested and didn't see the connection between school and life. People would say, "This is going to help you later." Well, later's a long darn time when you're a sixteen-year-old country Indian. I didn't have a clear understanding of how education could impact my life, and I got by with doing very little work, so I continued that pattern. Students like me need a lot of structure and not choices. Sports provided me with that accountability and structure. My high school coach Mr. Lawrence McDuffie made it very clear to me and my teammates what he wanted and what would happen if we missed practice or failed to put forth a strong effort, whereas in many high school classes when I didn't do my homework there was no consequence. I'd get a C and didn't care or think anything of it. Except for Mrs. Ann Phillips, the teacher who took me home one day in the sixth grade and forced me to do schoolwork under her supervision, I never had to stay after school for slacking off.

I needed structure and consequences, not freedom, which is also the case with many AIPCS students. My high school coaches, Lawrence McDuffie (Magnolia High), Francis "Boogie" Bass (Lumberton High), and Ralph Ortega (Sunnyside High), pushed me to achieve and kept me accountable for my actions. If secondary school administrators had the same philosophy and high expectations as the coaches who work for them, their schools would be more competitive in academics.

Let me share a story with you about Armante Washington, currently a high-achieving tenth-grader at American Indian Public High School. He came to American Indian Public Charter School in seventh grade with some bad habits, the most obvious of which was a pervasive laziness. It's hard to imagine this good-looking black teenager who now has poise, confidence, high grades, high test scores, and great attendance rates being a failure in class, but he was before he became part of our family.

Armante came to AIPCS with Cs, Ds, and Fs on his report card. He knew he was smarter than that, but Armante didn't motivate himself to do well at St. Elizabeth's, a local private school. His mom would get mad and ground him; Armante would promise to do better, but he never did. He wanted to make his mom happy, as most kids would in his situation. Minority boys especially want to make their mamas happy and proud and they're not shy to admit it, but Armante didn't know how to motivate himself in order to accomplish that. There were no strict rules at St. Elizabeth's, so he had plenty of rope to hang himself with.

When Armante first showed up with his mom, who wanted to enroll him at AIPCS, I said, "Since you didn't do anything in the seventh grade last year at your old school, I'm going to make you repeat it here." He was upset and hated the thought of being retained, but he needed a wake-up call in order to realize the consequences for being lazy. Like most of our students, Armante needed accountability and structure to do well. Without a doubt, if there were no discipline at AIPCS, the school wouldn't be anywhere near as good as it is in educating our student population.

Armante was raised by a single mom who believes in our educational philosophy. When Armante started seventh grade, he hated the rules and often had to serve detention, so he'd complain to her and say he wanted to transfer to a different school. That is a common reaction of newcomers to American Indian Public Charter School. Armante's mom kept him walking the line and said the discipline and structure were good for him. She wasn't about to let him leave because she knew improvement was around the corner.

Armante, as a tenth-grader, gets As and Bs in school, scores proficient and advanced in all his standardized test scores, and attends the prestigious Johns Hopkins University Center for Talented Youth program in the summer, where he recently took an engineering course. A visitor was impressed with Armante when, after she had spoken with him about his experiences at AIPCS, he stood up when she did and firmly shook her hand on his own initiative. It wasn't something she expected. Armante is proud now and acts accordingly. He no longer frequently serves detention, plays the fool, or acts lazy. He has a great future ahead of him and is a positive example for other students in our family.

American Indian Public Charter School provides students like Armante with solid structure and consequences for their choices. Consequences are easily enforced in self-contained classrooms. Think about it: If you had to spend all day with a particular student, such as Armante, you would make sure he followed your directions and did his work. We encourage teachers to take a "me or them" mentality. I want teachers to do whatever it takes to get students to pay attention and to work hard and smart. They know they have my support, so when a student or family member gives them a hard time, I'm there to back the teachers up. They are in control, not the students.

Teachers feel invested in their students when they have them for most of the school day. They forge strong personal relationships and want to see their students learn and progress. If you taught Armante every day for two years, you would grow close to him and recognize his intelligence and potential. He would also grow close to you. Mr. Berniker, his seventh- and eighth-grade teacher, tapped into his potential and pushed him to perform. Again, it's the structure of self-contained class-rooms and looping that creates a natural sense of stability and personal investment.

We do what's best for inner-city kids: poor, minorities, immigrants, non–English speakers, and some middle-class students who want more structure in school. When you look at the areas in which minorities succeed—sports, military, and church—you realize what they have in common. They are all highly structured and have serious consequences for stepping out of line. Public schools in the inner city, for all their talk of being culturally sensitive and aware, don't put practices in place that work for the demographic they serve. Instead of using discipline and consistent role modeling, they impose an impersonal system on students, which causes chaos. American secondary schools tend to offer students more choices and less control than many kids can responsibly handle, which is a recipe for increased student underperformance and failure.

In addition to the structure it provides, another benefit of the self-contained classroom is streamlining. Have you ever walked into a secondary school and noticed employees all over the place: teachers, librarians, security guards, counselors, administrators, teacher aides, curriculum specialists, attendance clerks, advisors, computer special-ists, janitors, and consultants? At American Indian Public Charter School, which now has 225 students, we have 1 secretary, 1 administra-tor, 3 sixth-grade teachers, 3 seventh-grade teachers, 2 eighth-grade teachers, 1 P.E. teacher, and 1 resource teacher who works 75 percent full-time. These 11.75 people are the only employees you'll find on a daily basis at AIPCS. Most districts hire too many staff persons and become bloated, especially with non-classroom employees like clerical workers, aids, administrators, and consultants. I say if the principal needs a "coach," you should fire the principal and hire the coach. Fur-thermore, overhiring full-time staff who work outside the classroom is very costly. A school's finances should be focused on teaching.

While our teachers are given lots of autonomy in the sense that they aren't required to undergo formal evaluations—believe me, I know which teachers are doing a good or lousy job—or attend frequent meet-ings or volunteer for extracurricular programs, they do have a lot of work. It is absolutely more work to be a self-contained classroom teacher in middle school than it is to teach one or two subjects. The eighth-grade teachers, for example, have to teach English, algebra, U.S. history, and physical science. The AIM-Ed system is not designed to convenience adults. We do what's best for kids. I realize, however, that to get what you want, you have to provide incentives.

In order to attract smart, hardworking teachers, we pay starting teachers $7,000 more than they would make in Oakland Unified public schools and provide bonuses for perfect staff attendance and good standardized-test results. I want AIPCS, AIPHS, and AIPCS II students to have the best teachers available to them. That's why we hire teachers who demonstrate high academic achievement in college/graduate school and who have the ability to follow our model. I pay our starting teachers significantly more than the district does because I believe in them and reward them for their hard work and for following the model, which enhances the lives of our students and teachers.

Another aspect of the self-contained class that I love is the effective use of time. Do you realize how many instructional minutes schools lose when students rotate classes frequently throughout the day?

Think of all the time that is lost when students write down their homework, pack up their books and materials, and wait for the bell to ring before exiting class. Let's say that process takes five minutes, and a student has six classes, all with different teachers. That's thirty instructional minutes down the drain each day. Furthermore, in some schools using class rotation, it's easy to ditch the next class. In a self-contained classroom, there's no way to walk out the door without a teacher knowing. Assuming students plan to attend their next class, let's take into account the time it takes them to walk there, sit down, unpack their materials, and wait for the teacher to take roll. In schools where the students are disruptive, it takes additional time to get them to settle down. Let's be conservative and say that process takes another five minutes per class, resulting in another loss of thirty instructional minutes. That means schools using six periods of class rotation lose an hour of instructional time a day, which is about the equivalent of one academic class or one-sixth of a typical school day. How can less time learning and more time rotating classes serve students' best educational interests?

# chapter six

# Looping and the Extended Family

"In elementary school, I missed over fifty days of school some years. I would fall asleep in class. I didn't pay attention. At this school, we are like a family. We work through things because we care for each other. I'm working hard to keep my grades up. . . . This is why we are the top middle school in Oakland."

—Sally Mitchell, a former AIPCS student of Sioux Indian descent,
as quoted in Free to Learn: Lessons from Model Charter Schools by Lance T. Izumi
and Xiaochin Claire Yan, 2005

In order to maximize instructional time and provide even more structure and a family atmosphere at American Indian Public Charter School, the students not only stay with the same teacher all day in a self-contained class, but the teacher follows them from one grade level to the next. A sixth-grade teacher follows his students to seventh grade and then to eighth grade. During the years when the school included ninth grade, teachers would continue teaching their students through ninth grade.

Not every teacher stays for the entire three- or four-year loop. I don't expect all of them to. Contracts are yearly; some teachers leave after one or two years or are fired before they even finish their first year.

No teacher in the years I have been principal of American Indian Public Charter School has taught for more than four years. We generally hire young, intelligent people who are full of drive. I want them to put their time in at the school and then go on to do other great things.

I'm not interested in hiring people who want to work at American Indian Public Charter School for the rest of their lives. I ask new teachers what they would like to do in the future, because I want to help them in their path of choice, whether it is school administration, law, business, or the environment. As with the students, I want to provide our teachers opportunities to grow. I hope all the teachers take some insight or lesson from the school and apply it to their future endeavors. Several teachers have become school administrators who run their own schools. In some cases, they have replicated the AIM-Ed model, which academically benefits the students they serve.

Having students stay with the same teacher year to year is structured, personal, and efficient. The students are used to their teacher, which bypasses the "breaking in" period. The teacher doesn't have to spend time evaluating each student. He or she knows what each student needs to work on, what some students might try to get away with, and how to motivate each student. Looping makes good use of instructional time throughout the school year and between each school year.

Most important, self-contained classes and looping are part of the bigger framework of building relationships. I'm always telling teachers, administrators, students, and family members that they need to build relationships with each other. Staff members serve as coaches. They're training our students for success. The staff leads by example by being dependable, intelligent, dedicated, and consistent. Our staff is clear about expectations and thorough in enforcing them. Do you remember the coaches, teachers, family members, or other role models who had a strong impact on your life? I sure do. At AIPCS, we work to create a personal system built on that type of reliable role model relationship, not a shifting class rotation where no one sees each other for more than forty minutes.

I'd like to share with you some words from Isaac Berniker, a former seventh- and eighth-grade teacher at American Indian Public Charter School, who reflects on the self-contained classroom, looping, and his relationships with his students:

> Being assigned to teach all subjects was intimidating at first. I was especially concerned about having to teach history because it wasn't a subject I felt particularly strong in. It took me a few weeks to get into a rhythm and pattern, and then I was fine and felt comfortable teaching all the subjects. I really enjoyed having the kids

with me all day because I started to develop great rapport with them. In a self-contained class, I could get so much more done because I knew where we had left off, what the students could handle, and where we needed to go from there. There is so much more control in a self-contained classroom because you aren't confined to a certain time period and subject. In a self-contained classroom, students really bond with the teacher and with each other. It is always amazing to me how good the kids are to each other and how happy and cheerful they look. With the structure, strictness, and smallness of the classes here, there aren't opportunities to form cliques. The class becomes like a family in the micro sense. Being around the students is the most fun part of the job. They make me laugh every day. I really liked looping because it gave me the opportunity to continue working with the same great group of kids. In some cases their academic improvement was incremental or part of a slow process, and in other cases the improvement was so significant it was unbelievable.

The students were so excited about their test score results on STAR. Some of them are still so excited by how much they improved and by the feeling of experiencing success. That was definitely a new feeling for some of them. I was blown away by how good they got at math by the end of eighth grade [after two years of teaching them]. When they started to get nervous for the upcoming STAR test in algebra, I reminded them, "You guys are really good at this." They all tested either proficient or advanced in algebra. It was such an awesome class accomplishment. [That was also a school record.] It's great when my former students approach me and show me their current ninth-grade report cards. They work so hard and are proud of themselves and what they have achieved.

I attribute their success in school to hours and hours of work. The kids here practice. They read. They do math. They write. They take notes. They study. They write. They practice. They do math. Hours and hours and hours and hours in school, homework. You have to get better. They come to school every day. Rain, shine, not feeling well—they come. They sit there. They listen. They do work and if they're having trouble, we get them help with tutoring. It's not magic. They've done it so many times that when they see the question on the test, they know how to do it.

I worry for my students [who went on to larger public schools after finishing eighth grade at AIPCS]. My impression is that the schools are so big, and there are a lot of kids there who have no interest in doing well. They're just kind of there. Who is going to stick up for Pauline? Who is going to challenge her? Who is going to help her if she is getting picked on? No one. Not with two to three thousand students at Skyline. . . . Who knows if Daisy, who is so smart, will pursue college at all? She wasn't doing anything over the summer, so I gave her books to read. Her parents and the others who don't speak English might not know how to gauge whether their children are being challenged enough. They don't know how to navigate the American education system.

When students leave us, we know their academic foundation will help carry them through less structured school settings. Mr. Berniker, who now teaches at American Indian Public High School, was very attached to his AIPCS students and protective of them. Do you think he would have that attitude if he only saw those students for forty minutes a day for a year?

Since American Indian Public Charter School students are together for three years and are often taught by the same teacher during the duration of that time, each class becomes its own clan. Students get really close to their teachers, such as Mr. Berniker, and each class takes on its own unique identity. Each class is a small family within the larger family. I consider the use of the self-contained classroom and looping to be an extended family or tribal model, which provides stability. Our school credo states:

The Family: We are a family at AIPCS.
The Goal: We are always working for academic and social excellence.
The Faith: We will prosper by focusing and working toward our goals.
The Journey: We will go forward, continue working, and remember we will always be part of the AIPCS family.

Notice how the credo starts and ends with family. That's very important to me. Students memorize the credo in the beginning of the year. I often visit classrooms in September, handing out money to the students who can recite it. The credo is also placed on the wall of every classroom, along with a copy of the student contract, which lists the school rules. Students carry in their notebooks copies of the credo, student contract, and mission statement.

We reinforce at American Indian Public Charter School the concepts of accountability/structure, high expectations, hard work, and family. The teacher is a surrogate parent, and I am the grandpa who showers my grandchildren, the students, with praise when they are good and scolds them when they are bad. I tell the students to treat their classmates like brothers and sisters. They will not always like some of their "family members," but they need to work out their differences and get along. They are a family who will be together for three or four years at American Indian Public Charter School.

The looping system and the concept of the extended family, which are key components of my educational model, reflect an American Indian worldview. Dr. Albert Wahrhaftig, an anthropologist and longtime friend of mine, talks about how tribes use external structures to control behavior, which is in opposition to nontribal societies. Dr. Wahrhaftig points out that white people in America are conditioned to rely on their conscience, on an internalized sense of right and wrong, as their "basic control mechanism." In a tribal society, this internalized moral code does not exist; the structure of the tribe and one's relationship within it is the control. Wahrhaftig says a tribe consists of "a constellation of relationships in which members must exist." In other words, members of a tribe are expected to behave in a certain way depending on whom they interact with. Ostracism is often the biggest punishment in a tribe. When studying Cherokees in their communities, Wahrhaftig noticed how elders would withdraw eye contact from children when they disapproved of their behavior. This sent a strong message to the children, who are conditioned to fear exclusion.

Wahrhaftig says, "We have destroyed these tribal structures, so now reservations are hotbeds of incest and suicide and alcoholism." I believe this could also be said of inner-city ghettos. Structure provides control. Remove the structure, and there is no control of human behavior. American Indian Public Charter School is set up according to a tribal model of extended family that leads to productive human relationships with boundaries that provide a system of control. The structure at AIPCS in which students stay with the same teacher throughout the day and over the years motivates the internal control of behavior, and the "constellation of relationships" maintains order, the kind necessary for sustaining a successful school in the inner city of East Oakland, California.

The structure of public secondary schools in America, with its focus on internal motivation and assembly-line education, isn't working in the inner city. Educators in places like Oakland need to create strict boundaries and high expectations for student attendance and academic achievement. There need to be consequences for acting like a fool and being lazy for both students and educators. Most high schools in Oakland are more like circuses without a circus leader than places of education. There are often no textbooks, curricula goals, or enforcement of rules. These students are only prepared to take such courses as general math, while affluent families in the hills send their children to private schools so that they can take AP calculus and AP English. It's easy for secondary students in Oakland to skip class or never even show up to school. They move from one teacher to another, and most students don't know the principal. They are not provided a school environment in which to build solid relationships with any educators. Oakland secondary schools could make major academic and social improvements by simply reducing class rotation and/or implementing self-contained classrooms. It would be a lot of work for the teachers, but it would be great for the students. Could it be that secondary schools are designed for educators and not students?

# chapter seven

# Family Involvement

"Why do I want my son to go to American Indian Public High School? For one, it's a sense of security for me to look across the street and know where my kid is at. For two, the school doesn't have a reputation for kids driving their cars and gambling and carrying weapons—the things that the high school kids are doing. It's a sense of relief for me as a concerned parent that my child is in a safe and good environment. Also that the school has high test scores. They have great credibility. It's a smaller school and the kids have less rope to hang themselves with. And they have a lot of guidance over there. They have teachers that aren't afraid to chastise them, and they get on them and set them straight. . . . I believe structure is very important because without structure and guidance, kids'll be lost. . . . The high schools now are scary. They were scary when I was there, so I can imagine. Because when I was there kids was packing guns and driving big cars and doing a lot of things that's ungodly and just degrading. . . . Other high schools in Oakland probably have guidelines, but they probably don't hold to them. You know what I'm saying? They probably say no this, no that, but do they really mean it? And I really don't think they care. A lot them's just passing these kids. They're there for a paycheck and not really for the kids. . . . I think a lot of the teachers has that attitude like if you want to come and learn, okay, maybe I'll teach you and if you don't, don't worry about it. . . . I see my son get frustrated with the homework, but I see him with a challenge now."

—*Dennis Mars, Sr.,*
*AIPHS parent, 2007*

"My daughter's teacher at Oakland High was telling us how the kids stroll in late with ice cream and we're, like, you're letting them do this. So the school's not giving them any structure, and it's going to hurt them later in life. See the structure they're giving them at American Indian, it'll help them. . . . I was on the PTA at Sherman, and I learned that parents have a lot of say. We can control things. When I asked the assistant principal at Oakland High why the kids can have electronics, he said because the parents fought for it. You know Dr. Chavis wouldn't have gone for that. We need to have two or three Dr. Chavises at each school. . . . The sense of respect has gone out the window. My pastor said in a sermon, 'We ruined our children.' It started back in the '60s with all the freedom stuff. What's happened is—you know how something starts simmering and it simmers and it starts dripping and dripping and all of a sudden it's overflooded? Well, we're in a flood right now. . . . Now with our children we have no control. We want control back, but it's almost too late. Drugs got heavy. Parents stopped being parents. And a lot of the boys are in jail. . . . Kids are angry because they don't know anything. They don't know how to fill out an application. They feel embarrassed; they don't feel important; they're ashamed, so they're, like, the best way I can deal with you is to cuss you out. They're ignorant. . . . And there's competition out there. We've got a lot of foreigners coming over here and they's kicking your butt. They taking over! You need to open your eyes and wake up and look around you and look at who owns everything right in your own community. . . . I told my daughter Roshea, 'You've got to know and believe that the reason you got where you are is because you had people like Ms. Simmons and Dr. Chavis encouraging you. You had them encouraging you constantly.'"

—*Priscilla Wilson,*
*parent of former AIPCS students, 2007*

We guarantee the families whose children attend our school that if they support our educational model by allowing us to educate how we see best, their children will be prepared to graduate from college. What we ask for is some trust and loyalty to AIPCS's mission.

In order for the school to function properly, I do *not* believe in requesting or relying on "parent involvement." We are not going to burden the family members of students who are barely making ends meet or tell them they are responsible for the school's success or failure or that they need to raise money and volunteer. That is hogwash. The staff and I are responsible for the school's success, and I am responsible for its fiscal stability.

How do educators expect poor parents to take time off of work in order to volunteer in schools? Many of the parents are uneducated and/or non–English speaking. My stepdad is illiterate, and my mom was only able to go to school for one month a year between planting seasons until she was about twelve years old, when she stopped going to school completely because she was needed in the fields. Why would schools want to put the onus on people like them to improve children's education? Isn't that the school's job? A colleague of mine saw a sign outside of a middle school in the heart of a poor, first-generation Mexican neighborhood announcing a shadow day in which parents follow their children through one school day. Do you think those parents can afford to take time off of work to do that? It featured a quote about taking responsibility for the outcome of your own life. Shouldn't schools take responsibility for their students? Isn't that their role and function? "Parent involvement" is often a scapegoat for educators working with minorities. It gives them someone to blame other than themselves for the lack of learning taking place in dysfunctional classrooms.

All we ask of family members is that they make sure their children get to school on time with a lunch and in dress code. My staff and I will do the rest. It is our job and our responsibility to provide an academic education for our students. I am not going to expect family members who can't speak English or do basic math to help their children with algebra homework. If a student needs extra help, we provide free tutoring at AIPCS, which releases a great deal of pressure on our families.

I disagree with the term "parent involvement" because it focuses on the nuclear family and disregards the extended family, which is so important in minority and rural communities. My grandparents played a large role in raising me. Many minorities have incredibly strong relationships with relatives other than their moms or dads, and many live with a grandma or other relative. A large percentage of our students either don't know their fathers or don't have much contact with them. I seek the person in the family with whom I can have the most productive relationship. If a student's dad ain't worth the air he breathes, I'm not going to waste my time trying to talk sense to him. It's all about finding the people who understand what you're trying to do for their child and are willing to support you.

I think the type of family involvement we have at AIPCS is very similar to that of the white middle class of the 1950s. When you ask a white, middle-class baby boomer from the earliest part of his generation about what happened to him at home if he caused trouble in school, the story usually went something like this: After the student got punished in class, the teacher called home and reached his parents, who grounded him. His parents made it clear that his behavior would not be tolerated at school or at home and that it was an embarrassment to their family to have to be called by the school. The parents said if they heard again from the school that their son was screwing off, he was going to be one sorry young man. He knew his parents meant what they said.

That was the type of involvement typical of parents two generations ago. Families didn't question the teachers' judgment or make excuses for their children. It was about support, not interference. Men and women who are now about fifty or more years old in this country remember how their families believed in the mission of the local schools and supported their use of discipline, which they thought was good for kids. The families built relationships and trusted the judgment of educators.

Most children were raised to mind adults then. As a child, you might not have liked what Grandma told you to do, but you obeyed. It was about respect and knowing your place. Children didn't bother complaining about what had happened to them in school, either. They knew their family members weren't going to take their side. Heck, my mama didn't even want to hear my version of the story. You put your head down and said yes, sir, or yes, ma'am. You were considered an embarrassment to your family when you did something to warrant a call or visit at home from the school. Adults in the community took care of children by making them walk the line.

At American Indian Public Charter School, the style of family involvement is more like the kind that today's fifty-year-olds experienced when they were growing up, which is something our families understand and respect about the school. Often when students get a detention or are made an example of at AIPCS, their families take the attitude of, "You deserved to get in trouble and have to deal with the conse-quences." I have had parents tell me to swat their kids if they're acting like a clown. I'd rather embarrass them in front of the other students, because it becomes a teaching moment. Many of our families are of the "old-school" mentality. Mexican families, for example, are accustomed to strict schools because the grammar schools they attended in Mexico didn't play around.

Pretty much across the board, the families whose children attend American Indian Public Charter School want the structure and disci-pline that the school provides. They don't want their kids goofing off, acting like fools, and not working. Who would want that? Unfor-tunately, that's what they get at most Oakland secondary schools. Fam-ily members drop by AIPCS all the time asking how they can get their child into our school. Some come in, and their kids are only in third grade! They'll say their son or daughter is not learning or behaving in school, and they want more structure and accountability. They like the rules and discipline that AIPCS offers.

Andrea Lloyd, for example, the mother of sixth-grader Mariah Smith, said she was drawn to the school because she liked the rules, the homework, and the uniform policy. She shared her belief that all schools in Oakland should be run like AIPCS because they aren't strict enough, the class sizes are too big, and the kids are rowdy. Ms. Lloyd prefers that Mariah be in the same class with the same teacher every day in-stead of rotating classes, because she hopes the extra attention of the self-contained classroom will lead to academic improvement. Mariah was below grade level before she came to AIPCS. I assure you that will not be the case when she graduates from AIPCS.

When asked by a visitor if my ranting and swearing bothered her or made her question the learning environment her daughter is in, Ms. Lloyd replied, "Dr. Chavis is a cool person. He's not doing anything that I don't do at home or that the students don't hear on TV or in the neighborhood. Some kids need that tough love."

Ms. Lloyd's opinions about strictness, homework, and tough love are ones I hear every day from folks dropping by.

What are the main reasons families want their kids at American Indian Public Charter School? (1) They know our students are taught academics and that we're the best school; (2) they believe their child needs discipline; and (3) their friend or relative went here and highly recommended it, so they want their child here, too. I love the No Child

Left Behind Act; without it there wouldn't be as much concrete data for the families to access. Now they can compare schools' academic performance and then pass the information on to friends and relatives. The school's popularity in the community has mostly come through word of mouth and the media.

Once students are admitted, we won't be flexible about the rules, which occasionally creates an uproar. When families come and create drama you don't need, you need to make it clear where the door is and what their options are. People think since schools exist to serve students, when families are unhappy that means we need to do something about it. Well, sometimes ghetto and/or educated families complain about ridiculous things, like wanting their child's cell phone back. We have a policy that any student whose cell phone goes off or is visible will have it confiscated until the end of the school year. We also have a policy that says families are not allowed to drop off lunches to their children. These two policies are clearly written in the student contract, which is signed before students are admitted to the school and then sent home again on the first day of school after being discussed extensively in class. There is no way these policies catch anyone off guard.

The most common family complaints have to do with cell phones and lunches. No family member has ever come to me and complained that his or her child is not learning enough. Believe me, if families have legitimate issues, we listen. But when mamas come in hollering about a cell phone being taken or a lunch not being delivered, I don't waste my time with them. As far as I'm concerned, if they're unhappy and want to withdraw a child from school over something so silly, there's something wrong with them.

When we allowed families to drop off lunches, the office became a mess of brown paper bags and excuse-making parents. It was a headache. As a result, I made it a rule that students had to bring their lunch with them to school if they wanted to eat. I figured if a student forgot his lunch at home and didn't like feeling hungry all day, he'd remember to bring it with him the next day. Some loony adults will try to say we're responsible for the child's health if he didn't have a lunch or we're responsible for the child's safety if we take a cell phone. Our rules are clearly explained in the student contract and in person several times. It's called personal responsibility, which we teach the students. Why is personal responsibility a scary idea for some family members?

It's interesting to me that the families who are non-English-speaking immigrants rarely complain or blame the school. They have a different mentality than their American-born or second- and third-generation immigrant neighbors, who have made it a habit to spoil their children on the one hand but lose track of the bigger picture called education on the other hand. Unlike the first-generation immigrants who remember how tough life was in another country, the others can get so up in arms about a confiscated cell phone that they opt to pull their child out to regain the phone rather than waiting until the end of the year and giving their child a good education along the way. The administrative assistant, Ms. Sophath Mey, and I protect the teachers and students from the rare times when irate or irrational family members barge through the door wanting to have it out with someone.

There are options for families who have a problem with my method of education, which involves embarrassing students for inappropriate behavior and providing structure, discipline, and respect. I have been known to cuss out a few family members who want to meet the savage in me. American Indian Public Charter School is a charter school, so families opt to send their children here. Once enrolled, if families have issues with AIPCS, they can always transfer their children to another public or private school. There should be school choice for all families.

When people write letters of complaint to the school, I enjoy scribbling notes on the more inflammatory and nonsensical ones. I have often written on their letters, "Are you a fool, an idiot, or a drug addict?" and then sent them back. In most cases it seems they belong to the first two categories.

Families don't get very far with me when their complaints are ridiculous. When a dad gets crazy about a detention his child clearly deserved, I don't want to waste my time talking to him about it. I am a pragmatic leader, not an ideologue, like many of the weak secondary school principals. I know how to deal with fools of all races and languages and walks of life. If you allow yourself to get bogged down by them, you neglect the important task of educating children.

Though we serve mostly children of low-income families, a few middle-class students attend. They have the highest likelihood of leaving because middle-class parents love to schedule a meeting and share their feelings on how things should be done in a school. They try to micromanage too much for my taste. It's never the middle-class child who is the problem—it is the parent.

There is a wooden sign in my office that some eighth-grade students carved as a gift for me in 2003. It states, "Family members, what have you done to help American Indian Public Charter School be the best school?" The question is adapted from a Mormon message President John F. Kennedy modified and made famous with: "Ask not what your country can do for you; ask what you can do for your country." A couple teachers found the sign puzzling when I first put it up. They knew I didn't buy into the parent involvement advocated in public schools. The gist of what I was saying became clearer when I had the teachers deliver a memo to all of their students that congratulated the families who subscribed to the school rules and criticized the families who refused to abide by the rules. The memo, dated March 16, 2006, featured the subject line "AIPCS rules and selective memory." It read as follows:

I respect the parents who support our staff and accept the consequences when their child breaks the rules. You are preparing your children to be successful in school and life. You can stop reading this now!

Why do some parents of AIPCS students have selective memories? If your child brings a cell phone to school and it is taken by a staff member, you will not get it back until the last day of school. You have the option to withdraw your child from AIPCS. We will return the cell phone and accept students who will follow our rules.

Is there anyone in their right mind who believes I am going to change the rules of American Indian Public Charter School because of a sad story, an argument, or a cussing out? I grew up with a whole family of crazy Indians and I can act like a fool with the best of you. I am always nice to people who are nice to me.

Why do some of you love to threaten that you are going to the school board to get me fired? Will you please get me fired? I have already retired in Arizona and get a monthly check. I would love to spend more time with my wife, children, and grandchildren and collect another check.

Once again, I respect families who reinforce to your child the importance of following the rules.

Students who transfer to other schools usually do so because of decisions—often irrational—their families make. Some students become like nomads when they leave AIPCS. Nickie Wildhorse was a sixth-grade student who did not do her work and disrupted class, so we retained her in the sixth grade. After a couple of months of repeating sixth grade, Nickie's mom decided to withdraw her from American Indian Public Charter School. Within a year, she attended three other public schools and dropped out of each one.

Our students are somebody when they are at AIPCS. The rigid structure held so firmly in place ensures they receive the attention and guidance needed to succeed. When their families reject that structure and enroll them in a different school, many never graduate. Families tell me there are no cracks to fall through at our school. There aren't many schools in Oakland where that statement would hold true. Most Oakland Unified schools fail to provide students with the basic writing, mathematics, and human-relations skills they need to be productive members in our modern society.

Generally, I have great relationships with our students' families. Most of them are thrilled when they find out their children will attend American Indian Public Charter School. Families frequently drop by the school to visit, bring food to share, express their appreciation, and just chat. I laugh and talk with them about how well their children are doing, and they are genuinely happy with the safe, structured, academic environment we provide. We have great family involvement at American Indian Public Charter School.

Families realize that part of the school's safety and control comes from my method of dealing with fools that I learned from my grandpa. Sometimes you must be willing to match or outdo people's hollering, ranting, and acting a fool. Being kind and tolerant can send the message to some families that you are a weak school administrator. My method prevents undisciplined students, families, and visitors from undermining the school culture of structure and academics that the vast majority of our families want.

# chapter eight

# Meet the Escobars

"I'm really grateful to Dr. Chavis for what he's done for other people's kids. My family is living proof. I've seen them go so far."

—*Julia Escobar,*
*mother of three children who attend AIPCS and AIPHS, December 2007*

In 2000, Julia Escobar needed to find a suitable school for her son Marco for sixth grade. After being turned away by several Oakland public schools, Ms. Escobar did not know what to do. The school year was well under way, and Marco was not enrolled anywhere.

Ms. Escobar had heard about charter schools and knew they were generally small, which she thought would be good for her son, who has a learning disability and mental condition. She had heard about AIPCS from her friend Stacy Moreno and decided to pay a visit.

When Ms. Escobar entered the office with Marco following her like a little puppy, I chatted with her and asked her where Marco went to school and about her family. It's interesting to me the difference between the way most middle-class whites and poor minorities make their initial introductions. Whites often cut right to the chase. They introduce themselves and inquire about the business at hand. Minorities approach the business at hand in a circular fashion. Some say I go around the block before I get to the point. I am indeed guilty. Minorities ask questions and share stories that get to the core of family and their background.

I usually find the humor in things when I'm with someone. For example, I might ask, "How you doing, dear?" to a woman who walks into the office with a baby in her arms and proceed to joke about the baby's size. That will get her to talk about the baby's birth, which will lead to me talking about my children and grandchildren. We put each other at ease and show ourselves as human beings before moving on to practical matters. Anyway, it's just the way I do things. It was that way for my mama, grandma, and anyone else I grew up with in our small Indian community of Saddletree, North Carolina.

While talking with Ms. Escobar, I noticed that Marco, who hadn't said a word, was tall for his age and stiff as a board. It was like his body parts had been sewn together by a 350-pound lineman. I came to the conclusion that he was the Mexican-Indian movie-star version of Frankenstein by the way he moved and walked. I said, "Boy, we have to get you in P.E. to limber you up a bit." He did not say a word and just looked down at the floor.

I often ask students to read to me a few lines from a book, newspaper, or anything else that's around when we first meet. It gives me insight into their reading ability. When I asked Marco to read a paragraph, he couldn't. So I pointed to a "c" and asked him what letter that was. He said he didn't know. He could recognize an "a." With the exception of his name, Ms. Escobar said, her son couldn't read or write a lick, and he had just been passed on to the sixth grade. Can you imagine how this troubled his mother?

My first thought was that Marco was mentally retarded. I knew for a fact he had some kind of learning problem. I've noticed minorities won't put a name or label on what's mentally wrong with their relatives; they'll say he's got a problem or he's not right. My mom says that about my sister, that she's different. It's just an interesting cultural difference of describing a person. Middle-class people will talk about how their child has a condition and how he is taking medication that the doctor is monitoring. In our family, we don't have a fancy name to put on what's wrong when a person's not quite like everybody else. So we just say he's different, which is true!

To this day, if you ask Ms. Escobar or one of her children what's wrong with Marco, they'll say they don't know or that they don't know how to pronounce the word that identifies his condition. Let's just say I knew Marco had some serious learning problems, and his mom reminded me of some of my people. In my heart I had no choice but to help Marco and his mother.

That day in the office, Ms. Escobar said she didn't know what to do with her son, who had been turned away from other public schools and clearly needed a lot of help. She asked me if I would take him. I said absolutely and told her I wouldn't let her down. I said, "Marco just needs to try his best. I love a kid who tries." I could tell she was relieved and happy. Can you imagine the feeling as a single parent of not finding a good public school that will accept your child because you don't live in a certain neighborhood and have a child with learning problems? Ms. Escobar certainly didn't have the means to send him to private school. It would be a hard situation for any family to deal with. I told Ms. Escobar to bring Marco to school the very next day. He needed to get started. We had some real work ahead of us. Heck, thinking back on it, I should have made him start right on the spot.

In his first year at AIPCS, Marco was like a lost person wandering around in his own world. It was difficult getting him used to coming to school on time and following the classroom schedule. I was trying to get special education resources for him, but with all the bureaucratic mess and the paperwork and the waiting, we didn't receive special education from OUSD for the boy until almost two years had passed. Though it was a long delay, I must say Oakland Unified has a great special education program with a talented, dedicated staff. Jean Simpson, Melinda Madigan, and A. J. Robinson have done excellent work with our students over the years. In addition, my friend and colleague Tom Hanson set up AIPCS's special education program and did an evaluation of Marco before we got help from the district. When we got Marco approved, I worked with the special education staff to get government subsidies for him. Normally I don't tell families to apply for financial assistance from the government. I believe in hard work! But I knew that it would be a challenge for Marco to live on his own as he got older. He was going to need financial support.

Marco's first year at the school was my own first year at the school. We were both in survival mode. Marco was beyond introverted. He looked unhappy and didn't talk to anyone. In fact, in general he was unresponsive—to the students, to the teacher, to school, to everything, really. I wanted to see some life in him, to get him to smile, to talk.

Marco would see me every day that first year of sixth grade, but he could not come up with my name. He'd say, "Who are you?" I'd tease him that it was about time he started to recognize me. About one year later he eventually did and said, "Hi, Dr. Chavis," with a shy smile when he walked by. Marco later told me he wasn't used to seeing principals around. I don't think he realized that principals could be caring human beings. He either rarely saw his elementary school principals or didn't know who they were when he did see them. They must not have taken much time out of their day to get to know Marco. It was their loss.

For most of his public elementary education, Marco was placed in bilingual Spanish classes. He could speak Spanish, but he couldn't write it. He was even worse off when it came to English. Obviously Marco couldn't do sixth-grade work like the rest of the students if he couldn't read or write. We mainstream all our special education students, meaning we put them in the same class as all the other students their age, but we have modified goals for them. In Marco's case, we started by trying to get him to recognize all the letters of the alphabet and to understand the sounds those letters make when put together. By being in a classroom and hearing the lessons from his sixth-grade teacher and hearing his classmates talk, Marco's listening comprehension improved. It was a start.

Marco began to look a little more at ease and aware of others and started getting used to the class routine. He started making more eye contact. After a year of small academic and social strides, I thought it would be best to retain Marco in sixth grade and have him repeat the year with his younger sister Roxana, who would be starting the sixth grade. I told Ms. Escobar that I wanted to retain Marco so he could be with Roxana and have a chance to improve academically. She said, "I trust you to do what's right for my son." It was great that she put her confidence in me and let me do my job with her children.

Marco and Roxana started sixth grade with Ms. Yamauchi, who would be their teacher for sixth, seventh, and eighth grade. Marco grew to really like Ms. Yamauchi, who he stayed in touch with via e-mail after graduating from American Indian Public Charter School in eighth grade. This was the same boy who couldn't even identify a "c" when he first came to AIPCS. The personal relationships created in a self-contained classroom and the structure provided by being with Ms. Yamauchi each day for three years was great for Marco and his sister.

Marco wasn't happy about being held back and having to be in the same class as his younger sister, however. He didn't want to be with her because he was older and found it embarrassing. I couldn't care less that he was embarrassed. I did what I thought was best for his education at AIPCS. Marco and Roxana were seated next to each other in sixth and seventh grade. Roxana frequently helped Marco with his class work and homework. It helped Marco to have his sister there because it made it easier for him to focus.

Early into Marco's second year of sixth grade, I addressed his class like a father who needs his children to understand that their special brother deserves to be treated with respect. I said that Marco was born with a lot of heart. He was a great boy, nice to everybody, never got into fights. I said they were born with a lot of brains, but they could benefit from his heart. When it came to heart, he had something special that they should all strive toward. They were lucky to be in the presence of such a genuinely nice boy. I told them they'd better take care of him and treat him with respect, because if they ever let anything happen to him or they did anything mean to him, they didn't even want to imagine what I'd do to them. I put them in charge of protecting and teaching Marco.

Young students like these sixth-graders want to please their teachers and principals, do what has been asked of them, and be recognized for being good, so they really took Marco under their wing. They were nice to him. None of them picked on him. I could tell he'd been picked on before at his other schools, and Marco told me about some of it. He said kids used to hit him on the head, imitate him, and laugh at him. I know that sounds mean, and it is, but sometimes kids in elementary school don't realize they're being cruel. They think they're being funny. The AIPCS students knew I wasn't going to deal with any of that nonsense from them. I truly believe that Marco and people like him are advanced when it comes to matters of the heart—of being nice, good, pure people; the rest of us are often special ed in the same category.

Marco started to warm up more and more to me. He'd often come to school late—probably because his mom worked nights and had a hard time getting him to class on time—and he'd bring me food. He loved to cook and said he wanted to be a chef at Taco Bell, which was a block away, so he could cook and take care of his mom, whom he thought worked too much. One day during Marco's second year at AIPCS, Marco walked into the office fifteen minutes late for school with a plate in his hands covered with tinfoil. He said sheepishly, "Dr. Chavis, I brought you food." I said, "Marco, you're late again. You're just trying to bribe me, aren't you?" He grinned at me and said, "I cooked eggs and tortillas." That boy loved to cook eggs. I laughed as he handed me the food and said, "Thanks, but get your late ass to class, boy." He smiled and said, "Ohh-kay," and shuffled out with his head bent slightly to the side.

I remember one day in sixth grade Marco took a test, got everything wrong, and then asked Ms. Yamauchi, "Can I do it again? I'll do better." What more could you ask of any student? Ms. Yamauchi was great with that boy. She kept working with him on his language arts, and slowly but surely he learned. By the end of that year (two years at AIPCS), he could read and write! We were so proud of him. This was the boy who didn't know the alphabet when he started.

I loved seeing Marco's sense of humor develop. By the start of seventh grade, Marco acted more and more comfortable around other people, even though he was still really shy. He started to smile and laugh more. Because I knew he loved Mexican food I would take him to a Mexican restaurant down the street called Gerardo's. He'd get so excited when I told him where we were going. One day when we were in line at Gerardo's with the smell of carne asada and cilantro rising behind the counter, I said, "Do you have any money, Marco?" I was just teasing him. He said no. "How are you going to pay for this food?" He just looked at me. I said, "Well, if you don't have any money, you're going to be stuck here washing dishes all night in order to pay for it." He said, "That's okay," and smiled. I laughed and said, "Well, today's your lucky day because I'm going to pay for your food." He grinned so wide I thought he was the happiest lunch companion I'd ever had. Some of his other classmates would get jealous and say, "How come you always take Marco out to lunch and not us?" I'd reply, "If you worked as hard as him, I'd take you out to lunch, too."

By the time Marco made his way to eighth grade, he had come a long way. He could not only read, write, and do more independent work, but he also had made huge strides socially. I'll never forget the day in eighth grade when Marco got a detention for talking in class. I was so proud of him. Usually I'm mad when students talk when they're supposed to work. This time, I was excited that Marco had talked loud and long enough to actually be considered disruptive. That was progress!

To me personally, Marco is our greatest accomplishment as educators at American Indian Public Charter School. He went from not knowing the alphabet or how to communicate with other people to being able to read, write, smile, and have conversations with all of us. By the middle of eighth grade, the boy was a hit with all the students and staff at AIPCS.

Toward the end of Marco's eighth-grade year, I brought him up in front of the whole school one lunch period. I asked everyone to quiet down so I could say a few words. All the students attending American Indian Public Charter School turned toward Marco and me standing in the center of the gym. I said, "I just wanted to bring your attention today to Marco Escobar here who works so hard. This boy is incredible. The improvements he's made since he first came to this school are outstanding. He succeeds because he works harder than anyone else. Can you guys work as hard as Marco?" The students hollered "yes" in unison. I continued to banter and made the students assure me they were going to work hard like Marco. By the end of lunch, the gym was resounding with the sound of the students clapping for him.

When Marco graduated from eighth grade American Indian Public High School didn't exist, so I wanted to help his mom find the best high school possible for him. The special education teacher recommended Mandela High School, which was part of the Fremont Federation, a cluster of small high schools in Oakland Unified School District funded by the Gates Foundation.

When I hear the names "Mandela High" and "Fremont Federation," and they're located in the Bay Area, what is the first thought that comes to my mind? Ideological nonsense. Nonetheless, I accompanied Ms. Escobar, the special education teacher, and the principal of Mandela High on a tour of the school. The history classroom we walked into had only one set of textbooks that were passed out each period to the students and then collected at the end of the class. The students could not take the books home. How were they going to do their homework effectively? A twenty-foot chain-link fence surrounded the campus like a penitentiary. The principal tried to walk us from Mandela High over to another school on the same campus, but she forgot the key to the gate, so we were penned in like sheep. At that point she asked me what I thought of the school. I said, "Well, it reminds me of the prison Mandela was in in South Africa." The principal had no response and just smiled. I told Ms. Escobar later there was no way she should send Marco to that crazy place.

After visiting more schools, Ms. Escobar chose San Lorenzo High School for Marco. He is now nineteen and in twelfth grade in a special education program there. He's going to graduate this year. He passed the math part of the CAHSEE (the California High School Exit Exam) but not the English part. As always, Marco tries really hard. I believe he will pass the CAHSEE and earn his high school diploma this year. I know he is getting a better education at San Lorenzo High School than he would ever get at Mandela High School.

Ms. Escobar often shares with me how happy she is with Marco's progress. She recently told me, "Now Marco can read at least at a ninth-grade level. He has the skills to be able to work out of the home. He's a shy, introverted person. I'm not going to be here forever, so my children need to learn how to be independent." I have confidence Marco will do just fine and have a good life. I have said a hundred times that Marco's kindness and dedication to hard work is an example for us all at AIPCS.

Marco says he wants to join the military after graduating high school so he can help our country, a desire I respect. Many people believe minorities are only interested in the military because we are desperate for money or have no other options. I do not buy this pigheaded thinking for one second. We join the armed forces because we love our country. I think minorities overall are militaristic, nationalistic, and ready to display loyalty to the United States. Deep down we believe everyone is out to get us, so we're prepared to defend our homeland and ourselves. That mentality, along with a desire to show strength and courage, motivates many minorities to enlist. Minorities are overrepresented in the armed forces compared to whites. The military would be lucky to have a young man like Marco serving.

My uncle Carl Walter Bell said to me one time that the American flag is an Indian symbol. I was a little boy sitting on the porch listening to my uncle and Grandpa Calvin, the drunk philosophers, talk. My uncle explained that the blue in the American flag represented the sky, the white was the creator, and the red—"That's us," he said. My uncle was a World War II veteran, and like many Indians, he internalized the American flag and made it a symbol of his own. When he fought in the war, he fought for his people, his land, and his country. When I was a graduate student at the University of Arizona, Dr. Robert K. Thomas, a Cherokee Indian, shared the same story with me about the American flag. Per capita, American Indians have the highest record of service of all the ethnic groups in this country. Over forty-two thousand American Indians served in the Vietnam War, and over 90 percent of those troops were volunteers. So when minorities like Marco, who is Mexican-Indian, want to enlist in the armed forces, don't assume they're doing it for money, because they've been duped, or because they have no other options in life. Those are all popular portrayals in leftist, antiwar politics. For many minorities, it is an honor to serve their country. In turn, we must honor them by respecting their wishes, which is indeed true tolerance.

The entire Escobar family, not just Marco, is very special to me. I'd like to share a little with you about the other family members to give you an idea of what their lives and AIPCS experiences have been like. I view the Escobar family—though unique in their own way—as representative of many of our AIPCS families with the challenges they face and the successes they've worked hard for in our country.

I see the sacrifices Ms. Escobar makes for her children, and it motivates me to do anything I can to help her. Ms. Escobar financially supports her four children by working graveyard shifts from 5:00 p.m. to 1:30 a.m. as a janitor for Kaiser Permanente. She has worked like that for the past twenty years. In order to make it easier for her children to get to school, they stay at their aunt's house part of the week, so Ms. Escobar can't spend as much time with them as she would like. Ms. Escobar came into Texas from Mexico as a young girl and was pregnant by age sixteen, like my mother, and dropped out of school. Later, she moved to California and worked odd jobs for minimum wage. Now, in addition to working as a janitor, Ms. Escobar buys and sells old used cars at auction.

When Ms. Escobar and Roxana asked me for guidance about Roxana's high school plans, I was eager to help. The charter high school Roxana had attended, Uprep, was shut down by its own board at the end of her junior year when Oakland Unified School District began to investigate allegations of cheating on Uprep's STAR tests, faulty transcripts that inflated students' grades and/or claimed they took courses they had not, and fraudulent attendance records that would have led to higher funding than merited.

Though American Indian Public High School was up and running, we didn't have a twelfth grade to offer Roxana. We had opened AIPHS the year before with ninth and tenth grades with the intention of adding grade levels when our students advanced. We were about to kick off our second year in operation, with eleventh grade as the highest grade level. When I looked at the classes Roxana had taken and saw she was behind our students as far as the academic track she was on, I realized we could enroll her in the courses our eleventh-graders were taking. She would have enough units and courses to satisfy the high school graduation requirements, would meet the requirements for college admission, and would take new classes.

Roxana spent about four hours a night on homework that year. Because she hadn't been challenged academically for three years, she had catching up to do. Ms. Escobar would often come home from work at two in the morning to find Roxana up studying Mandarin, a language requirement for our AIPHS students. Roxana is diligent and the type of person who believes in finishing what she starts. She could have chosen an easy high school in Oakland and had dances and football games and all the rest of that. Instead, she chose a khaki-pants-and-white-collared-shirt uniform, strict rules, and difficult academics, because she knew that's what she needed.

When Roxana sent her first college application to Cal State East Bay in the fall, she wondered what would happen. Imagine her delight and her mother's excitement when they received news ten days later that she'd been accepted! Over the course of the next few months, however, I started realizing that even though Roxana had received an offer of college admission and was ahead of the game compared to most Oakland teens, she was below our AIPHS standard. It wasn't her fault; she hadn't been given the proper training at her other high schools. I thought she would benefit from repeating twelfth grade, and I said that to Roxana and her mother. I made it clear that she had met the graduation requirements and been accepted to college, but I thought it better for her to take another year of courses with our twelfth-graders in order to strengthen her academic skills. Ms. Escobar said, "I know you'll always do what's best for my children, so that's what we will do." Roxana agreed to it as well.

After another academic year, Roxana will be even better prepared for higher education. After she finishes at American Indian Public High School, I am confident she will be ready to bear the honor of being the first person in her mother's family to go to college. Roxana's achievement, and what it will mean for her and the Escobar family, makes me really happy and proud. When our students graduate from college, they not only change their own lives but also enhance their families' lives and serve as role models for the other students at AIPCS and AIPHS.

Meanwhile, Alex, the third Escobar sibling, who had been quite a work in progress, made great strides as an eighth-grader at American Indian Public Charter School. Unlike the hardworking Roxana and Marco, Alex started sixth grade needing a reality check. He had been used to goofing off and being lazy at Hawthorne Elementary School, so when he got here he found out the hard way that I didn't play. I told him he was an embarrassment to the Escobar family, to Indians, and to Mexicans when he was lazy as an old, mangy dog. That boy was always in detention, sweeping the hallway, and cleaning up around the school during his sixth- and seventh-grade years because he didn't want to work in class. I have a process of trying everything in my power to motivate a student: rewards, payments, praise or detention, Saturday school, cleaning, and shaming. With Alex, nothing was working. I used to bring him up in front of the whole school to make an example of him. Though Alex didn't like the embarrassments, he didn't change. The clincher with students like Alex, when all else fails, is retention.

When I told Ms. Escobar Alex would have to repeat seventh grade, she supported the idea, which was rare. Imagine that: Ms. Escobar agreed to my suggestions to retain all three of her oldest children. Most parents hate the thought of keeping their child back a grade, but I don't do things to please parents if it's not in the child's best interest. I don't push students on to the next grade who haven't earned it just so they can be with their friends. We all want things in life, but have we earned them? That is the key. Students have to earn their success and not just get moved on to the next grade because someone feels sorry for them. I don't feel sorry for the students who act like fools or are lazy. I treat them like fools. They respect me for being consistent with them.

Alex's retention was his turning point in school. It was the wake-up call he needed. Alex accepted responsibility for not doing his best and vowed to be a better student by working harder and controlling his be-havior. His grades went from Ds and Cs to Bs and As. When his STAR test results came back in August 2007, everyone's mouths dropped open. He had been below basic in sixth grade and basic his first year of seventh grade. Imagine his surprise, then, when he tested advanced in language arts and math his second year of seventh grade! Alex's mom was so shocked, in fact, that she called the school to see if Alex was trying to pull a quick one on her. Neither of them thought he would ever score advanced in school.

Alex has gone from acting like a fool to acting like a winner. Now I treat him like a winner, and he loves it. He's become a positive example to other students rather than the class clown. Alex volunteers to work with the new students who come into AIPCS with his former attitude toward school.

Educators love talking about making their schools into communities, but few of them can really live up to what they say and do the work it takes to create a community. I can honestly say we've created a community at American Indian Public Charter School. Families like the Escobars send all their children here and expect us to do right by them. They get to know our staff and see me as a family mentor and elder. They refer their friends and family members to the school and tell them to send their children to us. It's rewarding to me that these great families choose American Indian Public Charter School.

Ms. Escobar told me how impressed she is with how much her children have learned, matured, and succeeded. When her youngest son, Brian, is old enough to go to AIPCS, she plans to enroll him as well. Brian, like Marco, has a mental condition. It'll be tough, but I know our staff can do just as much for Brian as we did for Marco.

Ms. Escobar said one day, "You know, Dr. Chavis, it takes two mules to pull the cart. It takes the kids pulling and you pulling to make things happen." I absolutely agreed and pointed out that the excellent staff and supportive family members help pull the cart, too. It's a joint effort. Marco, Roxana, and Alex forged ahead with their own effort, with the support of their mom, and with the help of dedicated teachers and administrators at American Indian Public Charter School and American Indian Public High School who have high expectations and prepare students to achieve them. Those involved at AIPCS work as hard as any team of mules who have ever pulled together.

# chapter nine

# High Expectations and an Academic Focus

"If you go to this school you can expect many doors opening for you."

—*Irene Vega,*
*a seventh-grader at AIPCS in 2007–2008*

I believe most people tend to live up to the expectations you have for them. When you have high academic expectations for students, they will work hard to fulfill those expectations. When you have low expectations, students will not work hard and will meet your low expectations. Educators can moan and groan that the system is unfair, racist, classist, that their students' upbringing has not properly prepared them for the academic rigor of middle- and upper-class neighborhoods, that immigrants cannot learn English well enough to compete with their American-born peers, that some cultures are not conducive to learning through rote reading and writing. I've heard it all. You provide students with all kinds of reasons why they cannot succeed in school, and they will ultimately live up to your low expectations and prove you right. I love to prove the excuse makers wrong and have my students outperform everyone's expectations of them.

Many educators in Oakland do not believe their students can excel in math. They put them on a remedial math track, where they stay throughout their education. How do you get better at math if you are always given limited exposure to it and the impression that you will never excel at it?

For the 2007–2008 school year, 2,624 ninth-, tenth-, and eleventh-graders in Oakland Unified took algebra. Ninety-seven percent of them failed the algebra STAR exam at the end of the year. That means 3 percent, or about 79 students, tested proficient. Of those 2,624 ninth-, tenth-, and eleventh-graders, 0 percent tested advanced! How is that possible in any school district in America? Could it be that Oakland teens are all dumb? No. They are just fulfilling low expectations. How do I know? Because we had poor American Indian, Asian, black, and Hispanic students from Oakland taking algebra for an hour and a half every day in eighth grade at AIPCS for the 2007–2008 school year, and 100 percent of them tested proficient or advanced in algebra. All of our eighth-graders take algebra. They have no other choice.

All the ninth-graders at American Indian Public High School take geometry. In 2007–2008, the STAR results revealed that 86 percent of our AIPHS ninth-graders tested proficient or advanced in geometry, and 79 percent of our tenth-graders tested proficient or advanced in algebra II. In OUSD, only about 24 percent of ninth-grade students took geometry. Of that small percentage, 22 percent of them were at grade level. My friend and colleague Larry Martinez of Tucson, Arizona, worked with us to incorporate a high school core curriculum that focuses on mathematics and literature. I'm glad we implemented Mr. Martinez's and many other people's ideas at AIPHS, because it has paid off in academic rigor and success.

American Indian Public High School students far surpassed their Oakland peers in STAR test scores for mathematics, English, science, and social science. We have the same student population as OUSD. Most of our students are minorities, poor, English is not their first language, and their parents are not college-educated. So, what's the difference?

We believe in our students, we have a structured game plan and extremely high expectations, and we demand success. We stick to the AIM to Educate model because it works. We do not play the victim card at our schools. I don't want to hear that crap from the students, families, teachers, or any staff who work with our students, because I know that low expectations yield low success rates and cheat students.

When I conducted research for my doctoral dissertation in education at the University of Arizona, I learned firsthand about the power of expectations. My dissertation examined the teacher-student relationship as perceived by Lumbee Indian students who attended segregated Indian schools versus Indians who went to integrated schools.

I discovered that most Indian students who attended segregated schools loved the experience. I had heard so many negative comments about Indian schools in university classes, but when I started observing and reflecting, it became obvious to me that the Indians who went to Indian schools were more successful overall than the Indian students who went to integrated schools. During the time of my research, the data indicated if you were an Indian who had attended an integrated school (as opposed to a segregated Indian school), you were more apt to be in prison, unemployed, and lacking a high school diploma. It was the exact opposite of what educators were saying and what I had been taught to believe.

I started to realize part of the reason Indians did poorly academically in integrated schools was because the staff at those schools had low expectations for them. They expected Indians to be the worst students, and the Indians lived up to that expectation. The expectations for Indians at the Indian segregated schools were higher because the staff members were invested in having their students, who were all Indian, excel, and they wouldn't make excuses for the students when they faltered. Indians in the segregated schools were expected to meet the academic and behavioral requirements set out for them.

I worked on my dissertation at night and taught social studies at Phoenix Indian High School in Phoenix, Arizona, during the day. Phoenix Indian was an all-Indian boarding school with about six hundred students from different tribal backgrounds. One good thing about working with all Indians is they could never complain about race and say they were discriminated against. Who could they say the teachers were giving preference to since all of them were Indian? Working at Phoenix Indian High School gave me insight into my research and reversed my view of the existing stereotypes regarding Indian schools.

These experiences and observations made me change my perspective on what I'd been taught in education classes. I came to the conclusion that many professors in the college of education were more centered on their left-wing liberal views than on what actually works in practice with minority and poor students. The data convinced me to question their assertions. Before that, I bought into multiculturalism, self-esteem, and all that education propaganda. I had been sitting in college classes thinking to myself that I was just a dumb Indian hick from North

Carolina who could not deconstruct the biased data in scholarly journals or know that much about education, so what the professors were saying must be true. They'd say we need to make students feel good about themselves. They said when you teach them about their culture, students will feel good about who they are, and if they feel good about who they are, they'll want to read and write and learn. It seems logical if you don't know any better, but most people who can barely read feel great about themselves. Having self-esteem hasn't helped their literacy. My own family of brothers, sisters, cousins, aunts, and uncles serves as an example of that. Many Indian elders who live on a Navajo reservation know a lot about their culture. Does that qualify them to get into Harvard or Stanford University?

This radical change in perspective put me on the path to becoming the "crazy," enlightened educator I am today. My dissertation committee told me I had to change my dissertation to say that it only applied to Lumbee Indians. Maybe they wanted me to say that the Lumbees were an exception and that my claim that Indian students did better in all-Indian schools didn't apply to other tribes. I went along with it and got my dissertation approved. If my findings had been the opposite—that Indian students did better in integrated schools—do you think the committee would have advised me to limit my claim to Lumbees? That was a major turning point for me. I became enlightened, not disillusioned. I started to question the sacred cows of education: parent involvement, volunteer work, more money for schools, culture, self-esteem, bilingual ed, and minority holidays. (At AIPCS, we celebrate minority holidays, such as Martin Luther King, Jr., Day, by staying in school and working hard like Dr. King did instead of taking the day off.)

When I went against the grain, I started having disagreements with my fellow graduate students and professors. I still do. Most public school educators do not see eye to eye with me. I didn't agree with the philosophy of victimization then; I don't agree with it now. I have no problem badmouthing educators who cheat minority students with their pity, community circles, bead making, general math for twelfth-graders, bilingual education for twelve years, sheltered English immersion, and low expectations. Can you think of a better way to screw over minorities in education and dumb us down?

We get the watered-down academics, the victimization, and the teaching of culture, while most middle-class students get rigorous English, math, science, and history courses. Is that logical? Where did educators come up with this idea that minorities are so fragile? We are resilient people; we don't need kid gloves; we need a sound academic education and educators who prepare our children to work hard and be as smart as any other group of people.

When whites disagree with minority educators and their liberal dogma, they're labeled racists. When I disagree with minorities and liberal do-gooders, they say I'm trying to be white. Hell, how does a hardheaded Indian like myself turn white? Do they think I'm God and can change my race?

When I finished my Ph.D. program, I decided to pursue my ideas about high expectations and academic rigor. I got a job as director of Indian education at Coolidge Unified School District #21, in Coolidge, Arizona, which was located close to the Gila River Indian reservation. The Indian education program employed mostly social workers, who had been focusing on culture and counseling without achieving academic gains. I shifted the concentration to language arts and math, which was the first time I ever did that in a school. A language arts and math focus are at the core of AIPCS's curriculum, as you'll see in a moment. The Indian educators at Coolidge Unified were shocked by my decision. I said the students can do art and Indian language after school, but during school they need language arts because they can't read, and our Indians are the lowest academic performers in the district. I wanted the students to improve in core academic subjects.

The left-wing liberal teachers at Coolidge and a couple Indian parents fought the new program because they weren't used to an academic focus, but eventually they agreed with me, and the program proved successful by the end of my second year, when, on average, the test scores for the American Indian students in reading, science, and math went up in seven out of nine grade levels tested. I set high academic expectations for those students, and they lived up to them. I also employed language arts and math educators, whose effective teaching led to student success in other subjects.

I would wager money that the expectations I have for my students at American Indian Public Charter School are higher than any other secondary public school principal's in Oakland. My expectations are both simple and ambitious. I think every student can attend school on time, improve academically, and get in good physical shape through our P.E. program. I expect every student to become proficient or advanced in language arts and math by the time they graduate from AIPCS in eighth grade. I guarantee families that if they let us do our job and follow our AIM-Ed model, their children will be successful in our school and prepared to graduate from college.

At American Indian Public Charter School, the curriculum focuses on language arts and math, because when you build on students' English and mathematics skills you lay the academic foundation for students to succeed in science and history. In general, the students who test proficient or advanced in English and math also test proficient or advanced in most or all of their other subjects.

Students of all grades at AIPCS start each morning with an hour and a half of language arts followed by an hour and a half of math. Those first three hours are sacred. I don't want families withdrawing their children for doctors' appointments during that time, and I don't allow assemblies or school-wide activities to occur then. The focus on language arts and math are a core component of the American Indian Model to Educate.

Our history and science classes each comprise about fifty-minute periods, while P.E. lasts forty minutes. Do you think less instructional time on history and science lessens the students' understanding of those subjects? If you look at the STAR test results for the eighth-graders, you see that it does not. For the 2007–2008 school year, the eighth-grade results went as follows: 96 percent of eighth-graders tested advanced or proficient in language arts, 100 percent tested advanced or proficient in algebra, 86 percent tested advanced or proficient in history, and 98 percent tested advanced or proficient in science. I use the eighth-graders as an example because they are the only grade at AIPCS that takes mandatory, end-of-the-year STAR exams in all four core subject areas: English, math, science, and history.

When students strengthen their writing and reading skills through intensive language arts instruction, they gain the skills necessary to succeed in other classes. Reading, writing, and speaking skills carry over into all the other subjects. A great advantage of the self-contained classroom is the opportunity it gives teachers for incorporating each subject area into the curriculum. They can say, "Remember last week in English when we worked on topic sentences? Well, we are going to use those skills today in history when we write a one-paragraph summary on the construction of the Great Wall of China."

Many AIPCS students live in homes where another language is spoken. Spanish, Cantonese, and Vietnamese are the most common primary languages of our students. Because the students aren't learning or using English at home, it is very important that they develop and practice English skills in school. That's part of the reason we spend so many instructional minutes in reading, writing, and grammar every day. In my perspective, most of our Asian, black, American Indian, and Mexican students can certainly use more work in their reading and writing.

While language arts skills provide students with an ability to read, write, and speak English proficiently, mathematics opens the door to the other end of the academic spectrum of math, science, and engineering. I want our students on an academic path that keeps every college and career option open to them. All eighth-graders have to take and pass algebra with a C or better so that they can progress to geometry, algebra II, precalculus/trigonometry, and calculus in high school. Those math courses are mandatory at American Indian Public High School. Students who graduate from other high schools with only general math and algebra under their belts are not prepared to attend college. At AIPHS, all the students have to take the four years of math courses named above and four years of science: earth science, biology, physics, and chemistry. It is our goal that our students will enter college with the ability to pursue mathematics, science, or engineering, as well as the liberal arts.

At American Indian Public Charter School, we lay the foundation for mathematical intelligence from day one. By spending ninety minutes a day in math, we accomplish at least two academic years of math in one school year. We have an extended school year that includes mandatory summer school because we know our students benefit from more practice time. We are always working. Summer school is required of all our students and lasts for three weeks. We now also have a second session of summer school that is focused on algebra and mandatory for all AIPCS seventh-graders. Additionally, many of our students take part in other summer programs, such as the Johns Hopkins University Center for Talented Youth (CTY) program and Stanford Academic Institute of Learning (SAIL). Our students spend more time learning mathematics and language arts than other youths in Oakland, and it shows in their academic results.

Our extended-year calendar leads to at least 196 days in school. During each of those 196 days, the students spend ninety minutes on math, which means in one school year they spend a minimum of 294 hours of class time in math. Compared to the hours of instruction other

California students receive, our kids are way ahead of the game with their abundant math practice. For example, if other California middle school students took forty-five minutes of math a day for 180 days a year, that would equal 135 hours of math instruction, which means our students would more than double their amount of math instructional time. The Center for the Future of Teaching and Learning reported in July 2008 that eighth-grade students in California ranked forty-seventh in the nation for their performance on the mathematics tests issued by the National Assessment of Educational Progress. Could it be that most California middle school students are not spending enough time learning math?

In sixth and seventh grade at AIPCS, our teachers strengthen the students' problem-solving and pre-algebraic skills and get them ready for algebra. The teachers strive to cover all the material in the math textbook by April 5 of each year and then review it before the state tests in the beginning of May. This provides ample practice and reteaching time. We now have at least two adult math specialists who work with struggling students in small groups during P.E. or after school. In addition, responsible students with good math skills from our high school receive fifteen dollars an hour to tutor their younger peers. Ninety minutes of math class a day, an extended-year calendar that includes summer school, a mandatory second session of summer school for all seventh-graders in algebra, and tutoring services ensure that 100 percent of eighth-grade AIPCS students are proficient in mathematics.

There is an elective period that falls at the end of the day, except for students who have P.E. then. During the elective period, teachers can review material they did not have time to cover earlier in the day. The elective period serves as a catch-up time or a flexible instruction period.

AIPCS students participate in P.E. every day except Friday, the early release day. Today, P.E. classes consist mostly of running and strength exercises. Ricky Stoker, a health and P.E. teacher from the high-achieving Jack Britt High School, which serves about two thousand students in Fayetteville, North Carolina, and is headed by Conrad Lopes, redesigned our health and P.E. curriculum in 2005. With the new program in place, our students surged to the highest level of physical fitness on the state test.

I want the students to get in shape. Visitors to a P.E. class will find students running on the blacktop or gym floor, doing push-ups, lunges, sit-ups, or wall squats. With only forty minutes for P.E., you can't afford to waste time. Students do not change clothes, which probably increases the amount of exercise time by ten minutes. As our current P.E. teacher, Mr. Eng, has noticed, many of the sixth-graders who enter AIPCS overweight slim down by the end of the school year.

In reference to AIPCS's exercise regimen, Paul Strand from CBN (Christian Broadcasting Network) noted, "It's like what you'd expect if the Marine Corps ran your local middle school." Just as with its academic education, AIPCS is back to basics when it comes to physical education. Diet aside (because I can't and won't regulate what students eat), how do children get in shape? Like adults, they exercise, get their hearts pumping, and break a sweat. AIPCS students performed in the top 1 percent on the state physical fitness test for the past two years (2007 and 2008). We believe in a well-trained mind and body.

At American Indian Public Charter School we offer some extracurricular activities, but they are not the focus of our program. Students interested in learning to play the violin, clarinet, or flute can take lessons after school with one of our music teachers. We have had sports teams in the past, such as basketball and soccer. Now boys' rugby has become the main athletic program, because I want our poor and minority students to participate in activities people wouldn't expect them to. You don't think of blacks, Mexicans, Indians, or Chinese when you think of rugby, right? It gets people's attention and makes our students stand out. Our twelfth-grade students are required to take golf.

So much of what we do at American Indian Public Charter School revolves around rigorous academics and standards-based teaching. I laugh when critics of the No Child Left Behind Act say the current legislation forces educators to teach to the test. Educators are supposed to teach students the standards. The tests then verify the standards have been taught. It's an accountability measure. The standards aren't random, inane facts, as some critics like to portray them. The California Department of Education defines the standards as "the knowledge, concepts, and skills that students should acquire at each grade level." The standards vary by state, grade level, and subject, but to give you a sense of what they are, here are a few seventh-grade California standards:

**Mathematics**
Number Sense 1.3. Convert fractions to decimals and percents and use these representations in estimations, computations, and applications.

### World History and Geography: Medieval and Early Modern Times

7.1.1. Study the early strengths and lasting contributions of Rome (e.g., significance of Roman citizenship; rights under Roman law; Roman art, architecture, engineering, and philosophy; preservation and transmission of Christianity) and its ultimate internal weaknesses (e.g., the rise of autonomous military powers within the empire, undermining of citizenship by the growth of corruption and slavery, lack of education, and distribution of news).

### Life Science

Cell Biology 1b. Students know the characteristics that distinguish plant cells from animal cells, including chloroplasts and cell walls.

### English-Language Arts

1.0. Writing Strategies Organization and Focus. 1.2. Support all statements and claims with anecdotes, descriptions, facts and statistics, and specific examples.

If teaching standards like these to seventh-grade students is considered "teaching to the test," then I'm all for teaching to the test. Do you see how educators who don't want to be held accountable for the standards-based approach to teaching mislead the public with loaded terms, such as "teaching to the test" and "high-stakes testing"? You teach the grade-level concepts to students, many of which will be tested in the end-of-the-year standardized exams. By giving students these tests, the No Child Left Behind Act attempts to make individual states accountable for providing an academic curriculum at each grade level.

Schools that frequently give their students practice tests (and truly teach to the test) miss the point. You want your students to feel comfortable with the layout of the tests and to know skills, such as how to narrow down an answer in a multiple-choice question. For this reason, we do test prep once a month for a couple of hours at American Indian Public Charter School. But there is little use in administering practice test upon practice test, which administrators at some failing schools require of their teachers, without systematically teaching the standards. You teach the standards and you give students occasional practice tests to prepare them for the test format. I get pissed when I read complaints from educators attacking the standards and mandatory testing. Some educators think they should be able to teach whatever they want whenever they want. They don't like grammar, so they don't teach it. But that is not what's best for students. In education we have to do what benefits students, not what conveniences adults.

I find it irritating and unprofessional when educators cry and moan about the unfairness of standardized tests. Some will say the tests do not accurately measure what students know. A law student might make the same claim about the bar exam, but he or she must buckle down and try to pass it anyway. In our society, we use the SAT, the driver's exam, and the sobriety test as measurements from which to gain information. They may not be perfect, but what is the alternative? Would our society be better off to have no standardized measurement for anything? The type of educators who want to play around in a world shielded from academic accountability and test results don't inspire much confidence in me. Sure, at times we would all like to do as we please, but generally that does not jibe with our competitive, free market capitalist society, which we need to prepare students to succeed in. Do you realize China is a communist country yet they prepare their students for standardized tests, competition, and free market capitalism in their country?

I understand the frustration felt by teachers who have students way below grade level and are expected to get them testing at grade level. They must get the students to improve, but teaching them seventh-grade standards when they only read at a fourth-grade level is very difficult. Often the problem is not with the teacher but with the school structure or principal. Students are pushed on to the next grade level who don't deserve to be promoted. I've reviewed transcripts from eighth-grade students who want to enroll at AIPHS. They'll have Ds, Fs, and one C in eighth grade and yet they were graduated from middle school. For us, a C− is a failing grade. How can these students be passed on to high school when they aren't academically ready for it? They haven't earned their way, but their sorry principals don't have the nerve to hold those students accountable by having them repeat the grade. I take a different philosophy. We'll retain students in a heartbeat and make them earn their way upward to the next grade level. The students who transfer in for high school have a difficult time; however, they learn to adjust to the American Indian Model of Education.

Two things low-performing schools often have in common is a lack of textbooks used by the teacher and a lack of good leadership. How do principals expect teachers to cover the standards without a central text? Sometimes they say the lack of textbooks is due to a lack of funding. But if you look into it, you'll find out that thousands of dollars have been pumped into consultants and staff development instead of books. Does it make sense to hire consultants and work on staff development when you aren't providing staff members with the curriculum resources they need to teach effectively? Priorities often are out of whack in inner-city education. The worst excuse from educators who don't use textbooks, which is one I often hear, is that textbooks are too boring for the students. They prefer to use more "creative" sources. Try teaching algebra for a year without a textbook and you'll see why 3 percent of high school students in OUSD are passing the course.

I recommend to principals seeking ways to improve students' academics that they adopt high-quality textbooks aligned with their state's standards as their core texts. Because the standards are incorporated into all the lessons in the textbook, teachers do not need to look up each standard and design lessons for it; the textbooks have already taken that into account. Good, standards-based textbooks provide teachers with a foundation to build on. It is like having a guide or blueprint. In addition, our teachers incorporate their own ideas and outside sources into the curriculum. All our language arts classes, for example, feature a series of novels as required reading in addition to our state-approved course textbooks for each student.

Good books, good teachers, good leadership, family, high expectations, accountability/structure, self-contained classrooms, a taste of free market capitalism, a back-to-basics education focusing on English and math, a structured environment, and an extended-year calendar with mandatory summer school have been a recipe for academic success at American Indian Public Charter School.

Just look at our students' steady academic improvements over time.

# chapter ten

# The Quest for Improvement

"I think of Dr. Chavis as being somewhat like the Peanuts character
Pigpen. You know, the kid who has a cloud of dust surrounding him
wherever he goes? Instead of dirt, though, Dr. Chavis seems to travel
around with an overabundance of energy because he doesn't rest,
and he always seems to be on some sort of mission. Every day of every
year, there is a sense of urgency. There is a need to improve, to grow,
to strengthen. It is fine to celebrate successes, as long as you are
prepared to recalibrate your goals before the party is over. He is
clearly a coach at heart. His philosophy stems, in part, from the
athlete who knows that every day he is not improving himself is a day
the competition is gaining ground. Every year, he implements a new idea
to improve the schools. Satisfaction seems rare and fleeting. Complacency
is outside of his vocabulary. He is unwilling to just strengthen the weakest
link. He wants to strengthen every link, every day. And if you aren't on
board, you'd better get out of the way."

—*John Glover,*
*AIPCS II site administrator and former AIPHS teacher, October 2008*

As stated before, at the end of my first year as principal the school
scored 436 on the Academic Performance Index (API), which was a
long way from the California Department of Education's benchmark of
excellence, 800. Though we had a tough row to hoe, 436 showed an
improvement over the past, when AIPCS didn't even qualify for an API
score.

Moving into the second year (2001–2002) as principal, my goal was to be the most improved school in Oakland. The state of California set as American Indian Public Charter School's growth target an API score of 454, which would have been a modest improvement. Instead, we hit 596, a score increase of 160 points! American Indian Public Charter School was not only the most improved school in Oakland, the original goal, but it was the most improved middle school in the entire state of California! Our API score increases also made AIPCS the fourth-most-improved school overall in the state. We were on the move, and nothing could hold us back but ourselves.

That year, 2002, about one-half of our seventh-graders tested on par with the national average in both language arts and math, compared to two years before, when none of the school's seventh-graders met the national average. The *Oakland Tribune* reported: "At the American Indian Public Charter School, Stanford 9 test scores went through the roof. . . . The school improved its standing in some areas more than any other Oakland public school this year."

The National Charter School Clearinghouse wrote on its Web site about the 2002 results, "These accomplishments took place among a student population where 96 percent of students qualified for free/reduced lunch, 5 to 20 percent of students were homeless, and all were minorities."

Even though AIPCS students had made incredible leaps in the course of just two years, I was not complacent at the end of the 2002 school year. I set out the next year to be the top charter middle school in the city. For 2003, American Indian Public Charter School's growth target, set by the state, was 606. Once again, our score far surpassed the target, as the school reached 732 on the Academic Performance Index, an increase of 136 points. That made us the best charter middle school in Oakland.

My fourth year at AIPCS, 2003–2004, I said we would be the top middle school in the city. I also wanted to break 800 on the API, the California benchmark of excellence. This would place AIPCS on a whole new playing field. This would make us part of an elite club—the Ivy League of California's K–12 education.

I told everybody who would listen that our students and teachers would lead American Indian Public Charter School to the victory score of 800. I was so sure of it. That fall, the official results came in, and AIPCS scored an 813 on the API, making it the best middle school in

Oakland. In fact, American Indian Public Charter School became the first secondary school in Oakland to ever reach 800! I was thrilled; however, I soon set new goals for the next year.

In 2005, at our staff retreat in Portland, Oregon, I explained why I'm so competitive about test scores and wanting the students to succeed. I told the teachers, "I know I'm always saying, 'Beat, beat,' but American Indians, blacks, Hispanics, and poor whites have been beaten down for years by the secondary public school system. I can be tough on our kids and do whatever it takes to get them going, but they are succeeding. And they know it. And I know our students are proud of what they have accomplished at our school."

My ambition to constantly make the school better mirrors a strong Lumbee belief in the importance of continuous improvement. In the *Lumbee Pride* newsletter (July–August 2005), a letter from the tribal administrator, Leon Jacobs, made clear that the tribe must always seek ways to make life better for its people. He used the term "continuous improvements" frequently throughout his letter. The preface to the letter acknowledged that "continuous improvements" had become a rallying cry for the Lumbee tribal offices. They wanted the slogan "to resonate throughout all tribal programs."

Like my tribe, I work to instill a culture of hard and smart work and academic improvement at the school. I make sure the official texts of the school reflect that culture. One part of the AIPCS credo says, "We are always working for academic and social excellence." The credo concludes with "We will go forward, continue working and remember we will always be part of the AIPCS family." The school's official notices and memos feature the slogan "A School at Work" at the bottom. These lines from the credo and the slogan represent the belief behind the Lumbee Indian phrase "continuous improvement."

I tell the students and teachers that my goal is for each student to improve from one year to the next. I measure this mainly by looking at the state standardized test scores and what the teacher says about the child's work ethic. I want each student's scores to rise, and if they don't, I want to know the reason why. I never stop pushing. I never sit back, congratulate myself, and consider the job over and done with. I am always thinking about how the school can do better, how it can beat all of its competitors and beat itself. I am a happy workaholic through and through. I'll have all of eternity to rest when I'm dead, so I might as well work now to enhance the education of our students.

For my fifth year at the school (2004–2005) I wanted to be the top middle school in Alameda County. AIPCS was the third highest middle school in 2004, behind Lincoln Middle School in Alameda and Piedmont Middle School in Piedmont, respectively. I also wanted to break 900 on the API. I held assemblies that year and told students I wanted to beat the rich kids' asses in Piedmont, an affluent town neighboring Oakland. I told them, "If you're a minority, people expect you to be dumb. This year you're going to prove just how smart you are. You're going to whip the rich white kids up in the hills of Piedmont and become the best damn school in the county."

The school came up close but short on both goals. AIPCS came in second for middle schools in the county, beating Lincoln but lagging behind Piedmont, which scored 918. American Indian Public Charter School's score was 880, 20 points below the targeted 900, and 38 points below Piedmont Middle School.

The weakness in the school's performance that year was the eighth-graders. I let the eighth-graders spend too much class time preparing for the SSAT, a test that is used to get students into private schools. It was my fault! I accept the blame because I'm the one who fell asleep at the wheel. I learned from my mistake. The effort to get the eighth-graders into private schools stemmed from the lack of good high schools in Oakland. I wanted to give my students, who I had put so much energy into, the opportunity to continue receiving a quality public education. American Indian Public High School wasn't open yet, so there was pressure to come up with alternatives. To this day, many of the graduating eighth-grade students who do not attend American Indian Public High School have received scholarships to prestigious prep schools in Oakland and across the country, such as Bishop O'Dowd, Head-Royce, College Prep, and Taft. The organization A Better Chance has also provided some of our students with the opportunity to enroll in various high-achieving high schools outside of Oakland.

I reset the goal for the 2005–2006 school year to beat Piedmont Middle School. My motivation was to whip those wealthy white and Asian kids up in the hills with our scores. I'd tell everyone we wanted to be the best in the East Bay Area. You have to keep expanding in scope. In my mind, the goal had already grown to being the best middle school in the entire Bay Area, not just the East Bay. I sent a memo home to families informing them of the school's appearance as an exemplary institution on *20/20*. We were featured as a positive example of student achievement among many negative ones on John Stossel's "Stupid in America." I wrote in the memo:

> American Indian Public Charter School students are featured in
> the news because they are proof that poor people, minorities and
> any other group of people who work hard and give their best
> will be successful in life. The goal remains: we want to score over
> 915 on the Academic Performance Index, and be the best school
> in the Bay Area.

When the test scores became official, AIPCS hit 909 on the Academic Performance Index, losing to Piedmont Middle School by 1 point! We finally beat them at the end of the 2007 school year, when we scored 950 and they scored 928.

Based on its test scores, American Indian Public Charter School ranked in the top 1 percent of all public schools in California in 2007, the same year AIPCS was awarded the prestigious National Blue Ribbon Award. The National Blue Ribbon Award, which is given yearly to the top 250 public or private schools in the nation, is the highest honor bestowed upon a school by the U.S. Department of Education. Not bad for a bunch of ghetto-poor darkies led by a sharecropping Indian from the segregated South.

# chapter eleven

# The Emperor Who Wore No Clothes and the Boy Who Called Him Out

[Reflecting on what Oakland Charter Academy (a middle school) was like before Mr. Lopez took over as principal and changed the focus from culture and fun to academics and accountability. Oakland Charter Academy uses AIM-Ed.]

"Before Mr. Lopez got there it was all parties, and let's go to Wendy's and let's go to Starbucks. Most of the time it was the teacher's idea. There'd be times when we'd walk into class and the teacher would say, 'I don't feel like going over what I had planned for today,' and we'd be, like, 'Okay! We don't either.' So we'd go for a walk or to Wendy's or something like that.

"At the time, I was, like, this is the best school ever; they let us do whatever we wanted. I mean, there were kids making out in the hallways, and the teachers would just say, 'Get a room.' That was basically all they did. Then Mr. Lopez got there and everything completely changed. And we hated him for it at the beginning. All we had known was party: party this, party that. Let's have a party for this. Let's go sell nachos outside. Let's go have all these weird tournament thingies where kids from other schools would come and start problems. So Mr. Lopez gets there, and he gets rid of all of that. It was just strictly academics.

"My grades were horrible before Mr. Lopez took over: Ds and Fs. I think my GPA was .75. At the same time, I remember we would get As just for being in class. The teacher would walk around stamping homework that could have been from three days ago.

"At the time I thought they were the best teachers ever. I heard my friends at other schools complaining about schoolwork and how they didn't feel like doing their assignments or essays. And I was, like, you know what, I don't have to deal with that. But once I realized how much I was missing out—to this day when I see little sixth-graders and seventh-graders walking around with their math books and their language arts books, I'm, like, I didn't have that. Like their social studies—I read their books and I find them so interesting just because we didn't learn anything. I think about it, and I realize that the staff before Mr. Lopez really deprived us of an education. They didn't help us at all. They took away from us by not teaching us what they were supposed to.

"They seemed to care about personal problems. We had community circles. We'd all sit around and talk about feelings or issues and family. Basically that's all we really did. We were close to the teachers because they asked about things that were going on at home or things of that sort, so it's like now when I think about it I felt like they deprived us of our education, but at the same time I don't feel a lot of resentment toward them just because I did feel close to them."

*—Deana Perez, an eleventh-grader at AIPHS in 2007–2008 and graduate of Oakland Charter Academy*

---

My approach to race and culture at American Indian Public Charter School is nothing like the victimization and babying of minorities preached in teacher credential programs and implemented in public schools. I prefer hiring smart, uncredentialed teachers because many credential programs brainwash educators to teach in a way that is soft, ineffectual, and focused on nonacademic topics, such as self-esteem and multiculturalism. I prepare my staff to see the logic behind the AIM-Ed system in working with our students. By law they must enroll in a teacher credential program; however, we train teachers to use our model before too many shantytown ideas are pumped into their heads during the credentialing process.

University credential programs do not adequately prepare teachers to teach their subject matter. They spend too much time on methodology, not content. In colleges of education, most professors of education know very little about math, English, or science, especially the professors focusing on secondary school instruction. They can preach convincing sermons on pomp and splendor but little on academics. What would be the chances of finding an education professor who could actually teach math or English effectively in an urban ghetto middle school for a year? I look for intelligence when hiring teachers. I figure when a candidate graduates from Dartmouth with good grades, he most likely has the knowledge and work habits that need to be imparted to our students. Some people say, "Well, just because they are smart doesn't mean they will be good teachers." I ask, "Does that mean we should hire dumbies and hope they can teach?"

President Barack Obama has indicated he will push for an additional $80 million to train public school teachers. In California, teachers must complete a five-year higher education program to qualify for a teaching credential. Then, once they are employed by public schools, millions of dollars are spent on teacher training for these college graduates. If you've spent five years in higher education and you still can't teach, how is more money going to help you? Could it be we need to restructure the colleges of education instead of wasting more money?

I'm always telling people, "I don't have time for this nonsense." So much of the terminology and practice in education is nonsense. Do you know the story of the emperor who wore no clothes? Professors of education and educational consultants who enjoy promoting culture, self-esteem, group work, and dual-language-immersion outhouse methods are not working with our students. These ideologues say the emperor looks good in his clothes. I'm like the little country hick who is shouting out, "The emperor is as naked as a blue jay at birth." I expose them for the below-the-salt four-flushers they are of children. Could this be why many of them disagree with me?

Students must learn to read, write, and do math. This is the academic justice our students need in order to succeed in society. I post a list of rules in my office called "Common Sense and Useful Learning at AIPCS." (This is also found in the appendix.) Here are some excerpts:

> Squawkers, multicultural specialists, self-esteem experts, panhandlers, drug dealers, and those snapping turtles who refuse to put forth their best effort will be booted out.

I do provide psychological evaluations to quacks and Kultur specialists on a sliding scale. See me immediately for such rates.

Our staff does not subscribe to the back swamp logic of minority students as victims. We will plow through such cornfield philosophy with common sense and hard work!

In an interview with the *San Francisco Examiner*, I was asked my opinion about the perception (misperception, in my opinion) that poor minority children are never told they are worth anything and they constantly receive negative messages from society, so they need self-esteem programs. I told the reporter, "I've been in education for thirty years. I've never met a child who came to school in kindergarten or first grade with poor self-esteem. I've never met one. They come to school feeling great about who they are. But once they get into school and they start taking all these cultural classes and self-esteem classes, at the end of the year when they can't read, they realize, 'I'm fucked.' That's when the identity problems start. Schools create identity problems, not families. I've never met a parent who said, 'I want you to teach my child culture.' Culture courses were created for educators." Why? Because they're easy to teach, and there is no accountability.

I look at the following excerpt from Matthew in the Bible and relate it to education:

> *Watch out for false prophets. They come to you in sheep's clothing, but inwardly they are ferocious wolves. By their fruit you will recognize them. . . . Likewise every good tree bears good fruit, but a bad tree bears bad fruit.*
> *Matthew 7:15–17, New International Version*

The false prophets of inner-city public education, such as Pedro Negara of New York University or Linda Darling-Hammond of Stanford University, promote multiculturalism, social justice, self-esteem courses, and bilingual education. They tend to be against standardized testing and accountability. They enjoy claiming schools don't have enough money; however, that's another reason teachers unions, school administrators, and school board members love them. These false prophets wear sheep's clothing by having the title of education professor and claiming to care deeply about students, especially minorities. In some cases, their intentions may appear good, but their practices are bad. Their fruit, the test-score data, graduation, and attendance rates, are lousy and proof they are false prophets. How has self-esteem, social justice, and multiculturalism led to higher academic success for students in Oakland Unified School District? What inner-city public school has Negara or Darling-Hammond ever led that has student test data that confirms their methods prepared students to succeed academically in school? AIPCS families such as those of Althea Glover, her sister Donna Glover, and Barbara Mercado have a better understanding of what it requires to educate minority, inner-city children than any of these false prophets.

My mentor as a graduate student in education at the University of Arizona, Dr. Robert K. Thomas, a Cherokee Indian and anthropologist, encouraged me to read books on different groups of people, not just blacks, Mexicans, and Indians, who were often the focus in education programs. What I learned from reading about the Irish, German, and Turkish experiences is they had the same problems we had in life. It became obvious to me that while education programs in America pitied the "poor blacks and Indians," they were neglecting the larger historical picture. The English had been slaves, and the Romans said the English were lousy, lazy, and dumb, just like the Southern white plantation owners said about the blacks and Indians. The Romans did not allow the English to read or go to school.

I could see a systematic approach to keeping people down that wasn't just about color. Ethnic cleansing, religious tension, and forced removals of people have been taking place since the beginning of recorded history. How can people be free to fully participate in our global society when they are illiterate in English reading, writing, and mathematics? The Romans understood this concept very well. That is why they forbade their English slaves to be taught these academic skills.

In college, many education programs train students to see minorities as victims. I fell for it for a while, but I eventually came to my senses. When I did come to my senses, there was no turning back and other minorities in education disliked what I had to say. I once took a job as an assistant professor in the Ethnic Studies Department at San Francisco State University. Can you imagine how my politically incorrect and straightforward ways went together with the liberal administrators at San Francisco State University? It was like oil and water. I worked at SF State for five years. I incorporated lessons on how to do taxes and run a business into my courses. What ethnic studies programs in America offer business courses to students? How can you talk about Indians and blacks without including business if you want us to empower ourselves? Many ethnic studies programs teach victimization and can be summed up as follows: blacks have been enslaved; Mexicans have been discriminated against; and the Indians had their land taken. It's all about look what happened to us, pity us. How is that supposed to help minorities?

First of all, it's important for minority students to learn about other people. The blacks, Indians, and Mexicans in my classes would say, "We didn't come here to learn about white people." I'd say, "Well, you don't know enough about white people in the United States to write a miniature paragraph that could fit on a gum wrapper. They run the world; we don't. If you want to really understand how the world works, you've got to study these people." I would teach a semester course that would spend time on each ethnic group, such as Greeks, Jews, the English, Germans, Irish, blacks, and so on. We'd study their various experiences in America and what they went through. My students started to see how these groups were similar. They'd say, "Wait a minute, whites were slaves?" Students were always shocked to find out that white people were slaves or that blacks had owned slaves in America. When college students are exposed to these truths, it causes them to question some of their urban legend beliefs.

Some students enjoyed my classes, and some didn't. Students would complain to the department head about the section on taxes and the requirement that the students get a business license. They'd say, "We didn't come here to learn about business and white people."

My practices as a professor led to dissension among my colleagues. To this day, I always keep a watchful eye on educated, left-leaning liberal minorities, who can be more distracting to our students' success than a stinkbug at a beauty pageant. There are some whites who have appointed themselves the guardians of racial tolerance, which usually means they will label anyone a racist who challenges their belief system or threatens their income as stump hollerers of social justice.

Unlike many educators, I am not one to say we are all equal, because I do not believe for one second that we are. My cousin Rayman Ann lost a special ability when people attempted to fix her lot in life and make her more like everybody else. Rayman Ann was an excellent swimmer. She was born with twelve fingers and twelve toes, which were connected by thin webbing. Despite the way children tease each other for being different, we all watched in admiration when Rayman Ann swam effortlessly through the Lumber River waters, her brown arms glinting in the sun. The river was a place where she could reap the benefits of being born different.

My cousin Rayman Ann could swim from one side of the Lumber River and back before I could even swim one way across. It was amazing to watch. I think she could have been an Olympic swimmer, but when my cousin started getting a little older, teachers and doctors, with their good intentions, ruined her chances. When they saw Rayman Ann's hands and feet, they felt bad for her and perceived her as malformed. They didn't see what she could gain by being different. In an effort to make Rayman Ann "normal," a doctor (with the family's permission) removed her extra fingers, toes, and webs, as probably most doctors in America would recommend doing. The surgery went as planned and expected, but to me, what was the point in having surgery if the result was to have feet that look like huge blocks and hands that resemble curled-up claws? It was like cutting the webbing in a duck's feet. The claws would no longer hold together the way they're supposed to, and the duck would look deformed and be unable to swim.

That's why I call Rayman Ann the handicapped duck. Her feet are so wide and block-shaped that the only shoes that fit her are flip-flops. What little money she gets is used to keep the family together. I think it's a shame she had the operation in the first place. All the surgery did was exchange one unusual appearance for another. The hands and feet she was born with may have looked different, but they could have led her to greatness. Rayman Ann went from being an excellent swimmer to being just another Indian swamp-diving in the Lumber River. This all connects with my belief that educators and other professionals damage people's opportunities and natural abilities in an attempt to make us all the same. We give lip service to so-called equality and force people to be "equal," and the result is mediocrity. I can't accept these do-gooders who preach tolerance but who tolerate only their own perspective or way of doing things. At American Indian Public Charter School the students aren't all equal. Some are better at English or soccer than others; however, all our students have the same opportunity to get a good education.

The No Child Left Behind Act is a crucial step to ensuring a rigorous academic education for all students, something that every child in America deserves. Even though the legislation is a step in the right direction, many secondary schools still get bogged down by the soft approach to teaching preached in credential programs that finds its way into the classroom, where it ultimately yields low academic performance for minority students. The language used in education will provide some insight into the con game: "our pedagogy," "across the curriculum," "cultural diversity," "second-language learners," "the whole child," "a holistic approach," "scaffolding," and "implementing a caring curriculum." When you see these terms, you begin to understand where priorities lie in public education. We need to get back to common sense and basics, so we can educate students instead of obsessing over whether our approach is tender enough toward their feelings.

Lighthouse Community Charter School, an Oakland middle school, doesn't use letter grades. The teachers grade students in categories such as "curiosity." If you pass curiosity at Lighthouse and you want to transfer into AIPCS, does that qualify you for algebra? My friend and educator Ricky Stoker said maybe they need to change the lights at the Lighthouse Community Charter School because most of their students test below grade level in every subject. Maybe the lights are burnt out or they need a higher wattage of light, because the future looks very dim for the students based on their present academic preparation at Lighthouse Community Charter School. I agree with him 100 percent.

Not only do I strive for academic rigor, unlike many charter and public schools in California, but I also take a very different approach to race and culture than most educators. I grew up around Indians, blacks, and whites as a child and saw that there were good and worthless people of all colors. For me it's a question of hard work and respect.

I joke around issues of race and culture and use politically incorrect labels. Oakland Unified School District administrators found my use of the terms "whities" and "darkies" offensive. Their failure to educate darkies in Oakland is offensive to families and to me. It's humorous to me that the first time I heard the word "darkies" was on a college campus. I was a young boy goofing off with my friends on the grounds of The University of North Carolina at Pembroke. We were too young to even realize we were on a college campus. A man suddenly shouted at us, "You darkies, get out of here! You're trespassing!" He started to chase us, and we ran away laughing. From then on, we'd use the word jokingly. "Come here, darkie!" We thought it was funny, and we started to wear the word as a badge of pride. It became a symbol of our buddies; we were the darkies.

When I was a child, if a white person walked down the sidewalk toward me, I had to move out of the way and step toward the street side of the sidewalk. As an Indian I wasn't allowed in certain stores. I think it's funny when people ask me if this treatment bothered me. I say to them, "Does it bother you that the rich people get to sit in the front of the auditorium, and you have to sit in the back? It's your place, isn't it? It's what you can afford." Go to any sports stadium, and poor people will be sitting up in the blind seats, and people with money will have the great seats. What's the difference between then and now? It's a class system. It didn't bother me then; it doesn't bother me now. I could deal with the whites in the South who were up front with their views.

The emphasis on tolerance and social justice has resulted in many Asian, black, Hispanic, Indian, and white students acting like no-account fools. Walk down the street in parts of East Oakland and you'll see a bunch of boneheads strutting up and down the block with their pants falling off and fake gold coverings on their teeth. It's the elderly and hardworking people who have to step out of the way now. How can that be progress in America?

I prefer the mentality of the South, where I was raised, to that of the West, where I currently live. Indians, blacks, and now Mexicans are more likely to own businesses or property in the South. I consider Southerners much more "progressive" than Californians, because a Southern Democrat will vote Republican and vice versa, but a California Democrat will rarely vote Republican. I grew up in the so-called racist South, but I think Southerners are much more tolerant, and you know where they stand. They're forthright.

To give you an idea of the racial climate I was raised in, I'd like to share a story my grandpa Calvin used to tell me about the time the Ku Klux Klan came to our town. Since the Ku Klux Klan came to Robeson County four days after my birthday, I like to joke that as soon as I hit the floor, the shit started. The members of this Klan were from South Carolina, and they decided to cross the border into North Carolina, where they thought their Lumbee Indian neighbors were getting too uppity.

The Klan wizard "Catfish" Cole called our Lumbee people "mongrels" and "half-breeds." I don't need to run a DNA test to confirm his views are correct on my family. I laugh when some Lumbees brag a great deal in claiming they are full-blooded Indian even though they have kinky hair or blue eyes. Somewhere down the road there were blacks and whites in the woodpile with us Indians, as my friend says. I know my ancestors mixed, and so did every other group in America. It seems to me the darker the Lumbees are, the more adamant they are that they are "pure" Indians, and the more they dislike being called or mistaken for blacks.

It seems the Lumbee psyche is that a white person looks at you and thinks, "I know you say you're Indian, but we know deep down you're black." Could that be why Lumbees are absolutely obsessed with skin color and hair? Blacks are obsessed with their color and hair, too. Otherwise, how do you explain why there are so many beauty shops for Lumbees and blacks in Robeson County?

My theory of racial mixing is that the Lumbees who lived in what is now called Robeson County inhabited a swampland below sea level. It was very insulated and isolated, so it became a haven for outcasts and marginal people. Runaway slaves from Virginia and South Carolina and fugitive white indentured servants, for example, came into the swampy area the Lumbees lived in and mixed with us. We shacked up with each other and created children that can pass today for any ethnic group. We are the best parts of all the interracial relationships.

Catfish Cole planned to scare us Lumbees and half-breeds with burning crosses and white dunce caps and promised to gather five thousand members of his flock for a big rally on our turf. It was more like fifty white grit eaters who congregated on that field.

Grandpa Calvin and some of the other Lumbees decided to pull a fast one and attend the Klan rally. Let me tell you something about our people: When necessary, we are savages of the first rank! My favorite thing to say about the Lumbees is a remark that professor Dr. Robert K. Thomas made: "The Lumbees are a lusty people." The Lumbees are a loud, proud, live-life-to-the-fullest tribe who party hard, praise God with fervor, are hot-blooded, and have a way of finding trouble. Because we are always up for a good laugh and some excitement, that Klan rally played right into our hands. Grandpa Calvin and his buddies went down there with their rabbit guns, and the show was on.

Old Catfish, the Klan wizard, stood on the poorly rigged wood stage under a lightbulb hanging from an electrical wire. He sermonized about how Indians were getting out of line and overstepping their bounds, and that would not stand with the Klan. His flock cheered, pumping out their chests with pride, while their heavy-duty belts held in their guts.

Of course the Lumbees say the white Ku Klux Klan men started it. In actuality, according to my grandpa Calvin, it was his cousin James who fired the first shot at the makeshift stage. The startled Catfish hit the floor hard and looked for more cover than a white sheet and hood. Someone shot out the lightbulb, and the glass burst across the stage. The Indians kept firing shots in Catfish's direction as he clambered along the planks in a panic. Grandpa said Catfish squealed like a three-hundred-pound boar hog as he struggled to get away, to no luck. The other Klan members took off running.

Sheriff McCleod, who was white, came and arrested Catfish, and brought him before Lacy Maynor, the only Indian magistrate in the county. Mr. Maynor ordered Catfish to pay a fine and return to court at a later date. Catfish Cole was later convicted for inciting a riot and served a short jail term.

Do you understand what a great time it must have been for those ole Indians to whip a bunch of rednecks and not have to go to jail for it? That was one hell of a night for those Lumbee Indians. Hell, they talked about it until the day they died. Those not even alive at the time still talk about how hundreds of Lumbees broke up that Klan rally.

This will shock people, but Charles Davis McNeil, who was the head of the Klan in our part of the woods, Robeson County, was a friend of mine and an elder whom I greatly respected. He died in 2006.

See, things are often different from how we assume they would be. People hear Ku Klux Klan and they think of lynching and other hate crimes. While that was sometimes the case in certain parts of the country, it wasn't the case in other parts of the country. Mr. Charles Davis McNeil was a great man! He helped a black friend of mine named Ms. Coot Sinclair start her own corner store and paid her to hire black construction workers for him. Mr. McNeil was sick as a dog when Ms. Sinclair died. He helped pay for her funeral, and he also paid to have a great story about her life published in the *Robesonian* newspaper. Have you ever heard of active Klan members who supported blacks in business pursuits? Well, it happened. The South wasn't necessarily the cut-and-dry, black-versus-white place people make it out to be.

Mr. McNeil said he advised the South Carolina Klan to stay away. He said, "I told them not to come around these parts. Indians take care of Indians, blacks take care of blacks, and whites take care of whites in this county."

In Robeson County, the Klan believed its job was to keep white people in line. When white men were sleeping with Indian or black women, the Klan would come around and rectify the white men's behavior. Where I grew up, there was an unwritten agreement that when racial boundaries were crossed, there was hell to pay. I remember when white men got killed by Indians because they had been hoofing it up with Indian women at the Bloody Bucket jump joint, which also served as an interracial love nest. The general attitude on all sides was they got what they deserved. This may sound like a harsh approach, and it was, but if you think about it, the underlying attitudes are not that different from many still held today. For example, how many Jewish people want their children to marry gentiles? How many Hispanics want their children dating blacks? I'm not saying these attitudes are right or wrong; I'm just saying they exist.

In Robeson County, I never saw or heard of any cross burnings on minority property during my youth. The KKK in our area attempted to rein in the behavior of white people, not minorities. But Catfish's Klan from South Carolina had the attitude of, Wait a minute, that's not how we do things; we keep the blacks and Indians in line. What resulted was a clash of perspective and Klan policy, a true version of North versus South.

Mr. Charles Davis McNeil ran an auto repair and towing company, so to get a little revenge on the Klan leader from South Carolina, he impounded his truck. When Catfish went to retrieve it, McNeil asked him, "Who in the hell are you, son?"

"I'm Catfish. That's my truck, and I'm here to get it."

Mr. McNeil told him he owed twenty-five dollars, because the impounding cost was five dollars a day. Catfish said, "Boy, are you crazy? I ain't paying no five dollars a day."

"Yes, you are, son, if you intend to get that truck back."

As a final resort, Catfish said, "That's God's vehicle."

"Well, you'd better go see God then and ask him for some money," Mr. McNeil replied, "because you ain't getting this truck back until you pay me."

Thinking of this story always makes me laugh. What's interesting, though, is that things aren't always what they seem. People who aren't from the South and who have only heard about the Klan in history books would never think that one white Klan leader would harass another white Klan leader for attacking minorities, but that's what happened.

Mr. McNeil passed away in the fall of 2006 on the very same day I went to visit him at the rest home. He was a real history buff. Whenever I returned to Lumberton, Mr. McNeil would take me to a graveyard to talk about the past. In fact, he was known for maintaining tidiness around the graves of people of any race. After he died, droves of white, black, and Indian people attended his funeral to mourn his loss.

One of Mr. McNeil's great kindnesses was when he let my stepdad, Buck, run an antique business in one of his buildings rent-free for five years. The story of how this came to pass is quite entertaining to me.

Buck is a born-again Pentecostal Christian. As such, he believes that God gives him signs. These signs can come suddenly and without warning. One day he was riding in his old $150 Indian car down Second Street across from the Trailways bus station when he suddenly told my mom, Shirley, to pull over. Sensing the urgency in his voice, she did. Before my mom had even come to a complete stop, Buck leapt out of the car like a madman possessed by a spirit. He ran over to the building in front of him and put his hands against its walls. He stayed there a moment, his hands placed firmly on the building, and then he returned to the car. My mom, dismayed by his odd behavior, said to him, "You've lost your mind. I've always thought you were crazy, but this time you've lost your mind." He assured her he hadn't. He said, "God led me to this building and told me to put my antique business here."

Well, if Buck was to carry out God's word, he had some logistics to look into, such as who owned the building. When he discovered it was the building of his friend Mr. Charles McNeil, the Ku Klux Klan leader, he approached Mr. McNeil and shared his religious vision. Mr. McNeil, who was using the space for storage, at first gently refused to move his possessions. He eventually caved in and allowed Buck to take over the building by the end of the month, sealing Buck's belief that the event had been ordained by God. And that's how the white Klan leader helped out my stepdad, a Lumbee Indian who looks like the singer Charlie Pride and is the tightest man in the world when it comes to a dollar. He has short arms and deep pockets when he has to part with his money.

Mr. McNeil expected white people to behave a certain way, but he did not have anything against Indian people or anyone else who was honest and worked hard. The Lumbee Indians had our own secret society that served a similar function to the Klan; it was called the Red Man's Lodge. The Red Man's Lodge tried to keep the Indians' behavior in check. Now, let me tell you, that's a full-time job.

Coming from the background I did, I take lazy people on in a straightforward way. I don't tolerate loafers of any color. There was a spree of media attention on American Indian Public Charter School over a disagreement I had with a young black male named Unity Lewis from Mills College. He was scheduled to show up for a tour of the school with his classmates from Mills. They were in a race-relations class. Well, I gave them a realistic view of race relations, but they didn't want to acknowledge it. Unity Lewis was the only one who showed up late, and he had a coffee cup in hand, which indicated that he chose to get his latte instead of being punctual like everyone else in his group.

Now, I'm a real stickler when it comes to punctuality. Just ask my wife, Marsha. On our second date, she was fifteen minutes late, so I left. When she called, I said, "Look, I'm an Indian, and you're a Latin. I know how all that shit goes, but I don't believe in minority time. If this is going to work, I expect you to show up when you say you will." We didn't have any punctuality problems from that point on.

When Unity Lewis waltzed into the office at American Indian Public Charter School late with his latte, I told him he couldn't stay. He thought I was joking. I made it clear I wasn't. He said something like, "You don't even know me, homie." I told him I wasn't his homie, that his ass could go, and that there was no black time at the school. If I make my students serve detention for being even thirty seconds late, why would I tolerate him showing up fifteen minutes late to a meeting? I told Lewis that people had been making excuses for him his whole life because he is black. I'm sure Bill Cosby would have agreed with me if he had been at the school. I told the group they had a choice. They could all leave with Lewis or he could go, and the rest of them could stay. They chose to stay. He got in my face and I got in his, but he left. Later, Unity Lewis and some of his Mills College classmates and professor accused me of racism and said I was unfit to be a principal.

The school year (2006–2007) during which the Mills entourage filed their complaints and even went as far as contacting the NAACP, every single one of the black students in sixth and seventh grade at American Indian Public Charter School tested either proficient or advanced in mathematics. One hundred percent of them were proficient or advanced! Only 12 percent of black sixth-graders and 15 percent of black seventh-graders in Oakland Unified, on the other hand, tested proficient or advanced in math. Does holding a black male graduate student at Mills College accountable for his actions and educating black students at AIPCS make me a racist?

To me, Oakland is nuts with its "Kultur" critics and so-called tolerance. Some Pollyannas walk around crooning about how progressive and diverse Oakland is, while the high school dropout rate for blacks in Oakland Unified in 2005–2006 was 35.8 percent. The dropout rate for students identified as Multiple Ethnicities or No Response was the highest at 56.9 percent. These percentages just reflect the number of students who actually dropped out of school. They don't take into account how many students failed to receive their diploma. The estimated twelfth-grade graduation rate for all students in the Oakland Unified School District for the 2005–2006 academic year was 60.8 percent. That's according to the California Department of Education Web site; other sources project that Oakland Unified's graduation rate was much lower.

So, the culture specialists do not agree with my method, but we provide a great education for students of all races at American Indian Public Charter School, something that unfortunately is almost impossible to find in Oakland secondary schools. When you compare our API for the 2006–2007 school year, which was 950, with the average API for middle schools in California with similar demographics to AIPCS, you see a stark difference. Their average API, called the Similar Schools API, was 645. That means we outperformed other California middle schools with a similar student body by 300 points.

I believe we can score a perfect 1,000 on the API by the end of 2009 and be the number-one middle school in California. How's that for a principal labeled a racist leading a bunch of poor darkies from Oakland, California, to excel in the classroom? What left-wing public school administrator has prepared a student population such as ours to achieve similar academic results?

# chapter twelve

# You Are Judged by Your Race Whether You Like It or Not

"A lot of people are just shocked by Dr. Chavis's jokes about race. I think the first day I met him he called me a mutt or something. I mean, it's all lighthearted and I'm not offended by it, and people mistake my race—you know I'm half Japanese and half mixed European—and I couldn't care less. It doesn't bother me. It is a reality of the world, and the kids will be exposed to it at some point. At the school I don't think any of the kids are offended.

"I loved teaching at AIPCS from the minute I started because I was supported in everything I did. I knew even if I made a mistake Dr. Chavis would still back me and guide me to not do it again. And the kids were working hard, and we didn't make excuses for them, and we were driven by results, and we demanded results, and it was wonderful. It's my dream job really. I think to myself I'll never be able to teach anywhere else because I'll never be this satisfied with how a school is run. If there was ever a problem with a student, Dr. Chavis would say, 'Let's take care of this right now.' And that's a huge difference from the administration at my last school, where there was no follow-through, no support."

—*Janet Roberts, AIPHS site administrator and former AIPCS teacher, November 2007*

"I definitely think that people represent their race. Dr. Chavis is really honest, which is why kids respect him. The students are aware of their race, so trying to act like we don't notice it is a falsity. Dr. Chavis has created a school environment that no matter what your race or your socioeconomic background is, this is a free institution that you can come to

that provides structure and some of the best teachers to give you an
advantage in life. I really am an advocate of the foundation that Dr. Chavis
has laid here, and I think the students are extremely fortunate to be able to
get such a great education in this environment."

—*Mrs. Claudia Walker,*
*an eighth-grade teacher at AIPCS, November 2007*

---

The student body at American Indian Public Charter School is
diverse. I will use any student's race to motivate him to be a better
human being. I'm teaching children about the real world. Before I took
over AIPCS, the school was focused mostly on enrolling American Indians and promoting American Indian culture. I took a different course.
I made certain that any student who was interested had the chance to
attend the school.

On a radio program in 2005, I was asked by the host why the
school was called American Indian Public Charter School when only
13 percent of its students were American Indian. I asked the host if
students attending a school named after Martin Luther King, Jr., had to
be black. In order to enroll at a school called Walt Whitman Middle
School, would you have to be white or a poet? Why do people believe
a school called American Indian Public Charter School must have only
Indian students enrolled in it?

During my youth, the restaurants were segregated in North Carolina, but Hardee's and McDonald's didn't give a damn what color you
were; they served it your way. The fast-food restaurants became a place
for everyone who was willing to pay for the food. They represented
a free market economy. If you could pay, you could stay. I remember
the first time I ever saw a black, white, and Indian person in the same
restaurant together was at a Hardee's. People are interested in our
school because we have all races who work hard, are smart, and succeed against daunting odds. It's a great American story.

I use the different races to motivate each other at school. I can talk
smack about the whites, and the others will laugh; the students realize
the Mexicans aren't any better than the Vietnamese, the blacks, the

Indians, or the Chinese. They put their clothes on, they put their shoes on, they fail, they're lazy, and those who work hard tend to excel academically and socially. That's what students learn at our school.

My first year, the majority of students were American Indian, Hispanic, and black. By 2003, Chinese students started enrolling. In 2004, I got a white student. In October 2005, the racial composition of the school was 3 percent white, 27 percent black, 23 percent Hispanic/ Latino, 32 percent Asian, 1 percent Filipino, 1 percent Pacific Islander, and 13 percent American Indian. People have tried to claim that AIPCS has high test scores because of our Asian students. This is a common myth in education.

Our Asian students are our lowest performers! In 2008, our black, Mexican, and American Indian students outperformed our Asian students in math. Every single one of the black, Mexican, and American Indian students in seventh and eighth grade at AIPCS that year tested proficient or advanced in mathematics, which was not the case with the Asians. It is a myth that Asian students are superior to other ethnic groups in mathematics.

It comes back to expectations. People expect Asians to be good at math, so they often live up to that expectation. People don't expect blacks, Mexicans, or Indians to advance in math, so they often don't excel in their mathematics courses. We have high expectations at AIPCS for all of our students in all subjects, which show in our outstanding academic results.

A school providing great academic opportunities to students in the inner city creates more lasting diversity than all the promise of culture, self-esteem, and community circles ever will. Could it be that people from all racial groups want their children to get an education? How many people say they want their children to learn ethnic culture and become more involved in the community? That's what the brand of touchy-feely educators want, not families trying to make better lives for themselves in the inner city.

Getting accurate statistics regarding enrollment in the past is difficult. Two different official Web sites gave drastically different figures for the number of American Indian students enrolled at AIPCS in 2001. One site indicated twelve; the other claimed twenty-two. From memory, I think the latter is correct. This discrepancy is partly due to students claiming on their standardized tests to be a different ethnicity from what they had specified in their application.

People often misinterpret statistics. If you look at the number of Indian students attending the school, it has basically stayed the same over the course of my years at the school. Each year there have been about twenty American Indian students at AIPCS (if you use twenty-two as the first year's count, as opposed to twelve). As the school has grown in numbers from fewer than forty students in 2001 to just under two hundred students in 2006, the percentage of Indian students has decreased from about 65 percent to about 13 percent. Yet the number of Indian students in 2001 was twenty-two, while the number of Indian students in 2006 was twenty-six. The dramatic percentage drop from 65 to 13 is misleading. The raw numbers of Indian students enrolled essentially stayed the same for five years.

I don't tolerate excuses from or about American Indians. In 2005–2006, my Indian students got the most detentions because they broke the rules the most often. They had the worst attendance at the school, which was about 97 percent. That would be great anywhere else in America, but not here. These statements aren't racist; they're statistical facts. At the same time, my Indian students beat other Indians, whites, blacks, Mexicans, and Asians across America with their academic performance, hard work, attendance, and test results. The year I was hired at American Indian Public Charter School, only one female American Indian student in the entire Oakland Unified School District graduated from high school. It was such a big deal that the district's Indian Education Program paid for the student to have a graduation dinner with other Indians in the community. I remember thinking, "What a waste." That dinner cost over $900. Why didn't we just give the girl that money? She was going on to college. She could have used it. That kind of absurd spending is typical of public schools.

My buddies and I who work in education have found through experience that your own race will attack you the most. Al Sye, a black friend of mine who was principal of a predominantly black high school in Atlanta, said his people drove him to leave the school. Jorge Lopez, a Mexican friend and principal of Oakland Charter Academy, a middle school, said Mexican families give him the most difficult time. I guess it could be worse; all the parents could be hellions who attack us instead of just our own race.

Race is a powerful force. I had people use my American Indian race to motivate, criticize, or compliment me. Those moments have stuck. My track coach in Arizona taught me a lesson. I was lazy one day and jogging slow laps. My coach didn't like my goofing off, and he didn't want to hear any of my excuses. He said, "Why don't you just go home with all the other country-ass Indians? Do you know what everyone is going to think when you lose? 'He was just another lazy Indian.'" He caught me off guard, but I knew he was right. He ended, "Just remember one thing: when you die, the newspaper's gonna refer to you as a Lumbee Indian."

I try to get the same point across to my own students: you are judged by your race whether you like it or not. I'll tell a student who is misbehaving or doing poorly in school that she is making her race look bad. I told Leanna, an Indian student, who was screwing up in school, "Please tell me you're not Indian. I don't want you making Indians look any more like fools than we already are." I make the same type of comments to students of any race who don't do their work at AIPCS. I tell the Hispanics when they don't do their work that people are going to call them lazy Mexicans. When you are black, people will label you lazy, too. Is that fair? No. Is it reality in the United States? Yes.

One time I went into a ninth-grade classroom to tell two girls to stop being catty and making their people look bad. They weren't getting along and were causing divisions in the class. I went into the class and said, "I'm gonna have to pray for Ms. Clementine because she's a dumb white lady." They looked at me in confusion, and I said, "She must be dumb to get a degree from Harvard and come all the way to Oakland to work with a bunch of darkies who argue with each other. She can't be too smart." The students said, "No, Dr. Chavis, she's our teacher. She's a good teacher." I continued, "I don't think I'd want to come this far to teach a bunch of darkies who are bitching with each other. I brought her here to educate you—not listen to your nonsense."

One female student had accused another girl of talking behind her back. I looked at both of them and said, "Go tell your mommas I'm a fool. I want every one of you to go home and say I am crazy. How many of your families have said I'm crazy?" Some of them raised their hands. "Good. All your families know who I am. Tell everybody you know that your principal is crazy because then everybody in Oakland will know me. Nobody will know you unless they're talking about you, so when she's talking about you back there, good." The rest of the students started laughing at the two girls.

Students often laugh when I come into the classroom to set someone straight. They enjoy the drama and like to see their floundering classmates get dressed down in front of the class.

I believe students appreciate my straightforward approach to speaking with them. They respect honesty. They're used to adults lying to them, trying to con them by telling them we're all equal. Do you think a poor Mexican thinks he's equal to Kobe Bryant? It's not the reality they live in. They walk down the street, and they know if a kid is tough, he's going to beat them up and take their bus pass. They live in the ghetto, not the fairyland of tolerance that some educators paint. I think for many of the students this is the first time they've been in a school where a principal is honest with them.

While I don't believe equality exists in the real world, I work to make sure it exists at American Indian Public Charter School. During one summer school session, the P.E. teacher Mr. Hannibal took half of the ninth-graders to an Oakland A's game, while the other half remained at the school. The students who had attended eighth grade at AIPCS were taken to the game as a reward for their accomplishments that year. The students who had attended eighth grade at Oakland Charter Academy were left behind. When I heard about it, I was mad as hell. I went into their classroom the next day to apologize to the Oakland Charter Academy students.

I said, "I want to apologize to you. Something happened yesterday that was not right. Mr. Hannibal took all the students who were in eighth grade here last year to the baseball game and left the rest of you behind. And some of those students he took don't even go here anymore. And some of those students he took are sitting right here in this class, and they've been the ones who have been screwing around and not doing their work. It pissed me off the way you were treated by him. How did the rest of you feel who were left behind?"

The class was silent. I asked, "What, Mexicans don't know how to talk?" (Most of the students from Oakland Charter Academy were Mexican.) They laughed.

One good-natured female student named Ana said, "Well, they said this was their reward from last year, and so I thought they earned it, and that's good for them."

I said, "All right, honey, but did it feel bad to be left here yesterday while half of your class went to the A's game?"

The Oakland Charter Academy kids mumbled "Yeah" in unison. They sat hunched over their desks in the self-conscious form typical of ninth-graders hiding behind their long hair and embarrassed smiles waiting for what I was going to say next.

I gave the class a good, long pause, and I said, "You were discriminated against because you didn't go to this school last year. It feels bad to be discriminated against. Before I took over this school, only Indians were wanted here. I said heck no. That's discrimination. I said that any student should be able to come to this school who wants to get an education, and that's how it's been. Mr. Hannibal is going to apologize to you." I made sure he did that very day.

The students' faces brightened a little. I gave a tall Latino boy named Martin a playful slap on the back. "Now come on and help me carry some boxes." A few boys followed me out the door wearing sheepish smiles.

My motivations for getting into public education were not driven by race. I didn't go into teaching to save city Indians, that's for sure, or blacks, Mexicans, Chinese, or country whites. I went into education because that's what I enjoy doing. And I'm a strong believer that if you enjoy doing something, you're gonna be good at it. That's just it. I've always done for a career what I wanted to do. When I taught public school I enjoyed doing it, and then I got tired of it. When I went to the university I enjoyed it, and then after several years I got tired of it. I focused on my real estate business for a while. Now I'm involved again in public education. If I get tired of it, I'll move on to something else. That's just the way I am. I'll just walk off and say, oh, well, let's try something else this old Indian will enjoy.

I want to give young people the same opportunities given to me. I'm doing what other great people did for me. People helped me, and that saved me. You know what they say, if you can make the world a better place, you should. At my age you have to start giving back, because I'm on the downhill slope. I have taken care of my own garden, and so now I can help people develop their gardens. But I'm not going to help you when you're lazy or acting a fool. I enjoy being around students, talking to them, and rewarding the hardworking ones. Working with these students is not a job to me. It's more like my favorite hobby that I love doing.

Though I love working with children, I don't believe in babying them. That goes for my own children and grandchildren as well as my students. The best thing you can teach a child is family, accountability, discipline, hard work, and a healthy dose of risk taking. Once children get enough bruises, they won't be so risky. They'll start to think, make sound choices in life, and not embarrass themselves, their family, or their race too often.

President Barack Obama has been celebrated around the world as the first black president of the United States. Whether President Obama likes it or not, his legacy as president will always be tied to his race. He has already given millions of people hope that we can rise to greatness, and he has proven a person of any race can hold the highest office in the United States.

President Obama was born on August 4, 1961, took office as senator of Illinois on January 4, 2005, and was elected the forty-fourth President of the United States on November 4, 2008. My grandmother Lela would say he is blessed by the number four. With his election as president of our great nation, race is no longer an excuse for not achieving.

# chapter thirteen

# Poor? If You Say So

"It's important not to succumb to your environment. You don't have to be a product of it. You can be bigger and better than your surroundings."

—*Kimberly Faye McLeod,*
*the mother of an AIPCS student and an OUSD educator born and raised in Oakland*

When I was raised in Robeson County, the Lumbees lived in absolute poverty, yet I wasn't aware of being poor until college. To me, my family was normal; we were just like everybody else. Many American Indian Public Charter School students don't think of themselves as poor, either. Outsiders, however, would have a different assessment. They could look at data and see that the percentage of AIPCS students considered as socioeconomically disadvantaged (qualified for the Free and Reduced-Price Lunch Program, which we do not participate in) has been about 95 percent on average over the years.

In Oakland, the percentage of people living below the poverty line is about 20 percent. In Robeson County it's about 25 percent. But what does it really mean to be poor in this country? Many poor people in the United States have televisions, cars, and more clothes than they can wear. Poor people don't wander the countryside in torn, dust-covered clothing looking for work like they did in the 1930s. America wears a new face of poverty. There isn't a single kid at our school who thinks he's poor, because he can always look around and see someone else in his situation. Furthermore, people don't want to identify as poor because it can be perceived as a sign of weakness. In a country of great wealth, who wants to raise his hand and say, "I'm poor," unless it means getting a check?

Politicians are the ones preaching about poverty. They're the ones playing the poor card. Poverty is a political tool that both parties use to manipulate voters. Republicans will point at poverty as a drain on the system and a reason for less government. Democrats, on the other hand, point at poverty as a reason to increase the role of the government in order to pimp—I mean help—people. Republicans lean toward tax breaks, Democrats toward tax increases, especially of the rich.

This brings up another interesting question: Who is rich? I had lunch with my buddy the other day, and he started talking about how we should increase taxes on the rich. So I said, "Who do you consider rich?" He said anyone who makes $300,000 or more a year. I replied, "Well, you must make just under that then." This friend and his wife probably have a combined income of at least $250,000. While my buddy emphatically claims he's not rich, my own parents and our students at AIPCS would beg to differ.

Wealth and poverty are relative terms, and people tend not to claim to be one or the other, yet economists indicate the middle class is shrinking. So you do the calculation. It seems most people favor denial.

Looking back on my childhood, it's undeniable that my people grew up in total poverty compared to most other parts of the country. I didn't recognize that as a boy, but I can see it clearly now. In the 1960s, many Lumbees, including my grandpa Calvin, used mules for transportation instead of cars. In fact, I recall one family still used a mule and wagon up until 1975. The 1960s were kind of a reconstruction period for our people in Robeson County, if I could put it in context. That's when we became free. The Civil War freed the blacks in the 1860s. It took another one hundred years to free us from economic slavery in rural North Carolina and to give us opportunities beyond sharecropping.

Despite our poverty, Lumbees in North Carolina have a lot of pride. The "mighty state of Robeson," as some people call it, is the place the Lumbees call home. Robeson County borders on South Carolina and is the largest county in North Carolina in terms of land. Its population, however, is quite small compared to other parts of the state. Robeson County is the tribal hub of the Lumbee Indians, the largest American Indian tribe east of the Mississippi. If a North Carolina Lumbee asks you if you've been to the capital, he doesn't want to know if you've been to Raleigh; he's inquiring if you've visited Pembroke, Robeson County, our tribal headquarters.

The land of Robeson County is beautiful. When the dogwood trees are in bloom it looks like snow has descended in April. Lumbee legend says that because Christ's crucifix was cut from a dogwood tree, no dogwood will ever grow straight. Their trunks are cursed with crookedness, and at the edge of each white petal is a tiny red spot, symbolizing the blood of Christ that was spilled.

Green fields of tobacco run up to rows of Carolina pines that sway in the breeze and overhang the edges of ponds, where water spiders glide across the surface and Canadian geese turn under in search of food. Large yellow and black butterflies drift across the road, and wild wisteria wraps itself around the branches of the pines and drops down in purple bunches.

The Lumber River, from which the Lumbee Indians take their name, meanders through most towns in the county. Because it's a lowland area, streams and creeks flow across the land and gather in small ponds. Though the ocean is an hour and a half away by automobile, the presence of water is vast.

Among this idyllic country setting, there was much poverty and suffering. People are sometimes shocked to hear the conditions in which I grew up, which they say sounds like the third world or the Dark Ages; however, those were the 1950s and early 1960s.

You couldn't exactly call the place I lived in as a boy a house. A sharecropper's home was a one-story hovel. The dark wood was rotted and unpainted, and an outhouse stood in the backyard. If you were to hold a kerosene lamp up to the side of the house, the only lighting my family had, you would be able to see through the cracks in the wood into the interior. The house was not insulated. It was built about two feet off the ground and supported with blocks and tree stumps. My brothers, sisters, the dogs, and I would play under the house every chance we got. It was a home away from adults. Flat farmland stretched out in the distance. Each sharecropper shack was a quarter mile or more apart from its neighbor. As a lowland swamp, floods were common, and the soil was very rich, black, and fertile, allowing darn near everything to grow.

Around the sharecropper's shack where I grew up, you would see dirt instead of grass. My mom and Grandma Lela hoed and swept the yard all the time in the summer. They kept the grass away from the house to keep varmints out. They dug up weeds and maintained a radius of dirt around the home, so that snakes, bugs, and other creatures would not be a nuisance. Most Lumbee women have a big dislike for snakes.

At night my family would gather on the front porch to talk, share stories, and keep cool, especially in the spring and summer. We'd burn trash to keep mosquitoes away. The swallows, which nested in open gourds hung from wooden poles near the house, would also eat the mosquitoes and other bugs. Without the smoke or the swallows, those mosquitoes would eat you alive, boy. My grandpa Calvin, who never was much of a worker, would sit on the porch and tell some great stories.

We had few possessions. For clothing I owned two pairs of overalls, two plaid shirts, and boots called brogans. I didn't have any toys, so I used my imagination to turn a tobacco stick into a horse that I could ride off into the sunset. The highlight of the day was my grandpa telling scary stories on the front porch. We didn't have TV or radio.

There was a chicken coop in the backyard where we sometimes raised chickens for their eggs, and there was a garden, too. All the sharecropper women had their own gardens, where they'd grow vegetables for the family. My grandma Lela thought the garden was for women only. She'd say, "What's a man want to do with a garden? Next thing you know he'll want a dress." She'd be embarrassed to see me as a grown man tending to my garden in Oakland. I used to think that I would never want to farm or have anything to do with raising plants or crops when I was older. I hated that kind of work. But old habits die hard. I now grow corn, cabbage, tomatoes, garlic, and zucchini in my yard. My garden is weed-free, tidy, and green. Maybe my grandmother would be proud of me after all, and I sure don't own a dress, as many other males in the Bay Area do; however, I respect their choice.

I remember the women in the family would often sit on the porch shelling peas or shucking sweet corn. They would can vegetables in small glass mason jars to preserve food for the winter. We didn't have electricity when I was a small child. There was no inside plumbing. We got our water from a well in back of the house. There was a hand pump on the porch that would easily freeze up in the winter if we weren't careful.

My family ate a lot of lima beans, corn bread, rice, and potatoes. We didn't eat much meat or chicken. The chickens laid eggs, which ensured they could live another day. When we did actually eat chicken, it was a big treat. Maybe that's why I love chicken so much now. We ate a good amount of fish and rabbit. My mom didn't care for the taste of rabbit. She would boil it to get rid of some of the toughness and wild taste. She would roll parts of the rabbit in the egg mix, put some flour on top, and drop it in the frying pan. I loved to eat rabbit in those days.

My grandpa Calvin taught me how to trap rabbit. We built a box about eight inches high and six inches wide and kept one end open. We made a trap door using a stick and some string. Then I rubbed old fruit (which I took from trash cans at the stores) on the outside of the box and placed a piece of the fruit inside. When the rabbit went into the box for the fruit, his back brushed up against the stick, causing the trap door to close behind him. We'd pull the trapped rabbit out by its hind legs as it made a high-pitched "eee" sound. It made me wince the first time I heard it. We knocked the rabbit out with a club to the head. Later at home, we skinned it by cutting through the fur on its back and pulling it apart.

Grandpa Calvin and I would sell the rabbit's feet to black and white people who said they were good-luck charms. As a young boy, I thought this was a strange belief. The rabbit had four feet, and they didn't seem to bring him any good luck, or he wouldn't have got caught in my rabbit box. But I never shared my views with the customers, who paid me ten cents a foot in cash and felt good fortune was coming their way with a lucky rabbit's foot. I guess that's what they mean when they say the customer is always right.

I also used to trap birds a couple times a week. I could sell the birds and make some money. I remember once I caught an opossum when I was looking in a trash can for drink bottles to sell. I was on my way to school, and I thought it would be neat to bring that opossum with me to class. I put it in a gunnysack that was in the trash can, too, and took off, bearing my prize. An old man called Black Jesus crossed paths with me farther down the road and said, "Boy, what you got in that sack?" When I said I had an opossum, he didn't believe me. Black Jesus looked in the sack, and liking what he saw, he offered me fifty cents. I took the money, deciding it was better to have coins jingling in my pockets than an opossum in a sack.

Before Black Jesus could eat it, he would have cleansed its system. Opossums eat dead things. An opossum will crawl into the stomach of a dead horse and feed on it, for example. People would put them in barrels with the lids closed and some small holes for air and a pan for water. They'd feed the opossum with potatoes, corn, grains—anything they were growing in the fields. They'd have to clean the barrel frequently, too. Then after a few weeks of this, the animal's system would be cleansed. People said it would taste a lot better.

We were simple country people who sharecropped and raised our own vegetables and made extra cash doing random things like selling opossums. In some ways, the life we led was total peace.

Sometimes, though, it was full of hardship, especially when my old man was alive. I remember my biological father, Pappy Lowery, with spite. He died when I was a young boy. I have never been attached to him or his memories, and I proceed through life as if he never existed. I don't carry his name; I don't even refer to him as my father. When asked about my dad, I talk about my stepdad, Buck, being sure to leave the "step" part out of it.

My biological father, Pappy, was a mean drunk. One time he locked me in a closet while he beat my mom. I looked through the open spaces between the slats in the door, terrified and helpless and wanting so badly to protect my mom. Another time, when I was about three years old, he started to beat her with a stick. When I told him to stop, he dragged my mom into the outhouse, locked her in, and came after me. He cornered me inside, picked me up, and pinned me against the hot cast-iron wood-burning stove. I screamed as my butt and hands burned against the scalding surface. He held me there long enough to leave scars that are still visible.

After that incident, I moved back down the dirt road to my grandma Lela and grandpa Calvin's shack. I think I was an outlet for Pappy's shortcomings and frustrations. He was a fucked-up drunk, screwed in the head, and inadequate. I don't think he could stand my aunt and grandma telling him what to do, but that's what strong Indian women do in my family. He knew I was their favorite, being the first child, illegitimate, and annointed as the "blessed one" by Grandma Lela, who could see into the future.

If Pappy provided, he provided; if he didn't, he didn't. He didn't care either way. Sometimes when he came home drunk, my mom would lock him out. It was better to have him sleep around and gamble than face what he might do when he was home. The best thing that ever happened to my mom was his death, because living with him was no way to live. My dad Buck is a great man.

Pappy died after a drunk-driving accident that led to physical complications; in short, he was a drunk and died because of it. I was a young boy when the accident happened. In the late evening, my mom, my sisters, an Indian named John who hitched a ride, and I were crammed into the front of an old truck. Pappy never owned a car, so I assume he had borrowed his boss's old green Chevy. We started to go around a deep curve on Highway 41, where the Robeson County fairground is now located. The truck went off the road, flipped over, and landed in a gully about ten feet down.

I just remember lying in that gully after coming to covered in mud. I looked up. There were people standing at the top of the dirt bank next to the road looking down at me. My mom and sisters were shaken up pretty bad, John the hitchhiker was paralyzed, and I was in critical condition. I almost didn't make it. I stayed in the hospital for several months before I was well enough to leave. Pappy died later. It wasn't clear if it was because of the accident or cirrhosis of the liver. Either way, liquor got his ass in the end. When I heard he was dead, I was relieved. I found nothing redeeming about him. Unlike some children who excuse their parents' faults and continue to love them even when they are abusive, I have nothing good to say about that drunk and no good memories of him.

Not everyone who knew Pappy felt the way I did. My grandma Lela liked him at first. She changed her mind when she saw his mean, drunken side, but my grandma, like many folks who knew Pappy, had been charmed by him. He was a good-looking lady's man who liked to gamble, fight, flirt, and party. When I was grown, older women would say to me, "You're Pappy's son? Your dad was a fun guy."

"My dad?" I'd say. "He was a jerk."

"Oh, no," they'd tell me. "You didn't know your dad. He was a good man. Everybody liked Pappy."

It depended what side of the fence you were on. These people saw a different side: the fun, partying, gambling man who liked his women, cards, and liquor. I saw the other side: hungover, no money, nasty, violent.

I'm not completely unlike Pappy. I can be wild as a jackass trapped in a hailstorm when the situation requires it. I fought with fists, feet, and any other object as a young man. I was unfaithful to women and wanted mine and everybody else's in my youth. My aunt would say, "That boy is a backslider. One day he'll find God."

My aunt Mildred tried to warn my girlfriend Marsha about me.

Marsha was living in California; I had just taken a new professorial position in North Carolina. Marsha, who was trusting, thought I would remain faithful to her while we lived on opposite coasts.

Aunt Mildred asked Marsha if she really thought this long-distance arrangement would work. Marsha said, "Oh, yeah, sure." Mildred looked at her with a mix of pity and disbelief and said, "You know he's got that Lowery blood. That's bad blood." (Pappy was a Lowery.) Marsha didn't make the connection or take the hint. Mildred shook her head and said, "You're there. He's here. We'll see." Sure enough I found myself another woman. I was still a boy and first-rate backslider.

I realized my dad slept around, because when I was a young man, my mom wanted to know whom I was dating. She wasn't curious; she demanded to know the girls' names and families. I think my mom was making sure I wasn't going out with any of Pappy's illegitimate kids. It was a small community; there were all kinds of hidden interconnections to look out for, so Mom watched me like a hawk.

After Grandma Lela died, my mom had to fend for herself and face a harsh winter. My mom's my hero; this is a fact to me. I watched her struggle and sacrifice. One virtue I firmly believe in is loyalty to those who stand by you in tough times, and I will forever be loyal to my mom for all that she endured on my behalf as a child. I have indeed been blessed with a great life. It has given me the ability to provide a home and anything else my mother, Shirley, and father, Buck, need in their golden years of life.

I have been told many times by friends that it's unbelievable I was able to escape the poverty of my youth. Poverty became my great friend that motivated me to dream and work for a better life. I grew up with the belief that I was the richest child in the world. There were a few nights I went to bed hungry; however, I always had pleasant dreams at night and my days always seemed to include some type of adventure. Poor? Not by any of my standards as a youngster.

# chapter fourteen

# Sacrifice

"Regardless of who your parents are, what they did to or for you, a person
can take control of his or her education and move forward in life, but, son,
it takes a lot of hard work."

—*Patty Bell Hernandez,*
*Ben Chavis's aunt*

When Pappy departed, my mom was just a young woman. She had
me, her first child, when she was sixteen and had five more by the time
she was about twenty-one years old. When Pappy's body hit the muddy
dirt in Robeson County, she had six children to raise on little means. In
addition to sharecropping, my mom tried to make ends meet as a maid
earning between ten and fifteen dollars a week.

In those days, the Food Stamp Program did not exist. There was a
commodities program that provided powdered eggs, powdered milk,
and powdered mashed potatoes. The food had no taste, but it filled up
our guts, thank God. People could only qualify for welfare benefits
when the caseworker and local policy makers considered them worthy
of receiving it. Welfare was managed by the local, not the state or federal, government. The system was eventually changed because it was
considered racist and corrupt, as most caseworkers and welfare recipi-
ents were white even though most of the county residents were Indian
or black.

A social worker in Robeson County visited my mom at our home
after my grandma died and told her she had to give away half of us in
order to qualify for government aid. The lady told my mom to choose

the three children she wished to keep; the others would be put in a foster home. How could any mother be placed in such a situation in America? My mom was treated like an old dog with too many in her litter to feed. She decided to keep all of us and forgo the government assistance. As a result, we nearly starved.

It was a tough winter of little food. It was a cold and rainy winter. My mom probably weighed ninety pounds, and we kids looked like mere skin over bone. One day, there was only enough food in the house to make one piece of cornbread.

My mom told me, her oldest at about five years old, to gather wood and corncobs to get a fire started in the wood stove. It was early evening and raining hard. I set out across the dirt road in front of our dilapidated shack and into the woods. I picked up wood in the wet forest—I can remember it so vividly—the green vines running everywhere and time standing still. It seemed like it took forever. After gathering an armful of wood, I grabbed corncobs from the neighbor's pigpen. The rain soaked through my clothes, and it started to grow dark, but the hunger in my gut and the love for my mom took over my fear of the harsh cold and darkness.

I brought the wood and corncobs to my mom, who lit the old wood stove, the same one my dad had pinned me against in his rage. One parent turned the wood stove into an instrument of love and sacrifice, the other of torture.

Smoke filled the room as the wet wood struggled to burn. My mom placed the black cast-iron frying pan on the stove and cooked that one piece of cornbread as we children sat at the table waiting. She divided it into six pieces and sat and watched as we ate. When I was done, I said, "Mom, aren't you going to eat anything?"

She said, "Naw, Buddy, I'm not hungry."

I realized sitting there at that table that my mother was struggling and that I had to do something about it. That motivated me. I wasn't ever going to let my mom starve in my whole life. I think of that and what my mom did for us, and I'm supposed to feel sorry for these lazy losers who refuse to work in Oakland? She didn't eat nothing.

The next day I went and stole some eggs. I went down the dirt road. This farm was about a half mile away, and the owners were gone, and I went into that chicken pen and ran up on those hens clucking and sitting on their eggs. There was a snake in the chicken pen, and I'm thinking it's that snake or it's my ass, and I'm not even in school yet. So you wonder how I see the world? I see it from the eyes of that child who watched his mom almost starve for her children.

I had to lie to my mom about the source of the eggs because she was, and is to this day, a deeply religious woman. My mom did not believe in stealing no matter what the circumstance. She would have whipped the hide off me with what little strength she had left if she knew I had stolen the eggs. I told her a man gave them to me for helping him in his yard.

The eggs were just a short-term solution to a larger problem. The white family whom my mom worked for as a maid gave us clothes and other household items, but it took the help of my aunt Kathleen, my mom's sister, to stabilize the family. Kathleen was about seventeen at the time.

There was a country store a couple of miles from where we lived. At the store, people could get credit for food and other items. My mom didn't make enough money to receive any credit, but Kathleen had started dating Johnny Smith, the white store manager, who was married, and as a result she got free goods for the family. Kathleen's unexpected romance was a godsend for us. By dating Johnny she provided our family with food and the occasional ride into town. He was a nice guy who would come riding up in his car with candy for us kids. I remember sitting in his car and thinking how wonderful it was to be eating and driving around instead of walking.

In thanks for what my aunt and mom did for me and for the family, I give both of them money on a frequent basis and help them with anything they need. My mom and aunt didn't think about themselves; they thought about their family. Now how do you top that? You know the old saying: if you could walk in my shoes—hell, I couldn't walk in my mom's or my aunt's shoes. I have it made compared to the struggles they faced. How could life ever get any worse than the time I split that piece of cornbread among my siblings and watched my mother sit by, not eating?

Since I lived through that, these little trials we have today in America are nothing to me. The attitude I take is: you can't get me because this is so easy. I don't see the students at American Indian Public Charter School who are mostly poor Indians, blacks, Mexicans, and Asians, some of whom are the children of drug addicts, alcoholics, and inmates, as victims. Their families have welfare. They have food. AIPCS students wear nice shoes. I never had shoes in the summer. I went barefoot all summer, running around, working, and playing in the fields, because you weren't supposed to wear out your shoes. I just thought it was that way for everyone. I didn't even know we were poor. It was just a way of life, and I never heard my mom blame anyone for our problems.

Life has improved for my people. During my childhood most Lumbee Indians were sharecroppers who did not own land. They would tend crops, perform manual labor, and clean homes. Educated Lumbees could teach. Teaching and preaching were the two best jobs Lumbees could aspire to have until halfway through the twentieth century. When factories such as Converse and Temptation Hosiery opened in Robeson County in the 1960s, they sparked the beginning of an economic turnaround for our people. Those factories changed our lives. They were nonunion and couldn't care less about your race if you were a hard worker. Indians were not allowed in unions; neither were blacks or Asians. Historically, unions screwed minorities more than the KKK. Unions love to say they're for the working people; could it be they didn't consider us Indians people?

Along with the new wave of factories, I-95 changed the way of life in Robeson County. As the halfway point between New York City and Miami, Robeson County has become a convenient shipping hub for industrial and agricultural goods, such as tobacco (the county ranks third in national tobacco production). Looking down at Interstate 95, which runs through the heart of Robeson County, you always see a line of semis headed north and a line of semis headed south. With the freeway came trade and commerce, which led to more jobs and money, a desperately needed jolt to the economy. The combination of factory jobs and shipping lanes boosted the local economy back in the 1960s and helped it continue to grow.

Thank God for free market capitalism, private property, and public education in the United States. I was a poor Indian boy who was able to get out of the tobacco fields and pursue a life that turned out better than any dreams I ever had as a child in North Carolina. This is part of what I want to pass on to our students.

Today the poverty I see is the poverty of little or no mathematics and language arts skills. People deemed by the census to be living below the poverty line often have food and social services that they can rely on. How often do they receive a quality secondary education that prepares them for higher education? I believe if you gave a poor Oakland boy an hour and a half of mathematics a day and an hour and a half of language arts a day for 196 school days, like we do at AIPCS, he would outperform a rich boy who only received forty-five minutes of math and forty-five minutes of language arts a day. I would also wager that if you took a rich boy from an affluent area and put him in a low-performing school in the inner city for his K–12 education, he would end up academically remedial just like his poorer peers. Education is the key to providing students of all races and economic classes with equal opportunity to succeed in our society. I believe academic justice will lead to social justice.

I instill in our students that they should get an education and learn from the people and events around them without succumbing to the negative aspects of their environment. I want the students to be school smart, street smart, aware of the mistakes I made in life, and observant of the unsuccessful behaviors of those around them. Instead of being "victims," they can be "survivors." They can break the cycle of drug and alcohol abuse, stupidity, laziness, and irresponsibility to really achieve something wonderful in life.

My biological dad, Pappy, was a drunk, my grandpa Calvin became a drunk after Grandma Lela passed away, and my brother James is a drug addict. I am a social drinker and have never used drugs. My path in life has been radically different from that of my brothers and sisters. At times I can't relate to them on any level other than bloodlines and family. If you include the four stepsiblings from Buck, there are ten children total in the family. I'm in a different class than they are in relation to higher education. None of them graduated from high school; I have a Ph.D., though I'm still a country Indian who couldn't be brainwashed by the university. My brothers and sisters all live in Robeson County except two; one is forty miles away in South Carolina, and another lives in Missouri. Several of my siblings lost most of their teeth in their thirties, and two of them are on welfare. I'm the only child in the family with a university degree, and my mom still treats us all the same because we are the same in so many ways.

One time I teased my sister about the welfare check she was sitting around the house waiting for one afternoon. She snapped at me, "You're just as bad as the white man." I replied, "You'd better thank the white man because he's the one writing you the check."

The expectations for achievement in my family by middle-class standards are low. None of my siblings have died and only one of them,

James, the drug addict, spent time in prison. Those are indicators that my family is doing well.

James has been in and out of prison for various crimes. My brother Larry, the youngest in the family, is sick with AIDS. He's the best-looking of us all. He's going to die, but you know what? He has lived his life and made his choices. I can respect that. Larry was never cautious. When he came out, it was the '80s, and he knew about AIDS and condoms.

My stepbrother Wayne is my closest sibling. My relationships with my other brothers and sisters during childhood were more distant, mostly because of gender and age differences. The boys in my family didn't play much with the girls, and age gaps between my brothers kept me from being close with them. What's a sixteen-year-old boy going to do with his ten-year-old brother? My sisters had all left home and had kids of their own by age sixteen.

I didn't have my first child, Celeste, until my mid-twenties, or Lela, the second, until my thirties, which struck my brothers and sisters as strange. They thought I was gay. My grandpa Calvin told me I didn't have to be married to have children. I guess I was just on a different track from the rest of my family.

Success is relative. Where I'm from in North Carolina people say: that boy is doing good. All that means is you're not in jail and you're working. My niece told me what she looks for in a boyfriend; she said if the guy's got a job and a car, he's a keeper. I don't apply middle-class standards to my relatives or try to give them a middle-class lifestyle. I'm not responsible for people my own age. I take care of my parents and children. I believe in supporting the old and the young, but I have no patience for lazy middle-aged adults, even if they are kin. I almost never give my siblings money, because you know what I've found? People are generally unappreciative of handouts. Also, if people are always provided for, they won't learn to work hard or figure out how to succeed on their own. It's an honor to give my hundred-year-old aunt, Pearl Bowan, and other elderly relatives money as a gift. It means a lot to them because of the poverty they lived in during the past.

I am not leaving any of my children money when I die. They probably wouldn't appreciate the money, spend it wisely, or learn to thrive independently. I'm a self-made man, and that's the only model I live by at this final stage of my life. My daughter Lela is in college and manages some of our apartments to pay for her education. My children will have my contacts as well. I paid for my own college education while sending money home to my mom. From my perspective, my children have it made. The older ones didn't have to send me money when they were in school, and the younger ones won't have to, either.

I make sure to bring my children and grandchildren to Robeson County every year. I want them to know their family and history and partake in some Lumbee traditions, such as spot fishing each fall. As for the children at American Indian Public Charter School, I make sure to steep them in a culture rich in achievement, academics, free market capitalism, discipline, and family. I assure you they are preparing themselves with the skills needed to have a wonderful life and to pass their knowledge on to others. What more could a principal ask of his students who are giving their time every day to enhance their education?

# chapter fifteen

# Free Market Capitalism in the Classroom

"Whenever I was sick, I thought to myself that if I didn't go to school I would miss the hundred dollars, which kept me motivated. My attendance is still good even though we don't get paid at the high school. I come to school regularly, and if I'm sick I still come because I want to learn more. The second reason I come is if you miss five days you get retained."

*—Jose Mendoza, a ninth-grader at AIPHS in 2007–2008, and a graduate of AIPCS who received the perfect attendance money every year in sixth through eighth grade*

I am fond of saying I have no original ideas. I look at what works, and I adopt it. There's no point in reinventing the wheel when you can just find it and recycle it. The slogan I use at AIPCS, "A School at Work," was adapted from the slogan of Saddletree, North Carolina (where we have a family farm), "A Community at Work."

One of my most fundamental educational practices, paying students for perfect attendance, came from my third-grade teacher, Mrs. Helen Smith.

Mrs. Smith realized that students who attended school every day or almost every day did better than students who often missed school. She also knew her students (all Lumbees) were poor, so money motivated them. As Mrs. Smith later told me, she was willing to do whatever it took to get her students to come to school every day and to learn.

On my first day of class in the third grade, Mrs. Smith announced that she would give each of us three dollars at the end of the year if we had perfect attendance and recited three hundred Bible verses. That got my attention. Three dollars was a fortune! Before third grade, I had an atrocious attendance record. I used to go fishing or tag along with my grandpa Calvin instead of going to school. In third grade, with money motivating me, it was different.

Every day I'd be reading that Bible. You've never seen so many third-grade Indian children running around with Bibles in their hands. At first I stuck with the short verses, like "Thou shall not kill." That would count as one verse in Mrs. Smith's record book. We could approach her desk at any time and say we'd like to recite a verse. After using up all the short verses I could find, I remember memorizing long ones, like John 3:16, which I still remember to this day: "For God so loved the world that he gave his only begotten Son, that whosoever believeth in him should not perish but have everlasting life." The Lumbees love that one. I remember seeing a car dealer advertise in the *Robeson Journal* with John 3:16 written on his ad.

The Bible didn't rub off on me too much as a child. Some people misinterpret its purpose. In my opinion, few are converted to Christianity from reading the Bible. People usually become religious when something spiritual or tragic happens and they ask God into their lives. The Bible is a great guide on how to lead a good life. I've never thought of myself as a religious man, but I make sure to keep that to myself when I'm around my family, which is full of backsliders and Holy Rollers. The Bible fascinates me, though, because I love the stories. The Bible has all the elements of intrigue. It also teaches respect, discipline, human nature, and customs. While reading the Bible, I am struck by how often the word "property" appears. Private property or landownership remains of the utmost importance to us Lumbee Indians and to many groups of people throughout the world.

Proverbs is one of my favorite books in the Bible. It focuses a great deal on discipline and knowledge. It says in Proverbs chapter 1, verse 7: "The fear of the Lord is the beginning of knowledge, but fools despise wisdom and discipline." It's my belief that fear is good and keeps most of us in line. When people have no fear, they are dangerous to themselves and their community. Anyone who acts like a fool should be treated like a fool. There have been many occasions in my life when I have been a fool. I work to instill the discipline and wisdom in our students that will prevent them from making many of my mistakes.

At one point during third grade while keeping up on my Bible verses and maintaining perfect attendance, I almost missed a day of school, putting my three dollars at stake. See, I had wanted cowboy boots in the worst way. I kept begging for them and begging for them, so my mom finally broke down and bought me a pair the summer before school started. I felt like a bona fide cowboy for a couple of months, but then one day the bottom fell off of one of the boots. At first I tried to tape it back on, but that didn't work. My mom sewed the sole to the rest of the boot, but it fell off again. There was no way to save that boot from the scrap heap. It was winter, and I didn't have another pair of shoes. I knew the other students would tease me if I showed up to school with no shoes on. It didn't matter that the rest of the kids were poor, too. They'd still pick at you when they could. That's just part of growing up and learning as a child.

I thought, "How am I going to keep my perfect attendance and save face when I've only got one boot?" After thinking it through, I found an answer to the soleless boot dilemma. I wrapped my foot and ankle with a bulky rag and covered it with a white sock. I told everyone I had twisted my ankle and that it had swollen so much I couldn't put my boot on. Here I am reading the Bible verses and lying to my classmates because I was embarrassed I didn't have a pair of shoes to wear. They bought my story hook, line, and sinker.

I had to keep up the lie for a week, while my mom scraped together enough money to buy me a used pair of shoes at the Hodge Podge used-shoe store on West Fifth Street in Lumberton, North Carolina. But I never missed a day of school that year. In the end my discipline and hard work paid off in the sum of three whopping dollars.

When I was an assistant professor at San Francisco State University in the 1980s, I ran into Mrs. Smith in a restaurant one summer during my vacation home. I reintroduced myself and asked Mrs. Smith if she still gave attendance rewards, which I offered to pay for at that time. She said she no longer did. Her school's administration wouldn't let her use the Bible in her class. Thank God the principal didn't have such rules in my day. I might have been a third-grade dropout.

I respected Mrs. Smith's wisdom and the method she used to motivate us to attend school, so I offered her the chance to fly for free anywhere in the world. Though flattered and thankful, she, like several of the other teachers I have given the same offer to, politely turned it down. I think in most cases that the handful of teachers I have offered to buy flights for are uncomfortable about the idea of air travel. Robeson County is what they know, and that's where they feel at ease. I do enjoy getting together with many of them to this day. One summer Mrs. Smith called me up and said she wanted to take a trip to Charleston, South Carolina, with her daughter, who is an attorney. I was really excited to book their reservations at the Wentworth Mansion for July 28–31, 2008. Mrs. Smith's educational gifts to me as a teacher changed my life and affected thousands of students, educators, and families in Oakland, California, financially, academically, and socially.

I know her attendance policy made me a responsible student for the first time in my life. I saw how it affected my classmates as well. Most of the students received three dollars at the end of the year. Four students out of that third-grade class completed their university degree in education. Who says good teachers don't make a difference?

Realizing the power of money to young, poor Indian children, I set a similar policy in place at American Indian Public Charter School. Students who attend school every day receive up to $100 at the end of the year. I took Mrs. Smith's idea and modified it by striking out the religion. Instead of reinventing the wheel, I recycled it, altered it, and set it rolling again.

Since good attendance had been a goal and a challenge at American Indian Public Charter School, I adopted the method that Mrs. Helen Smith used on us at Piney Grove Elementary. I persuaded students to attend school by promising to pay them for perfect attendance. Currently at AIPCS, sixth-graders receive $50 at the end of the year if they never miss a day of school, seventh-graders receive $75, and eighth-graders get paid $100 for perfect attendance.

The money motivates most students to strive for perfect attendance. Most of our students, past and present, are poor, so the perfect attendance award is a significant amount of money to them, just like it was to me as a boy. Students who miss school due to attending a funeral, being in the hospital, or showing up to school sick and leaving with their homework after being checked out will still receive their perfect attendance money.

In addition to the individual rewards for perfect attendance, there is also a class competition for best attendance. A large, colorful board hangs in the hallway listing each class and its number of consecutive days of perfect attendance. If every student in the class is present, that day counts as a day of perfect attendance. In 2002, the class perfect attendance record was 31 consecutive days. That means every student in the class was present for 31 days in a row. In 2006, Mr. Berniker's seventh-grade class set an amazing school record with 180 days of perfect attendance! I put their class photo and attendance achievement on several billboards across Oakland so people driving by or walking through various parts of the city could see what those students had accomplished.

I love to see the classes compete with each other because I believe records were made to be tied or broken. I want our schools and students to get better year after year. And you know what? The attendance record was tied by Ms. Lee's sixth-grade class of 2007 and then broken by Mrs. Petel's class at AIPCS II. So far, the students in Mrs. Petel's class have not missed a day of school for almost two years since they started sixth grade in 2008. I believe they will be our first class to have three years of perfect attendance. Now that is a culture of achievement.

Our attendance policies have been incredibly effective. The year before I took over the school, the attendance rate hovered around 65 percent. During my first year (2000–2001), the daily attendance rate rose to 95 percent. The next year it climbed to 98 percent. For the past three years, the daily attendance rate has been 99 percent. For the 2006–2007 school year, for example, the attendance rate was 99.87 percent at both American Indian Public Charter School and American Indian Public High School. Do you realize the odds of both schools having the same attendance? At the end of the 2005–2006 year, over 85 percent of the graduating eighth-graders had not missed a single unexcused day of class in the three years they had been at the school. Those eighth-graders received $150 as a reward for their dedication.

Schools say we shouldn't be for profit. I intentionally put in the mission statement that we are preparing our students for success in a free market capitalist society. The way the secondary public school system runs today, it's outdated and should be replaced. We have a capitalist philosophy in America, so we need to prepare students to become thriving members in a free market economy.

I explicitly promote free market capitalism at American Indian Public Charter School. I believe if a drug dealer were to offer an AIPCS student money to sell dope, our student would think, "I'll make more by going to school every day and getting $100 at the end of the year." When AIPCS students who have no athletic ability tell me they want to play for the L.A. Lakers or the Oakland Raiders when they grow up, I say, "No, you want to own them and run the team." I believe fervently in the importance of private property ownership; you have to own property to have more control of your own life. Growing up, it was always instilled in me to buy my own land and to look for opportunity where most people would believe there was none.

One person's problem is another person's opportunity. I remember sitting with my grandpa Calvin on the porch when I was a boy one day and there was a fire in the distance. He looked at the black smoke billowing up against the horizon and said, "There's a job for somebody." That seems harsh, doesn't it? Oh, well. When schools are dysfunctional and failing to educate students, I see the opportunity in it for the American Indian Model of Education. That's why I love the No Child Left Behind Act. The incompetent people have to compete with me, and they can't. The left-leaning social-justice liberals who preach diversity and tolerance generally don't prepare students academically to be successful in higher education. I couldn't care less what sex or color someone is if that person runs a good school. To many wishy-washy administrators and teachers unions, I am despicable and racist, but there's proof that learning takes place at my school. Throughout the United States, we have dim-witted administrators running schools who waste and embezzle money and who get caught up in touchy-feely ideologies that produce very poor academic results. How often are they held accountable for depriving students of an education?

One time a white man drove by my house with a bunch of kids stuffed in a raggedy old car and, seeing me in the front yard, said, "Wow, I wish I was as lucky as you to have a house like this. Sure must be nice." That pissed me off. I said, "It's not luck, you cracker. I work harder than you do. If you worked hard, you could live like this, too." Since it wasn't the reaction the idiot was expecting, he quickly drove off without a word.

In America you can do anything if you will discipline yourself, work hard, and sacrifice. This philosophy is ingrained in my hard head. That's part of the reason I don't believe in giving anything away for free unless it's for the elderly, handicapped, or children who cannot work. Able-bodied people do not benefit from continued handouts in the long run, and they feel better when they work for what they get. When I lived in San Francisco, I frequently crossed paths with a bum I called Jamaica at the Church Street Muni station. When he asked me for change, I told him I didn't give handouts, so he would have to earn my money by entertaining me. He told me a joke, which made me laugh, so I paid him. Later when we would see each other in the Muni station, if he had a good joke to share, I'd give him some change, but if the man had nothing to say, I would continue on my way.

I don't see "homeless" people in the Bay Area; I see bums, transients, and drunks. When the politicians and social workers label them homeless, they get a government grant, which creates jobs for the left-wing opportunists who fight for causes that put money in their pockets. To my people, the Lumbees, you're an embarrassment to your family if you're a bum. Everyone who works in the household in some way has a place to stay.

I don't give my students anything for free. They need to earn everything they get through work. I will arrange a job in a local restaurant for any student who says his family cannot afford lunch. I don't just hand them money and say, "Here. Take it." No way. I give students bus passes when their families cannot afford them, but I make it very clear that when I'm paying for you to come to school, you'd better not be late or absent. I've taken back students' bus passes when they failed to live up to their part of the bargain. They can walk to school; it's their choice.

I sometimes go around to the classes and give money to students who have done their work and who have stayed out of detention. I'll come in and say, "Everybody who has done their homework this week and hasn't been given detention, stand up." More than half of the class will stand up. I praise those students and tell them, "If you work hard in life, you'll get the money. It feels good having money in your pocket, doesn't it?" The students grin and nod. I'll say to the seated students, "You guys want to be like these students, because they're getting paid." I walk around to the standing students, smile at them, make eye contact, say their names, congratulate them, and count off the bills into their hands. I usually give each student between three and five dollars. I carry a huge stack of one-dollar bills that makes the kids' eyes bulge out.

I also pay the students who earn perfect attendance money with stacks of one-dollar bills. When they walk down the aisle at graduation with a stack of one hundred ones in their hands, most of them grin ear to ear and are flustered about where to put it. It's great to watch the students enjoy their hard-earned money. They deserve every penny of it.

The mission statement explicitly states the school will prepare students for a free market capitalist society. Paying them is one clear case of that. The responsible students who do their work and behave receive money. Isn't that how it is in the real world? I instill in their minds that hard work equals pay and respect.

Paying students for perfect attendance serves several purposes. First of all, it ensures they attend school. Poor attendance is a major problem in many low-income, inner-city schools, and poor attendance leads to lousy academic performance. If students are not in school, how can they learn? Second, the attendance money also supports my free market capitalist viewpoint that hard work equals pay and respect. Third, paying children to be in school makes money for the school because most K–12 public school funding in California is tied to attendance. It's more cost-effective to pay students to attend school than to lose money for absences. California public schools are not given funding based on enrollment; they are given funding based on average daily attendance. That means the higher the attendance rate, the higher the funding. In Oakland Unified School District, the absence of a sixth-grade student for one day constitutes a loss of over $35. Paying a sixth-grader $50 at the end of the year for perfect attendance costs less than it would if that student missed two days of school.

Here's the catch, though. It is illegal in California to use public school money to pay students. It's fine, however, to hire your wife, girlfriend, or both, which many school administrators have done. Where is the logic in that? Because I'm not allowed to pay students with school funds, I pay the students out of my own pocket. I realize I'm in a unique position as a school principal. I give myself a salary of only $25,000 from the school and donate it back. I'm very proud to be the lowest-paid public school administrator in the state of California. The money I made in real estate and previous work experience gives me the ability to use my own funds to pay students for perfect attendance, hard work, and good behavior. I'm not the principal of AIPCS because I need the money. I'm the principal because I love working with our students. It's my dream job!

# chapter sixteen

# Schools Have Enough Money

"You could give public schools all the money in the world, and it still wouldn't be enough."

—*Ben Chavis,*
*as stated on ABC's 20/20 special program "Stupid in America"*

I hate it when educators say they don't have enough money to run their schools effectively. Schools don't need more money! They need better money managers. Taxpayers have been conned for years into believing the problem with public schools is that they don't have enough money. Schools have plenty of funding; the problem is most school administrators operate their schools with no business sense and therefore end up in debt. I'm a free market capitalist. A school is a business, and it should be run like one. I don't go for all the socialist mumbo jumbo that these ridiculous educators toss around.

I had to work with the debt I had inherited at American Indian Public Charter School due to the previous leaders' incompetence, not lack of funding. As proof of our ability to work with the funds provided by the state and federal government, we not only brought American Indian Public Charter School out of debt but also managed to maintain a 30 percent reserve at the school several years later. By law, I need to have a 3 percent reserve, but I go further to make sure the school is protected. Growing up in poverty is my advantage. I can get by with less, and I'm thinking down the road—not on what's here right now.

When a funding source is not permanent, I won't hire with that money. Why would I want to have to fire personnel when that funding gets cut? I learned not to hire with soft money from the superintendent of Nogales Unified School District in Arizona, Mr. Buck Clark, with whom I did an administrative internship. I realized the significance of Mr. Clark's advice when dealing with the ugly and unfortunate situation I encountered at Theodore Roosevelt Boarding School on the Fort Apache reservation in Arizona, in which I had to fire people when the school no longer had funding for their positions.

Through my budgeting success at American Indian Public Charter School, I have proven it's a myth that public schools need more money in order to achieve their academic goals. As a charter school, AIPCS receives less money per pupil than the regular public schools in Oakland Unified School District, yet we outperform them all. In 2005, the average per pupil expenditure for Oakland Unified School District was $8,675. For the state of California, the average per pupil expenditure was $7,077. The per pupil expenditure for American Indian Public Charter School in 2005 was $6,271. Even though that amount is significantly less than what the Oakland public schools receive for each of their students, I think we are given sufficient funds to provide students with a high-quality education focused on rigorous academics. As a business-minded principal, I allocate funding to what I deem most important: academics.

I favor simplicity when it comes to spending. I use Title I funding, which is federal money given to schools serving low-income students, on high-quality, standards-based textbooks and smart teachers. As stated earlier, one thing most low-performing schools have in common is they don't use textbooks tied to the state standards curriculum.

In addition to allocating funding to textbooks, I pay my teachers more than the average salaries offered by the Oakland Unified School District. A starting teacher at American Indian Public Charter School in 2008 received $45,500 a year, which was about $7,000 more than the district's starting salary. I want to attract the best teachers to our school. You get what you pay for; I can acquire smarter, more qualified teachers by providing them with a higher starting salary than they would normally receive elsewhere. Teachers past and present have come from excellent universities, such as Dartmouth, Duke, Harvard, UC Berkeley, Columbia, Cornell, Wesleyan, Stanford, and Brown. In addition to the higher salary, I usually give staff members a Christmas bonus and an end-of-the-year performance bonus for the school's success on the STAR tests.

Advice I'd give to principals interested in hearing it is that at first it is important to show your merit without accepting private money. That way, you prove your school can accomplish success while staying within the means normally allotted to schools. Then, once you are a high-achieving school, you can consider receiving outside money in order to expand and do even more.

Increased spending on public education in America has not led to better academic performance. Since 1971, the United States doubled the amount of money spent per pupil on education (adjusting for inflation), yet graduation rates and test scores stagnated. Regardless of what the data indicate, the myth that schools would do better if only they had more money still remains a strong political angle. Schools and districts continue to overspend and then turn around and blame their debt on a lack of funding and then ask for more money from taxpayers.

In 2003, the Oakland Unified School District was taken over by the California Department of Education because it had gone bankrupt. OUSD overspent its budget so excessively that it was forced to rely on the state for a $100 million bailout loan, the largest at the time of any school district in California. I and many others were furious with the superintendent, Mr. Dennis Chaconas, for doing such an irresponsible job regarding finance in Oakland Unified. Mr. Chaconas was asked to resign and given a severance package of $389,000, the equivalent of eighteen months of salary. Was his golden parachute a reward for driving Oakland public schools into enormous debt? The Oakland school board was stripped of its power, putting the California Department of Education in charge of the district.

I supported the philosophy of the first appointed state administrator, Dr. Randolph Ward, who was called in to oversee Oakland Unified after Chaconas was forced out. Many people in Oakland saw Dr. Ward as the enemy, a representative of the "big brother" state government, who was trying to close schools. I saw him as someone who attempted to return financial and academic sanity to the district. He looked at the bigger picture, but many of the OUSD go-getters for equality didn't agree with his methods for solving the district's problems. They couldn't manage their money, but they wanted to say Dr. Ward created their school system's troubles. How could you blame him for the low academics and poor financial management that had been going on for over forty years in Oakland?

Dr. Randolph Ward came to Oakland Unified School District with a good track record. He had turned the Compton Unified School District around after it was taken over by the state for fiscal irresponsibility. Under his leadership, Compton Unified became the first school district in the country to pay back its loan.

Unfortunately, after the 2006 school year came to a close, Dr. Ward decided to take the position of county superintendent in San Diego, and leave his post in Oakland, where he had been constantly attended by a bodyguard due to being threatened and attacked by people in the community who said they were concerned for the kids. If they were so concerned, these individuals would have made sure the students were properly educated and the district's finances were effectively managed. Because of their incompetence, Jack O'Connell, the California state superintendent, had to send Dr. Ward to Oakland Unified to clean up their mess. Do you see the urban ghetto logic these people use to interpret events in their lives and in the community?

People go cuckoo over public schools. They don't see the bigger picture, and they keep believing that American schools would improve with more money. The teachers union often spearheads the cry for increased funding in schools. They also strongly oppose the No Child Left Behind Act (NCLB), saying it is unfair and underfunded. The union opposes NCLB because it requires stricter standards for academic achievement and, therefore, threatens job security. The teachers union doesn't want competition. They want to maintain their control of public education wages and policies and continue collecting their monthly fees from educators.

Many folks believe teachers unions or associations are the problem with public schools. I disagree. The teachers union, like the Mafia, is paid by its members to protect their personal and financial interests. In Oakland Unified School District (with the exception of charter schools), all educators, including substitutes, are enrolled in the teachers union the day they are employed. The teachers union fees are taken out before one cent is paid to the substitute, who has no say in the matter. Who can blame the teachers union in Oakland (called the Oakland Education Association) for getting their cut of the money up front? I think that's great for them. A lot of substitutes have called it highway robbery. In the union's defense, it protects the interests of its members. A few years ago, I spoke with Ben Visnick, the president of the Oakland Education Association, about our teachers joining. He said it would be problematic. Our teachers are paid $7,000 more in their starting salaries than other teachers in the district, and from Mr. Visnick's perspective that was an issue.

What has happened in this country is we have pimped kids in the name of jobs and pay for adults. Politics in public education is all about jobs and money. Do you think the postal service wanted Federal Express to compete with them? Who wants competition in any business? The teachers union wants to protect their jobs and control the sector. I find it telling that so many teachers union representatives in Oakland, as well as Sheila Jordan, the superintendent of Alameda County, send their children to private schools. Does it sound like they have faith in the Oakland public schools?

The Oakland teachers union made it difficult for Dr. Randolph Ward to focus on turning the district around and to get back to fiscal sanity. For the pending three-year teacher contracts of 2006, Dr. Ward wanted to restore the 4 percent pay cut in teacher salaries originally set in 2004. The union not only fought the pay cut but also proposed a 3 percent salary increase. Dr. Ward and California State Superintendent Jack O'Connell said OUSD couldn't afford the salary increase without cutting programs, which they were reluctant to do. Dr. Ward also wanted to incorporate into the teacher contract the payment of one-half of 1 percent of teacher salaries to health care premiums. Teachers in OUSD were currently receiving free health care. The teachers union opposed the health care contribution as well. The average teacher salary in OUSD in 2006 was $53,000. One-half of 1 percent of $53,000 is $265. The union threatened to strike. The teachers union fought for months, taking the focus in Oakland public schools away from students and toward employees.

A tentative agreement between the teachers union and Dr. Ward was reached on April 20, 2006, the night before the planned strike. That agreement was a 6.25 percent teacher raise over three years, one year of free health care followed by two years of paying one-half of 1 percent of their teacher salaries, and the condition that the contract be retroactively dated to July 1, 2005. Some members of the union wanted to keep fighting for a better settlement. Because of the last-minute timing, it was believed many teachers wouldn't know the strike had been called off. As a result, school was canceled for the following day. A euphemism was patched over the whole affair as the day officially became a "student-free day." Now, think about this: forty-two thousand students in the Oakland Unified School District, mostly us darkies, stayed home getting dumber, while teachers went to Peralta Park to celebrate or debate the money they had won. Do you understand how we have pimped students in the name of public education jobs for adults?

As reported in Grace Rauh's *Oakland Tribune* article of April 21, 2006, "Teachers Reluctant to Celebrate Mysterious Tentative Agreement," Dr. Randolph Ward appeared briefly at the park where hundreds of Oakland's thirty-two hundred teachers union members gathered to barbecue and celebrate or complain. When Dr. Ward left, surrounded by three police officers and his bodyguard, some teachers chanted, "Hey ho, hey ho, Randy Ward has got to go." One teacher spat on the ground as Dr. Ward walked by. I can see why Dr. Ward wanted to head to San Diego.

Teachers unions have made such inroads in establishing employee protections that it's very hard to fire public school staff who are incompetent or to act with common sense without getting entwined in red tape. In Joanne Jacobs's article "More Money for Schools Doesn't End the Problems," printed in the *San Francisco Chronicle* on September 12, 2004, Ms. Jacobs writes about one father who reported that an obscenity, an incorrectly spelled "fuck," had been written at the entrance of his child's elementary school in San Jose, California. Someone in the office told him it would be taken care of. When he showed up at the school the next day and saw that the graffiti was still there, he decided to take matters into his own hands. He was a construction worker, so he took out what he needed from his truck and began to remove the obscenity. A school employee quickly approached him and told him to stop immediately. She said it was a union-protected job and he'd be arrested if he didn't vacate the premises. The graffiti remained on the entrance wall for two weeks, greeting the children as they entered the school each day. That father found out how much parent involvement and democracy schools really want.

Unions are just one part of the larger mess of public education. I'm a registered Democrat, but let me tell you something: Democrats are the ones who destroyed secondary public education in this country. The Republicans must take a portion of the blame, too, because in the 1960s with all the racial upheaval, they gave control of public schools to the liberal socialist Democrats (let's call them LSD). It was, like, okay, flakes, you can have this. Remember the War on Poverty and the Johnson era and the race riots? It was like the Republicans said we got to cool out these darkies. Let's give public education to the Democrats, and they can deal with it. That's my theory. Then the LSD went to the other extreme—from discipline and structure to schools without walls.

During the schools without walls movement, architects built schools without interior walls. Do you realize how ridiculous the concept is of educating two hundred to three hundred students in one open area while teaching different subjects? The open classrooms did not use detailed curricula or standardized tests. The students would move from one "interest center" to another, learning at their own pace with the assistance of the instructor, and supposedly "discovering" knowledge on their own. In practice this setup was not very effective for students. There were no mechanisms in place to guarantee that students were learning the basics. In short, educators did not have to be held accountable for the teaching of grade-level curriculum. Do you see how this set the stage for decades of lousy public education in this country?

Eventually there was a strong backlash to the schools without walls movement; however, the '60s-style approach to education, which valued freedom and creativity (code word in education for LSD nonsense) over structure and the basics, lingered and became so entrenched that it couldn't just be eradicated when the flaws of the system became apparent. Criticism of public education continued for decades before any significant legislation passed that moved American schools in the direction of accountability and standards. In the mid-'70s, with the Vietnam War dragging on and the economy tanking, critics viewed the public schools with a wary eye, claiming that academic standards had fallen by the wayside, while violence in schools had increased. This was indeed the case for minorities and the poor.

I remember in 1983, when President Reagan released the report "A Nation at Risk." It was loaded with information showing how America's public education system was failing our children. President Reagan's administration never implemented any effective educational changes as a follow-up, but it did get policy makers to focus on public education. Reagan's report set the course for George W. Bush's No Child Left Behind Act of 2002, almost two decades later. "A Nation at Risk" recommended emphasizing the basic subjects, like reading and math, adopting measurable standards, improving teacher quality, lengthening the school year, and increasing student expectations, all of which form the backbone of No Child Left Behind.

It's kind of funny to me when Democrats criticize the No Child Left

Behind Act and see it as Republican in nature, because NCLB was not only based on Reagan's findings but also on Lyndon Johnson's Elementary and Secondary Education Act of 1965. The 1965 education act was one of Johnson's Great Society programs that tried to bring equal opportunity to children of poverty by closing the achievement gap between high- and low-income students and between white and black students. It's also important to point out that the No Child Left Behind Act received bipartisan support in Congress, passing by a vote of 381 to 41 in the House and 87 to 10 in the Senate.

I have said many times, I love the No Child Left Behind Act! NCLB is the greatest education legislation that has ever been passed for the sake of minorities in public schools. *Brown v. the Board of Education*, the 1954 Supreme Court ruling that outlawed racial segregation in public schools, let us sit in the classrooms with whites; however, there was no accountability confirming minorities were getting an education. Now the No Child Left Behind Act ensures black, American Indian, Hispanic, handicapped, and special education students are provided the opportunity to compete with everybody else. If public schools don't provide that education, the state can close them down. Before, they would stop a school's federal funding if they didn't let minorities in the schoolhouse. It took fifty years for public education to do something! Blacks, American Indians, and Hispanics have been standing around in public schools being dumbed down for fifty long years. The No Child Left Behind Act says all students will get an education, or we'll let another organization take over. We need true equality in schools. The handicapped must pass, the poor kids must pass, and all of this must happen regardless of race. That's moving in the right direction to me.

No Child Left Behind increases accountability. The act requires all states to implement rigorous, standards-based curricula that hold all children to high levels of academic achievement. In order to make sure schools implement challenging grade-level standards, students take state and sometimes national standardized tests at the end of the school year that assess how well they have mastered the academic standards. The test results are broken down into categories, such as race, limited English proficiency, special education, and socioeconomic status. That way, schools can see where they need improvement, and the public can be made aware that, for example, the local middle school in their area has a great track record for seventh-grade math achievement with Hispanics but a low success rate with its African-American eighth-graders in English. NCLB's goal is to hold all public schools accountable for all of their subgroups.

No Child Left Behind sets yearly targets for schools. In California, the percentage of students required to score proficient or above on their math and English tests was about 12 percent in 2003. The number of students required to test proficient in English and math increased to about 23 percent in 2004. If a school failed to hit those benchmarks for both 2003 and 2004, that school would be penalized for not meeting its targets for two years in a row and would be placed on a five-year improvement plan overseen by the state. Here is where some critics of the law get upset. One option that the school has is a state takeover. Instead of opting for a state takeover, a school can replace some or all of its staff, reopen as a new public charter school, contract with an outside agency to run the school, or take the popular and vague option to do "any other major restructuring." As Nanette Asimov pointed out in her article "37 Schools Forced to Make Changes," published in the *San Francisco Chronicle* on September 20, 2005, "It does not appear, however, that the consequences will be dire. The government has withheld no funds, and the state has taken over no schools."

Another criticism of NCLB is that even when a school is doing exceptionally well, if it lags behind in one category, it is considered failing. While this is harsh, the law is called No Child Left Behind for a reason. Drafters of the legislation felt that education must meet the needs of *all* students. Novato School District in Northern California has some of the highest test scores in the state, but it failed in 2004 because it did not meet the requirement for English-language learners. Well, my friends, what color do you think those students were who were failing? Twenty-three percent of Novato's English-language learners did not test proficient in English, the minimum amount as required by the state. The superintendent was upset and commented that NCLB needed to be restructured. Could this mean she did not want to be held accountable for educating her local darkies? How do you think the students in her district felt who couldn't read?

What needed to be restructured was Novato's educational program for English-language learners. While the superintendent's frustration was justifiable to her—no one wants to be successful with whites yet considered failing when it comes to darkies—school districts need to provide everybody with a sound academic education. The subgroups that good public schools fail usually concern English-language learners, special education students, or minorities. Schools complain and say it's unfair they've been penalized for just one subgroup. Well, they're often evasive about what that one subgroup is, but if you look into it, it usually has something to do with minorities, non–English speakers, or poor students.

The percentage of students required by No Child Left Behind to be proficient will keep rising over the years until 2014, when 100 percent of students are expected to be at grade level. The plan is to educate all children, leaving none of them behind.

Do I think that will actually happen? No. Here's something you have to understand about policy: politicians set things up to grandfather when they've left office. With President George W. Bush gone, President Barack Obama and Congress will change the legislation and either lower the standards requirement or water the law down in some way. I assure you no politician or union member will be left behind.

In the meantime, No Child Left Behind is producing the results I love to see in public education. Test scores went up every year President Bush was in office. Graduation rates have improved, and reading levels have risen. Everybody wants to look at statistics in their own way, but to me minorities are at an all-time high with their test scores because we are once again emphasizing reading, writing, and math in public schools. We still have a long row to hoe, as my grandpa, the preacher Mr. Charlie Bell, used to say when we hit those cotton fields at six a.m. back in the day.

To me, the No Child Left Behind Act is based on the concept of a contract between the U.S. public schools and families. At American Indian Public Charter School, we believe each child will make significant yearly academic gains by following the American Indian Model of Education. At our school, we have our own contract between the families, students, and staff.

# chapter seventeen

# Sign on the Dotted Line

*What did you think when you read the student contract for the first time?*
"Oh, my gosh. It was crazy! I'd never seen so many rules before. You can't
do this; you can't do that. I dreaded coming here, but my mom said I had
to go. When Mr. Glover was explaining the rules on the first day, I
thought, 'How am I going to survive here?' I wasn't used to a strict school,
but I eventually adapted."
*So, here we are three months later. Are you still getting detention?* "Are you
kidding me? [Laughing.] I'm in detention right now. In the beginning of the
school year I got detention every day on a regular basis but then eventually,
when I started to adapt to the rules, I got fewer. I was bragging the other
day saying I haven't had detention for three weeks. Then last week I got
one every day [laughing], so I decided I needed to stop bragging."

—*Diana La,*
*a ninth-grader at American Indian Public High School, November 2007*

Anyone wishing to be admitted to the American Indian Public
Charter School has to sign the contract shown below:

## American Indian Public Charter School
### Student Contract 2008–2009

These rules and regulations must be followed at American Indian Public Charter School.

## Respect Self
1. Students must attend school each day on time.
2. Students cannot miss more than five days of school. (Students who miss five days may be retained.)
3. Students who are tardy five times during any semester will not get any money and must attend Saturday school.
4. Students will complete all homework and class work given by the teacher.
5. Students will not use drugs, alcohol, smoke, or chew gum.
6. Students cannot wear hats, makeup, jewelry, nose rings, or earrings.
7. Students cannot have personal electronic devices (for example, cell phones, pagers, Game Boys, or Walkmen/Discmen). If any of these items are found on your person, they will be confiscated for the remainder of the school year.
8. Student absences must be made up during Saturday school.
9. Students must follow the school dress code.

## Respect Others
1. Students will not use foul language, put-downs, or fighting.
2. Students will raise their hand to be heard and will not interrupt.

## Respect Facility
1. Students will not leave school grounds or campus.
2. Students are not allowed phone privileges, fast food, or parents bringing lunch to them.
3. Students are not allowed to have bikes, skateboards, scooters, cars, or loiter upstairs or downstairs.
4. Students will not have food or drink upstairs.
5. Students are not allowed on the stage.
6. Visitors must check in at the front office.

## Respect Staff, Guests and Volunteers
1. Students will follow staff and teachers' directions.

Those who choose not to follow these rules will not be allowed to attend AIPCS or any other after-school activities. No student will be given money if suspended from school. Families are guaranteed if they follow and support our model, their children will be prepared to graduate from college.

---

Student Signature                                    Date

---

Parent Signature

I often say, "This school is not for everybody." To make sure students and families know what they are getting into at American Indian Public Charter School, we set into place a list of strict rules to be followed called the student contract. Students and family members all have to sign it. Above is a student contract from the 2008–2009 school year.

Each year the story is basically the same: you will not be admitted to our school without reading and signing the contract. Students and family members sign the student contract in the application packet, on the first day of summer school, and the first day of the regular school year. They sign it for each teacher they have, including P.E. teachers, resource teachers, music teachers, and tutors. The idea is to constantly remind students and families of the rules they have agreed to follow with us. With their signatures scrawled on the line, they acknowledge that they have read the rules and agree to abide by them. Once accepted, when students don't want to follow the rules, they will get after-school detention, Saturday school, repeat the grade, or they may choose another school.

When I first drafted the student contract, there were fewer rules than exist now, and AIPCS had a more lenient dress code policy. In fact, the first year I was principal there was no student contract or dress code policy.

I realized the importance of starting with feasible goals and knew I couldn't turn the zoo into an academy in one year. I had taken over a school when it was at rock bottom, so it wouldn't make sense to implement severe policies and expect the students to adhere to them. We had to work gradually at becoming a great school. As the years went on and the staff, students, and family members steadily built AIPCS into an academic success, our policies became stricter. This happened in increments. The second year we went from having no dress code to requiring students to wear any white shirt and blue or black pants or skirts. We introduced the no jewelry policy the third year and eventually cut out makeup, bright accessories, logos on shirts, jeans, and colored jackets. Now students have to wear white collared shirts and khaki pants or skirts. Boys have to tuck in their shirts and are not allowed to sag their pants. Sweatshirts and sweaters have to be plain white and cannot have hoods. The dress code is part of our game plan.

Jose Ortiz began sixth grade at American Indian Public Charter School when I first became principal, so he witnessed the school transforming and the rules becoming stricter as he made his way from sixth through ninth grade. When Jose was a sixth-grader, there was no mandatory uniform or summer school. Jose's teacher, Carmelita, was strict, but the students weren't used to a school culture of hard work like the students Jose sees now when he drops by to visit American Indian Public Charter School.

Jose came to AIPCS from Calvin Simmons Middle School. His mom, Maria, wanted him to leave Calvin Simmons because of the gang activity there. Jose had tried to get into a middle school called Dolores Huerta, but it was full, so the principal recommended he try American Indian Public Charter School. Jose came to us with a 1.97 GPA. He says of his sixth-grade year, "As students we still weren't putting out our best, but it was a better education than I had at Calvin Simmons. On my first report card at AIPCS, I got a 3.67. It was a huge improvement."

Though Jose did much better at American Indian Public Charter School, he didn't like it at first. He says, "It was too small. There wasn't any liberty. At Calvin Simmons I could just walk out, and there was this place across the street where we could play pool. Here you couldn't sneak out. You couldn't go nowhere. It was kind of boring. I hated it too because on the first day I got a detention." He did indeed. Jose was one of many students to walk home the first day of school with a detention slip in his backpack to share with the family. We wanted to get the students' attention about following the school rules.

It took Jose time to adapt to a stricter school culture, which is a common experience for new students at American Indian Public Charter School. One day Jose walked up to me and said, "Was' up, Dr. Chavis?" I looked at him like, "Are you a fool?" and said, "We don't do that here." Jose wasn't the only one to get that response from me. The students were used to acting the same way in school as on the streets. They had never been put in their place or taught how to behave.

We don't allow students to act like thugs, and it took them time to get used to our expectations.

I immediately ingrain in my students my golden rule: *If you act like a winner, you'll be treated like a winner. If you act like a fool, you'll be treated like a fool.* The golden rule has stood the test of time at American Indian Public Charter School. It may have taken years to implement mandatory Saturday school, but the winner/fool rule has always been my trademark. It is a mix of kindness and toughness. I'll tell students how proud I am of them when they show dedication to their education. I'll joke around with them, smile, look them in the eye, and congratulate them. When a student's behavior is out of line, I deal with it swiftly and to the point. I do the same thing with adults.

Many students don't like me at first, but as I always say to the teachers, "When students think you're bastards in the beginning of the year, that usually means you're doing your job." The teachers I remember and respect the most were the ones who made me toe the line. The ones who let me play hell seemed cool to me at the time, but I didn't respect them. It was the same thing with Jose. He didn't like his teachers or me because we pushed him to work hard and follow the rules. Now he misses American Indian Public Charter School and says sixth through ninth grades were his proudest years in school. When he was a junior in high school, he came by to visit AIPCS more often than any of our former students. He'd watch the students and comment, "These kids have no idea how good they have it here." Now, that's a wonderful compliment from a former student.

When Jose started sixth grade, we didn't pay for perfect attendance, a practice that started the following year. I still used money as a reward, though. I'd pay the students a dollar or two for getting good grades or staying out of detention. Jose and his classmates were rewarded with tickets to a Warriors basketball game. On the last day of sixth grade, Jose won fifty dollars because his group at MESA, an after-school math and science program run by Jill Rogers, built the tower that resisted the most weight. Jose recalls, "I was little then, so fifty dollars to me was like wow, fifty dollars!" There's nothing like money to put a smile on the face of a young child who doesn't have many opportunities to acquire it. Think about it. Jose is nineteen now, but he still remembers how exciting it was to get fifty dollars in sixth grade. I felt the same way when Mrs. Helen Smith gave me three dollars in the third grade for perfect attendance.

In seventh grade, Jose and the students had stricter rules to follow. They had a dress code; their families weren't allowed to drop off lunches; they couldn't wear makeup. Jessica Bell, a black student who joined Jose's class in seventh grade, came to school the first day wearing lip gloss and eye shadow. Jessica, who now attends community college, recalls, "A girl came up to me in a panic, pointed to my makeup, and said, 'Take it off! Take it off! Take it off before Dr. Chavis gets here!' I was, like, 'What in the world is wrong with you?' I had no idea what was coming." Sure enough, her teacher made her go to the bathroom to remove her makeup, and she got a detention and later a talking-to from me. Jessica says, laughing, "My first impression of Dr. Chavis was he was crazy. I didn't really have any problems with him until he started to make 'Jessica rules': you couldn't have any color in your hair; you couldn't wear fake nails; you couldn't wear bandanas; you couldn't have writing on your shirt anymore." Most of my ideas for school rules come from students' actions or recommendations.

Jessica was an extremely smart student who loved to set fashion trends and get attention for the wrong reasons. I wanted her to stand out for her intelligence, but she wanted to stand out for her style. After Jessica dyed her hair blue, I decided I'd seen enough of that distracting look, so I made the rule that students couldn't have bright colors in their hair. Jessica and her classmates laugh about it now, but they were in shock when they first arrived at AIPCS. It wasn't just the strict rules but the fact that we enforced them. Other schools have rules, but their teachers, staff, and principals don't make their students follow them.

Lyzanna Chairez, who now attends UC Berkeley, as does Han Trang, an incredibly hardworking student from her ninth-grade class, first came to AIPCS in seventh grade, entering at the same time and into the same classroom as Jessica Bell and Jose Ortiz. Like Jose, she came to American Indian Public Charter School from Calvin Simmons. She remembers, "The first day we had a whole list of assignments, and I wasn't used to that. I wasn't used to discipline at all whatsoever. I had no discipline to sit down and get to work. At AIPCS, I think it was the intimidation I received—I was intimidated by Dr. Chavis. It was, like, 'I got to do this. He isn't playing. I got to go home and get my home-work done.' And the detentions really scared me. I'd get in trouble at home if I ever got detention. That whole system worked in my favor even though I didn't see it then, but AIPCS definitely played a very im-portant role in my life and education. I didn't see until now that AIPCS prepared me for college." These are the types of success stories that are possible by implementing rules and enforcing them at any school.

The regimen of homework and discipline intimidates students like Lyzanna at first, but they eventually thrive under it. In seventh grade, Lyzanna and her classmates had two to three hours of homework a night and had to learn to do math problems the right way by showing their work. Small responsibilities, such as showing your work on math homework, combine to create a disciplined student when measures of accountability are in place. It's all part of the training. My third year as principal, we started requiring all students to attend summer school, so they had even more time to learn accountability and core academic skills.

When Lyzanna, Jessica, and Jose entered eighth grade, the student contract expanded to say no jewelry. Many of the students tried to ignore the policy, so I let them know I wasn't a weakling or coward, like many of the secondary school principals they had before. I went into each of the classrooms with a pillowcase and had everyone take off their jewelry and dump it into the pillowcase. Then I tossed the pillowcase with all the students' jewelry into the Dumpster. That caused quite a ruckus. Families and students were up in arms. Some of them wanted to get me fired. The families had a meeting with the school board. They talked about how that "devil" Dr. Chavis had thrown away valuable jewelry that had been in their family since Columbus landed in America. I was surprised that so many poor American Indians, Asians, blacks, and Mexicans had so much valuable jewelry that they let their middle school children wear it to school. They all had selective memories regarding "No Jewelry" in the student contract.

I was disciplined by the board and vowed to change my ways and keep students' jewelry until the end of the year in the future. After that, there were no more jewelry problems at AIPCS.

During Jose, Jessica, and Lyzanna's eighth-grade year, I decided to address the sagging pants problem with the boys in a hands-on way. I brought pink mason string into the office and made the boys who loved to let their pants hang below their butts with their drawers sticking out come see me. I tied the pink string around their waists where a belt should have been and wrapped the string into a big bow in the front of their pants for extra embarrassment. I formed suspenders on some of the boys. Later, Johnny and Christian, two American Indian students who were repeat offenders when it came to sagging pants, were brought back into my office for a makeover. I took an electrical cord that had a lightbulb hanging off the end of it and tied it around Johnny's waist. He had to walk around all day looking like a mad electrician. Then I took a small electric heater and tied its cord around Christian's waist. Students laughed at the boys all day.

Eventually, no sagging became an official part of the boys' dress code at AIPCS. When they did sag, they would get detention, and sometimes I'd hitch their pants up like I did to the boys above. The policy changes were incremental.

During the spring of 2006, when I implemented a mandatory rule that boys had to tuck in their shirts, I noticed some teachers weren't enforcing it. This is a problem at most failing schools: the educators don't enforce the rules. Can you blame students for not following them? Letting the students break the rules was becoming a trend with some of the teachers that year, and I was sick of it. I worked part-time that year and left the day-to-day administrative operations up to Mr. Katz, who was letting those teachers have their way. Whenever I was around, I usually had a confrontation with one of them.

At lunch one day, a group of teachers were talking about the new dress code requiring boys to tuck in their shirts as I walked into the office. Mr. Bates, an eighth-grade teacher, commented to me that the students looked geeky with their shirts tucked in and joked that their appearance was offensive to the eye. I told him I was glad, and that I hoped the students looked like nerds, because I didn't want them dressing like gangbangers with their pants sagging and their shirts hanging baggy and long. I said to the group of teachers sitting around the lunch table, "These kids, when they're your age, they can wear whatever they want. I don't care. You're adults, and you've earned it. You're accomplished. You can dress however you want. You can have tattoos all over your cheeks," I said, pretending to grab my buttocks, "for all I care, but these kids don't have that privilege yet."

I was trying to joke around about the dress code, but I realized from the lack of response that most of them disagreed with me. Then I became irritated and said, "You know what, no one looks at the teenagers in Oakland and says, 'They may be a bunch of dumbasses, but at least they look cool.' I don't care what you think, and I'm tired of you guys helping the students undermine the rules. Some of you are letting them wear their shirts out. Mr. Bates, these kids can be anarchists like you if they go to a stick-it-to-The-Man college like you did, but they're not going to be anarchists here. How are these kids even going to get into your private college? You know, I've gone all over the state looking at secondary schools, and not a single one of them that uses a liberal philosophy with ghetto students is worth a damn. All this liberalism has screwed over minorities. You think they're poor and underprivileged and they can't cut it, so you give them an easy way out. It's people like you who have fucked over my people, and I'm sick of it." I walked out of the room and immediately came back in to finish "giving them hell," as my grandpa Calvin Chavis would have said.

I continued, "You know, I'm a Democrat, too, and sometimes when I look in the mirror I can't stand what I see because we haven't done anything for minorities in public education. All this left-wing liberalism has destroyed generations of minorities." I'm sure I could be heard proselytizing to the backsliders of common sense in the hallway until I walked out the front door.

A few weeks later I told Mr. Bates he had done a great job teaching his students core academics over the past three years, but he had failed them in one very important aspect: teaching them respect. His students had a reputation for their attitude and frequent defiance of authority. They were the worst-behaved class in the school. I said to him, "I know you like to teach your students to question and defy authority, but do you really think blacks, Hispanics, Asians, and American Indians need to be taught to question authority by a white liberal? Don't you think we do enough of that? Do you think we don't graduate from high school or go to college because we're all dumb? Don't you think there's a reason so many of us are in prison?"

I am trying to teach our students the rules of life and that's why I want their pants pulled up and their shirts tucked in. We need to teach students they are judged by their appearance, so they'd better give off the right image to society. Mr. Bates can dress pretty much any way he pleases, and no one will think anything of it because he is a white, upper-middle-class male with money from his parents. When our minority students walk around with their pants sagging and their shirts hanging out, whites and minorities are going to think they are losers or up to no good, and it has resulted in one of our former students being shot dead. That is just a fact of life as to how minorities are perceived, even by our own people. Do you think most people will admit these are their views? I think not.

I want students to think about their appearance both in and outside of school. A current tenth-grader named Jose Mendoza shared with me that when he's not in school and can wear whatever he wants, he thinks about how he'll be perceived. Keeping in mind the rule that if you look like a fool you'll be treated like one, Jose keeps his pants at his waist instead of sagging, like he often used to, because he doesn't want people to think he's an idiot or a gangbanger. He knows to an outsider, image is everything and we aren't often given second chances.

# chapter eighteen

# Guided by a Firm Hand

"At Montera [a public middle school in Oakland], I used to ditch class and wouldn't get caught. The teachers and principal either didn't care or they believed the lies we told them about where we went. Here the staff looks after you, and you know they care. My grades and behavior were much worse at Montera, and I missed many days of school. . . . My self-esteem is better here. At Montera, I would worry about how I looked and would constantly ask my friends how I looked or would check the mirror. Here [where we all wear the same uniform] no one cares what you look like, and we all feel equal."

—*Amanda Haick,*
*a tenth-grader at AIPHS in 2007–2008 and the high school's only white student*

"The staff pays more attention to us here. Everyone wants more freedom, but in some cases it's not good for you. I think the limitation on your freedom at this school is a good thing. You do less bad stuff. You know that teachers are around you, so you're not thinking of doing bad things like drugs."

—*Jose Mendoza,*
*a ninth-grader at AIPHS in 2007–2008*

As we improved academically year after year, I modified the existing student contract to make students more responsible not just in terms of dress code but in other aspects as well. My third year as principal we added the rule that any student who misses a day of school has to attend Saturday school to make up for that absence. It's no longer just a reward to be in school. You get punished for not having perfect attendance. I'm preparing students for the workforce. Saturday school is not held every Saturday but is announced with a few days' notice. I don't care what special plans students or families may have made for that Saturday; Saturday school is mandatory. Students come to school at 8:30 in the morning in uniform and with homework packets in hand and leave at 1:00 p.m. Teachers are not required to come. I oversee the students and get some of them to help me clean the campus and classrooms.

Jose Ortiz and hundreds of other former students witnessed changes take place between 2000 and 2007. He said in an interview, "Dr. Chavis was basically building this new school from scratch. Seventh grade was getting stricter; he enforced the dress code; he had new regulations. Eighth grade he had everything down, and ninth grade he was just flowing. It was basically a whole improvement, and it all paid off because we became the best school. Nowadays you've got Governor Schwarzenegger coming in twice. That's a huge improvement right there because I remember Dr. Chavis started from nothing."

My former students like Jose Ortiz think new students at American Indian Public Charter School will dislike the school at first and find it hard, but they will eventually come to appreciate it later in life, as Jose and his peers have. As Jose says, "When I graduated from AIPCS, I started thinking about it, and I started missing it too. I was, like, man, what if I were in the tenth through twelfth grade at AIPCS? Because you know, after that I started falling off." This line of thinking confirms that students realize the worth of a good public high school education as they move into adulthood.

Jose left AIPCS when he finished ninth grade. At the time, our high school, American Indian Public High School, didn't exist. It was for reasons like Jose's, Jessica's, and Lyzanna's experiences after leaving us that I knew we needed to open a high school for our students to continue on to.

Jose went to a small private school called St. Elizabeth's until his mom could no longer afford it. The academics were disappointing to him. Jose found the classes easy compared to AIPCS, and he found it difficult to be internally motivated. He says, "It was hard for me at first because I'm used to working under pressure. From sixth to ninth grade,

I always had Dr. Chavis and my teachers on my back, so I'd always push myself, and I really didn't fall off, but when I went to tenth grade, I started falling off because I had no one on my back. It was a private school, so they really didn't care what you did as long as you paid up. Just pay up and then you can stay."

One of Jose's teachers at AIPCS, Ms. Sullivan, found it surprising that Jose of all students came back to visit her so frequently after he continued high school at St. Elizabeth's. Jose was a student she had to constantly push to keep from being lazy. Because he tended to slack off, Ms. Sullivan was always on his back to get cracking and do his work well. She laughed and shared with me one day, "I assumed he would have hated me and thought I was mean because I was always on him. 'Jose, pay attention! Jose, get to work!' I was a new teacher then, but I realized as time went on that my students appreciated my firmness. They knew they had learned from me, and because I pushed them to do well, they saw it as I cared." Many teachers don't push their students because they may think it's not their job or worth the hassle that may result from being hard on students. But that is exactly what inner-city students need.

Ms. Sullivan describes Jose as a curious young man, especially in the areas of science and history. Jose has a low, kind of mumbly voice with a slight Mexican accent. That voice, the way he cocked his head, and his tendency to ask random questions would make his classmates giggle. He'd turn to them and say, "What, man. I think that's interesting," with an intonation like Cheech and Chong. Jose seemed to find his peers immature, but they definitely liked him. He has thick, jet-black hair and always wears glasses. Though Jose was really big for a middle school student, he had a very gentle way about him. He also had a tendency to fall asleep in class, so Ms. Sullivan was constantly keeping an eye on him and making him pay attention.

Jose equates discipline with concern. When his teachers at St. Elizabeth's, Unity, and Newark Memorial—all high schools he attended between tenth and twelfth grade—didn't make Jose put forth effort in their classes, he thought it showed they didn't care about him or his education. Jose and all students need consequences and accountability for their actions. Without rules and structure they flounder, like Jose did, going from one high school to the next.

Halfway through his junior year, Jose transferred from St. Elizabeth's, which his family could no longer afford, to Unity, a small charter high school in Oakland. Jose found his education at Unity mediocre, and he didn't live up to his potential there. By the end of his junior year, Jose's mom had decided she'd had enough of Oakland's violence and bad influences and moved the family to Newark, a city thirty minutes south of Oakland. Mrs. Ortiz didn't want her younger children to be raised into the same environment Jose had experienced.

That brought Jose to Newark Memorial High School for twelfth grade, which ideally should have led to better success and a better education, but Oakland followed Jose in the form of a sensationalized, gangbanger reputation. People assume when you come from Oakland that you're some kind of badass, but that is very rarely the case. Most of the teens are trying to look tough by dressing like thugs and talking the talk, but that's part of the survival culture of urban ghettos. Jose says, "In Newark you could get an education, but the students there were caught up in the ghetto image. Being ignorant was the thing that was in. When people found out I was from Oakland they tried to start fights with me to prove themselves. There were all these people trying to get at me, saying they were going to shoot me, or they were going to jump me."

Jose is a big guy but not a mean young man. Folks in Newark must have let their imaginations run wild, because I could not picture Jose starting a fight with anybody. It's not his nature. Apparently, Jose let his imagination get the better of him as well. Those kids weren't going to do anything to him, and he knows that now, but at the time Jose thought he was going to get jumped, so he started carrying a knife on him, and he got caught with it at school. He was arrested and charged with a misdemeanor. Jose says, "I realized when I came back to reality that they were all talk, they weren't going to do anything, and now I just tell these wannabes it's stupid to their face. I tell them they're embarrassing our culture. I say, 'You live in a nice place with no violence, so what do you have to do this stupid shit for?' I'm mad at my own people, too, because of that. That's why people start building this stereotype that all Mexicans are criminals, that they're all cholos and gang-affiliated. I kept it cool for the rest of the year, decided I didn't care what anyone thought, and started ignoring it when kids called me a gangster." This is part of the daily life that our students experience. Now you understand why many public school teachers in our city send their children to private schools.

Due to problems with his California High School Exit Exam

(CAHSEE), Jose wasn't sure if his graduation from high school was official until months after the graduation ceremony had come and gone. All public school students in California need to pass the CAHSEE in order to receive a high school diploma. Jose hadn't taken the CAHSEE in tenth grade like most high school students because he was in a private school. He should have taken it at Unity in eleventh grade but did not. At Newark Memorial, he took the CAHSEE, but his test was lost. When he realized there were no results for his exit exam, Jose had no choice but to take the CAHSEE again. The scores would not be released until after his high school graduation ceremony. He could walk the stage but didn't know if he truly graduated. Jose says, "That's basically showing that you have no care for my education if you're going to lose my exit exam and then I have to take it again. What kind of attention is that? Later in the summer I got the letter telling me I had passed, and I picked up my diploma."

Part of the reason Jose didn't enroll in a junior college after finishing high school was because he didn't know if he'd actually graduated from high school. I think he should have gone ahead and signed up for classes anyway. Students like Jose come out of high schools like the ones he's described, and they're lost. They don't know how to work the higher-education system because their families have never done it and no one has shown them how to do it. Instead of taking initiative, Jose got scared off by the cost of pursuing his two passions: graphic design and culinary school. He decided to put off pursuing either one because he was concerned about money. At the time of this interview, Jose worked at the store Tuesday Morning and said he was saving up for a car so he could transport himself more easily to school and work. I think he should have taken public transportation and gotten started on his college education. Jose claimed he would enroll in school the second semester. I hope he did.

Jose lives with his mom, stepdad, four sisters, little brother, and grandma. He's the second oldest. They all speak Spanish at home and came to America from Mexico. Jose's stepdad works in construction, and his mom helps with the business—buying the materials and handling the bills. Jose says, "They tell me to get an education. They didn't want me to work during high school. The problem with Latino families that move from Mexico to the United States is they tell their children to just work—work and support your family—and the sad thing is the families don't encourage their kids to go to school. That's

why some of these Mexican families just spend their whole lives working, and they're still struggling because they never were inspired by
their parents to get a college education like in other cultures. My mom
doesn't think like that. She told me, 'I want you to work but at the same
time you have got to get your education because if you're just breaking
your back, you're going to be struggling your whole life. You have to
get an education to have a better life.'"

Jose's mom is right. He is going to be okay. Jose has a good head
on his shoulders and knows what he's supposed to do, and that's part
of the battle. Like most of our students who do not thrive in an unstructured school environment characterized by choices and internal responsibility, Jose needed to be pushed. Our inner-city students do better in
school when there are rules, consequences, and guidance. Unfortunately
we didn't have the high school when Jose and his peers graduated from
American Indian Public Charter School. Nonetheless, Jose and his
classmates had an advantage over Oakland youth from lousy middle
schools, because at least they could take the academic training we provided them in order to compete in high school.

Students who are poor, minorities, and immigrants need structure
in school, and that is why the student contract exists. They may not like
all the rules, as Jose Ortiz pointed out—and believe me, most of them
don't—but they thrive under them. Jose Mendoza, the tenth-grader
mentioned earlier who thinks about how he'll be perceived when he
sags his pants, thought he was going to be entering "hell" when he read
the student contract and saw what he was getting himself into at American Indian Public Charter School. He realizes the discipline and structure are making him a better, more responsible student. That in turn
makes him feel good about himself and makes his family proud.

There is a cycle most students go through when they enter our
structured middle school. They don't like the rules and high expectations at first; they want more freedom, but then over time they realize
the freedom they had at their previous school didn't prepare them to be
successful in school or life.

# chapter nineteen

# Nate

"I wanted to be challenged, so when the work was harder, when the homework was longer, when the tests actually made me think, I enjoyed that. I went home smiling."

—Nate Robles,
former AIPCS student from 2001 to 2004

Nate Robles was an exception to most new students who enter American Indian Public Charter School: he wanted rules, structure, and high expectations. Nate, a Navajo, Yaqui, and Choctaw Indian, was in the same class as Jose Ortiz, Lyzanna Chairez, and Jessica Bell.

Nate was born with a nerve disorder called Charcot-Marie-Tooth (CMT). The peripheral nerves that would normally send signals to his legs, feet, arms, and hands don't function properly. Because Nate's peripheral nerves have degenerated, they can't sustain muscle growth from his elbows down or knees down. As a result, Nate's calves are smaller than my wrists. When I'd see him walk down the hallway toward me, his legs looked like thin stilts that couldn't bend, which made it easy for Nate to trip or fall. With less muscle mass and motor control, Nate also suffers from fatigue and pain. His hands don't have the full mobility of an average adult. When he writes, his hand wraps around the pencil like a claw, but CMT doesn't affect the brilliant ideas he's able to put on paper. We used to provide Nate with two sets of textbooks, one for school and one for home, because his legs couldn't support the weight of his backpack. As he shares, "It's been difficult. It's something I have to deal with as an identity issue, as a getting around issue, but I'm working through it."

Nate inherited CMT from his mom, who died when he was ten years old. They were very close, and he wishes she were alive for many reasons, one of which being that he'd have someone to relate to who also had the disorder. He's never met another individual with Charcot-Marie-Tooth, which he thinks would be helpful in dealing with its challenges, but he's promised himself that he'd never let CMT get in the way of his goals and life path.

When I first met Nate, I didn't know about his disorder. I saw a frail, quiet Indian boy in front of me. From his appearance, I figured he'd been beaten up at his old school and that's why he wanted to come to AIPCS. But when I started talking to him, I discovered an insightful young man who was tired of low expectations and unchallenging academics. He described the power structure at Roosevelt Middle School and talked about how he survived by hanging out with the kids who gambled behind the school building. They were tough black, Cambodian, and Vietnamese students who respected Nate for being smart and good at math. Because he helped them make wise decisions while gambling, they watched out for him. It was a mutually beneficial arrangement.

Nate had been pushed ahead a grade because the staff at Roosevelt couldn't provide him with the academic challenge he needed. He remembers, "I was struggling trying to figure out a way to not waste time. I was, like, this is not going to work. You guys need to step it up. I need to be challenged more. They didn't have any solutions because that's not something that they're used to dealing with, so they were just, like, go to the next grade, go to the eighth grade, and tell us how you feel there. But it was the same middle school. It wasn't operated that well. In the eighth grade kids would be smoking outside the classes and doing irresponsible stuff like that. The work was a little bit harder—but at the same time, I thought, 'I have to get out of this school.'"

Nate started talking with Mr. John Six-Killer, an American Indian man who had helped Nate's sister find the right school for her. One day Mr. Six-Killer brought Nate over for a tour. Nate liked the way AIPCS looked right away and thought it was an immediate improvement over Roosevelt Middle School.

At the same time, he was young and proud of being advanced a grade, so it was hard for him when I said, "Listen, you need to be back in the seventh grade because I'm going to provide academic challenges for you that they couldn't at your former school." Nate admits that at first he was skeptical, but other than having his pride hurt, his initial impression of me was that I was willing to go further than his previous educators to give him the challenge he required. Nate told me later he was impressed, and he noticed things didn't slip by me like they did his other principals. He figured he could find a safe, structured, quiet, and challenging learning environment at American Indian Public Charter School, and he did. Nate says, "I wanted to be challenged, so when the work was harder, when the homework was longer, when the tests actually made me think, I enjoyed that. I went home smiling."

The first few times he saw me use public embarrassment with the students, he wondered if I was going to get in trouble. He wasn't used to hearing the blunt truth from principals. Nate thought, "This guy's got guts. I'm impressed." He saw that what I was doing worked and that it created a safe environment. Hard work and integrity were rewarded, while foolishness and laziness were punished. Nate always thought it served students right to be made an example of when they were acting out or slacking off in class; he had just never seen it happen before at a school.

Midway through seventh grade, Nate prepared for the SAT in order to attempt to qualify for the prestigious Johns Hopkins University Center for Talented Youth (CTY) program. I brought him home with me the day before he was scheduled to take the SAT so that I could ensure he got to the test site on time. That Friday night there was a fiftieth birthday party for Cheri Ivy, the principal of Fruitvale Elementary School. I brought Nate with me to the party and introduced him to Jerry Brown, the mayor of Oakland at the time. I said to Mayor Brown, "I'd like you to meet Nate Robles, a star seventh-grade student at American Indian Public Charter School who is taking the SAT tomorrow." They shook hands, and after chatting with him, Mayor Brown realized Nate was indeed special and intelligent, and he said to him, "I want you at my school, the Oakland Military Institute. Here's my card." I looked at Mr. Brown, laughed, and said, "Hell, no! I'm not going to let you take my star student." He laughed. Nate, who had been quietly formulating his words, said to Mayor Brown, "I've visited your school, but you don't have Dr. Chavis." We all smiled at that one.

At the birthday party I continued introducing Nate to various educators and politicians. It's funny how when I told the blacks or Mexicans present, "This student Nate is taking the SAT tomorrow," they'd say, "You must be confused. He can't be taking the SAT. Do you mean the PSAT?" I thought, "Do they think I'm so dumb I don't know what the SAT is?" Mayor Brown, who is white, didn't question me about Nate taking the test. The darkies did. Do you see how racist we are against our own people and how our expectations can be so low? A young minority male taking the SAT—nah, the blacks and Mexicans thought there must have been some kind of misunderstanding.

That night, I helped Nate take the braces off his legs he wore for support as he prepared for bed. I was shocked to see how thin his legs were. Very little muscle was visible around the bones. He said, "Dr. Chavis, I had a great time tonight. Thank you for introducing me to all those people." I said, "When you get an education, you will meet those types of people on your own. Smart people like to be around other smart people."

When Nate's SAT results came out, he qualified for the Johns Hopkins University Center for Talented Youth (CTY) program. Nate was the first public school student in Oakland to gain entrance into CTY! The only other Oakland students who took part attended prestigious private schools, such as Head-Royce.

Nate was actually the only public school student in Oakland that year to take the SAT as an attempt to qualify for CTY. Other Oakland public schools could have signed students up for the SAT just like AIPCS did, but they didn't, probably because they didn't want to deal with the paperwork required. In the summer of 2008, two different Jamaican parents whose AIPCS students were taking CTY courses at UC Santa Cruz called me to say how ecstatic they were to see their children in the program, but one father, Mr. Bey, wondered why the only black children there were from AIPCS. Why didn't other Oakland or San Francisco schools get their black students into the program? He was frustrated public schools weren't doing more on their black students' behalf.

To me, Nate was the star quarterback of an up-and-coming football team. When he became our first student to qualify for Johns Hopkins University CTY, I made him the poster child of American Indian Public Charter School. I put together a propaganda packet about the school that included an article about him, and I presented Nate as a positive example to other students. The message he conveyed was that it's good to be minority and smart. I built the school culture and image of academic achievement around Nate. He was at the heart of our rising success.

It was physically hard for Nate to write, walk, and carry a backpack, yet he came to school on time and put his pencil in his stiff hand and got down to work. With the students who were slacking off I could say, here's someone who is handicapped, yet he works hard. You have great physical health, but you're being lazy.

The first time Nate flew by himself on a plane was on his way to Hood College in Maryland for the CTY program. He completed two summer sessions on the college campus and didn't have to pay a penny! He received a full scholarship. Nate said the best four summers of his life were the ones he spent in CTY. His second and third summers he took courses in logic and psychology at Lafayette College in Pennsylvania. The fourth year Nate studied marine biology on a college campus and on a boat in the Atlantic Ocean. He says, "Many of the things I learned during those summers still motivate what I do for my own personal research now."

Another fond memory Nate has is the AIPCS trip to Mexico. He, Jessica, Lyzanna, Jose, and other students in the eighth-grade class who earned a spot on the trip for their perfect daily attendance, excellent behavior, and GPA got to go on an all-expenses-paid trip to Mexico City. They visited Teotihuacán, where the remains still stand of a civilization that formed around the time of Christ and lasted longer than the Roman Empire. When the students got to the top of the Pyramid of the Moon, which may have been used for ceremonial purposes, it started raining and thundering. Nate has a deep memory of the rain coming down and the clouds moving over the ancient, mysterious remains. The trip inspired him to be a world traveler. Today's eighth-graders who earn their way are sent on an all-expenses-paid trip to Washington, D.C., after graduation as a reward for their hard work.

Nate's transition from AIPCS into Oakland high schools was "drastic." He says, "The genuine encouragement for you to succeed is not present in most other public schools in Oakland. That's one of the things that stuck out to me at American Indian Public Charter School, and it still sticks out to me now that I've actually experienced different high schools. I jumped around to three different high schools after completing ninth grade at AIPCS, because I felt like I'd accumulated such high standards that anything less than that was not good enough for me, because it wouldn't justify the work that I'd been doing. And so I went to Uprep in tenth grade and that was—how can I put it nicely—god-awful.

"There were folks strolling in and out. You didn't feel safe outside of the classroom, and that's not something that should be tolerable. And I felt that way almost the entire time I was there. There was a lot of intimidation. I thought, 'I don't have to deal with this'—and basically a pattern of that continued from school to school."

Nate transferred from Uprep, which, as was mentioned earlier, was closed down by its own board amid allegations of faulty transcripts, forged attendance reports, and cheating on the STAR tests, to another high school the second semester of his sophomore year. That school had many resources, especially in the way of technology, and lots of private funding. But Nate found it unstructured. He describes shady stuff happening there, such as frequent drug use and sex in the bathrooms. People smoked weed, did meth, and had sex in the stalls. Nate accidentally walked in on two people having sex in the boys' bathroom. These are the types of things that happen at many public high schools in the United States.

Nate really became unhappy and frustrated there when he was accused of selling drugs and cutting class. Nate declares his innocence to this day and says he was treated guilty as charged. He was constantly called into the principal's office, where he'd sit and wait hours sometimes before being seen and interrogated. He would miss classes as a result, and the teachers wouldn't let him make up the work. Nate says, "I didn't feel like backing down, and so I didn't. Basically it was a push out. I felt like I was disrespected every day by the majority of the faculty. I don't know why that was, though. I don't know why it was me. I got the feeling of, 'Oh, he's a bad apple. He's a bad seed. He's one of the lazy ones; he's one of the bad influences. Oh, yeah, look at you. You look like you're a bad influence on everybody.'"

There was no process for Nate to prove his innocence. It was like he wore a scarlet letter. Whereas at American Indian Public Charter School we interview students and use a process of deduction to hopefully arrive at the truth. For example, one time Nate was almost in tears at AIPCS when he discovered the drawing his older brother had done for him was missing. Nate's older brother is an amazing artist, who had drawn in pen an image of a supernatural world. Nate was really proud of it, and I warned him he shouldn't bring it to school. You always have to be wary with your valuables. That day when it went missing and he was upset, I went into the class, and by gauging the students' reactions and interviewing them I was able to figure out that it was Nate's best friend who had stolen it. I told Nate he needed to take responsibility as well because he had left the drawing out in the open and should have been more careful. Nate learned from that incident to take care of his own valuables and to learn who his real friends are in life.

After feeling wrongfully accused and disrespected, Nate transferred to Unity High School. All three of the high schools Nate attended are charter schools. Do you see how charter schools can fail their students just like the regular public schools? At Unity, Nate became fed up. He didn't feel he was learning enough and felt under too much pressure from himself and from others. He dropped out and enrolled in courses at a community college because he still had the desire to learn. It is frustrating to see such a talented, smart young man being a high school dropout.

The ghetto secondary school system is not designed for students like Nate. The ghetto secondary school system gives more money and attention to the fools than to kids like Nate who are bright and want to learn. When talking, at age eighteen, about his educational experiences, he stressed structure and rules more than anything else. What he sees as negative are situations in which no one takes the bull by the horns. He can't stand it when educators don't enforce rules and let chaos reign in their classrooms or schools. He felt best in classes where the teachers were in complete charge. Nate loves structure and discipline; like most kids he also tries to bend the rules, which is why he knows it's important to have teachers who enforce them and keep students walking the line.

There are some things that can't be controlled. Nate of all people understands that as every day he faces an incurable health condition that physically hinders him. He can accept that to some extent his condition is beyond his control, but it really bothers him when schools, which can be places of control, are not. This reminds me of the Serenity Prayer: "God, grant me the serenity to accept the things I cannot change, the courage to change the things I can, and the wisdom to know the difference." I try to improve our students' lives by giving them the structure, academics, and discipline under which they thrive. I can't by myself change the way the Oakland Unified School District runs, but we have opened additional charter schools in Oakland that use AIM-Ed and offer students the skills and knowledge necessary to succeed and pursue higher education.

Nate lives with his father, stepmother, and sister. He says it's not the ideal situation, but he loves his father intensely. His dad told Nate he trusted him and said, "Just always tell me the truth, and I'll always support you." Nate has never mistreated his father's trust and never plans to. They continue to have a really special, strong bond.

Nate says, "It's easy to find the negative in the city," but as he works in the nonprofit health field in Oakland while taking community college classes on the side, he's beginning to really appreciate Oakland. He loves its pride. He says, "We have so much room for growth in our young people. We have so much room for growth in our schools. It's like we're in the thick of it. The things they talk about in the news—this is where it's happening. Oakland is a perfect place for progress to start, and I see that so much more clearly every day."

As the credo states, our students and staff will always be part of the AIPCS family. Nate always has a place in our AIPCS family, on which he's left his indelible mark.

# chapter twenty

# Taming Wild Horses

"Therefore it is necessary for a prince to understand how to avail himself of the beast and the man. . . . A prince, therefore, being compelled knowingly to adopt the beast, ought to choose the fox and the lion; because the lion cannot defend himself against snares and the fox cannot defend himself against wolves. Therefore, it is necessary to be a fox to discover the snares and a lion to terrify the wolves . . . and he who has known best how to employ the fox has succeeded best."

—*Excerpt from chapter XVIII of* The Prince *by Niccolò Machiavelli*

One day in the fall of 2005, I called an American Indian student named Dean Vargas into the office at AIPCS. "Look at you: dressed like a fool." I pointed at his sagging jeans. I took some string and hitched Dean's pants up as high as they'd go. I said to him, "We take you in here and give you an education for two years and the counselor is giving you therapy. Now I'll be honest, I don't believe the counseling is working. You walk around looking and acting stupid. That therapy can't be going too well." I kept Dean's pants hoisted up high using two pieces of my pink mason string to form suspenders. Then I walked him outside for trash duty and put him to work.

These urban Indians can be dumbasses when they get the urge, just like everyone else. Dean is as hardheaded as a billy goat. One day he came to school with a knife. He said he found it on the street and decided to bring it with him to school. Instead of expelling him, since I knew he would have loved to go home, I did an in-school suspension and made him sweep and clean every minute of it, which he hates to do.

Dean's mom has issues, like most of us. She kept calling the police when she'd fight with her boyfriend (Dean's father), and finally the police realized the old boy wasn't a legal citizen, so they sent Mr. Vargas back to Mexico. She regretted that her actions led to him being deported, which was never her intention, but by then it was too late. Mr. Vargas was a good man. Dean and his brothers went downhill as soon as he was gone.

Dean needs a lot of structure and discipline or he will just run wild. He reminds me a lot of myself as a young boy. At American Indian Public Charter School, he had a decent GPA and qualified for the Johns Hopkins University CTY program based on his SAT scores. At Chipman, his former middle school, Dean did nothing. He was failing his classes, skipping school, cussing at his teachers, and testing below basic on his STAR tests. I made him repeat the sixth grade and put him in the class of Ms. Chang, who really made him work hard and improve. Dean constantly had some billy goat in him, but we reined it in more. He started to perform to his academic potential. In seventh grade, for example, Dean scored advanced in math and proficient in his other subjects.

Dean now attends the Chemawa Indian boarding high school in Oregon. It was good for him to get away from Oakland and the drama in his family. Dean is a very smart boy who will do great things as long as he puts his buck-wild tendencies to good use rather than crime. I enjoy it when Dean comes by to visit me on his breaks. Last summer, he worked with Tommy Seaton, a Navajo elder in the community, painting the interior of one of my commercial buildings.

I know many of my students and their families have had hard lives, but I'll never make excuses for the students. I expect the same from students who come from struggling families as I do from the students who come from more stable families.

I don't make excuses for my mistakes, either, and I made a lot of them. I called Dean stupid, but I would have picked that knife up too as a young boy. I was a mischievous kid, and I had a lot of billy goat in me at his age. No one is to blame but me. I used to steal anything from candy to cars in my youth. When people didn't pay me to watch over their cars in downtown Lumberton, I would steal their hubcaps and sell them. In college, I dined and dashed with my friends at Sambo's, a restaurant chain that has since been bought by Denny's. Those were the old days, and I was dumb as a gourd.

I'm not a moralist; I observe a situation and try to learn from it. I stole a car once with my stepbrother Wayne when I was a teenager, and we got caught. I never went into crime with him again, that country dodo bird, and that was the end of my car stealing. Crime taught me to carefully select my people, because they're the ones who could turn on you or get you killed. I think the same way when running the school; I choose my people carefully because they will either help you or hurt you. Also, you can't be afraid to discipline the ones who screw up. That's what I learned from the crowd that I hung out with in my youth.

When someone breaks into my car, I'm being paid back for my wrongs as a young boy. I didn't get it then, but I understand now that image is important. You are judged by your family. When you come from certain families in Robeson County with a bad reputation, you aren't considered worth a damn. As the saying goes, your reputation precedes you.

I will ridicule American Indian Public Charter School students who are stealing, cheating, or being lazy. I tell them, "You're too stupid to be a criminal." Truly smart people, though, stop their criminal ways before they end up in jail. When you encourage children to (1) stop, (2) look around, and (3) think about who is watching, they will be discouraged from committing a crime. Theft and other devious behavior in children is often a result of mischief. Many children are naturally mischievous. Instead of lecturing Dean to be a good boy, I challenge him to be smarter about the stupid things he does. I hope eventually he will realize he can hurt other people and himself or make good choices.

I told one particularly sneaky Chinese student named Jeremy Shiu that he had to learn how to con people. Why would I say such a thing? In order to get his attention, I needed a different approach. I said, "Before you do something, look to see who's watching. People want to think since you're Chinese you're a great guy. When you're nice, they're going to say you're a model student." Jeremy thought for a second and said, "Dr. Chavis, that's true. I need to think more." Getting him to question his behavior is a start. The Chinese have boys just as crazy and dumb as the rest of us. Jeremy will gradually move out of the stage of stealing and conning to become a contributor to society. My goal is to get students to think about their actions, which will encourage them to change for the better.

When I was a boy, there was the good side of the Lumber River and the bad side. The blacks and Indians lived on the bad side, which flooded easily, but the whites lived on the good side, which was built on higher ground. Shielded from the flooding, some whites kept their horses in stables along the river. More than anything else, I loved horses and always wanted to be a cowboy or a jockey. Unfortunately for me, by my teens I had grown too tall to race horses, so I started running. As a boy, I wasn't able to afford my passion for horses, so I found other means. At first I was content to ride a tobacco stick and pretend it was a horse, and of course there were the tales of the Lone Ranger and Tonto floating through my mind. But after a while, I wanted an actual horse to ride. At night, when no one on the white side of the Lumber River was watching their horses, I would sneak into the stables, choose a horse, and take it for a ride.

I did that for a while, but one summer I decided it wasn't enough just to "borrow" a horse—it was time for ownership. I took my favorite, a black quarter horse with a white blaze on its nose. To prevent the owner from recognizing it, I rubbed cheap black dye into the horse's white blaze, so that its coat looked completely black. I rode black lightning all over the county. I was probably the last Lumbee Indian raiding horses from whites in the early 1960s. The problem with using cheap dye was that when the rains came, the dye washed off, revealing the white blaze beneath the sooty black. After a rainstorm, someone spotted the horse and told the owner, who came and reclaimed the horse from where I kept him in the woods. Luckily for me, the owner never discovered that I was the thief. I was a wild boy who sought adventure and did stupid things, so I relate to students like Dean and Jeremy because I recall the bad decisions I've made in life. I believe none of the students I worked with during the past four decades were as wild as me.

My experiences with horses taught me something about discipline as well. When I was ten years old, I saved the money I made as a farmhand from hiring myself out over the summer and bought my first pony for twenty-five dollars. Its name was Buck, like my dad. It was the meanest pony who ever walked the earth. I learned how to tame him, though. Animals are just like human beings; they need discipline and structure. I started a training regimen that included tying a rope around Buck's flank and pulling the rope over and over again until he was so worn out that he would no longer buck or kick. Eventually the pony got tired from fighting back and realized there was no point in retaliating. Buck gave up and stopped lashing out.

Training a pony is not much different from disciplining students. The key is wearing students out and teaching them to realize there's no use in being defiant. There was a sixth-grade white boy named Adam— white people, you have your share of fools, too—who started off the school year talking smack to his teacher. He talked back because he could get away with it. After the consequences of detention, trash duty, and public embarrassment, he got worn out, realized he wasn't going to win, and became meek as a mouse. Adam was saying, yes, sir, and doing his work. But I had to talk with his teacher, Ms. Jessica Figlio. Adam didn't have a problem; Ms. Figlio did, because she let the boy get away with acting out. She needed to say, "I don't want to hear anything from you; get to work." Once students know you're not playing, they change their behavior. Who came up with the mule-headed philosophy that educators need to take the time to hear a middle school student's excuses for acting a fool? After all the listening and talking, when would a teacher have time to teach? The class day is too short as it is, and instructional minutes need to be utilized to their fullest in a secondary school.

As a boy I'd buy a wild horse, train it, and then sell it to someone who wanted a gentle horse. It's like the work I do at the school. I take new students who need to be broken in and trained because they've been left to run wild through the Oakland public school system. At the end of their stay, they graduate ready to prove themselves in their next endeavor, and their high school teachers love working with them.

Some students are self-motivated and self-disciplined. Others require external motivation. At our schools, that takes the form of rewards or punishments. When a student can't discipline himself to complete his homework, he'll be disciplined with detention. When the problem persists, loss of privileges, public humiliation, forced cleaning, or retention may follow. Some may call my use of public humiliation extreme; however, Oakland is an extreme city with a high homicide rate. I would rather embarrass them now than see my students get killed.

I know that some students who step through the school's door will do great work from the beginning. Others will need to be broken in, like I was as a child. I wasn't a motivated student, so I identify with those students who need somebody on their back all the time. The self-contained classroom lends itself to that kind of personal oversight and structure. Students who arrive tardy, are out of dress code, are disrespectful, or who do not have homework will receive a one-hour detention to be served the next day. I tell new teachers, "When a student even looks at you the wrong way, give him detention." It is not a democracy at our schools.

At the beginning of the year, I inform all the new teachers that their detention boards better be covered with names when I walk in or they're not doing their jobs. Our teachers need to immediately implement the no-nonsense discipline system in their classrooms. When all employees start working at AIPCS, they'd better give lots of detentions or they are going to answer to me.

I have no patience for weak or lazy educators. When a teacher is too easy on students, I have to step in and do the job. I've fired new teachers just days into the school year. Others I've threatened to fire, some of whom turned their performance around, and some of whom did not. Those who did not come around moved on to other jobs, and I hired people willing to educate our students. In some cases I've found it takes teachers a few weeks to adjust to AIM-Ed's use of structure and discipline.

Early in the 2005–2006 school year, I brought Armante Washington and Brian, an Asian student, who were acting like critter control clowns on a hog farm, up in front of their class. As they stood before their new teacher, Mr. Berniker, who was acting like the blind farmer in regard to their behavior, I told their classmates they were an embarrassment to their class and needed to grow up. Mr. Berniker was very uncomfortable. He told me afterward it bothered him to see his students being ridiculed, but he got the message loud and clear. Students will not respect you when you let them get away with disrupting class. They will walk all over you. How are we preparing our students for life when we let them play hell in school?

After a couple of weeks, Mr. Berniker caught on to my methods and started enforcing rules. And guess what happened? Armante and Brian started to respect him, follow his directions, and most important, they did their work. That's the goal—for students to be working. I want to see them bent over their desks, thinking, and writing. Students acting like clowns need to keep their mouths shut in class. I have no tolerance for anything that interferes with learning. Mr. Berniker went on to become an excellent teacher—his eighth-grade class had the highest academic performance of any before them—and his students loved him.

Mr. Berniker is an unbelievably hardworking and dedicated teacher and one of the best we have ever had. I enjoy teasing him and telling him I want my tribe to be like his tribe; that's why I give them so much math. Some minorities will tell me that I want to be white. I joke with Mr. Berniker that I'd take it even further and make sure I come back not just white but as a Jew because you guys are so smart. He laughs and then gets back to work. Armante and Brian became well-behaved, high-achieving students under Mr. Berniker. They enjoy serving as role models for other new students who attend AIPCS.

With the students, I try the nice way first. I pay the ones who do their work, stay out of detention, and have perfect attendance. I compliment the hardworking students, telling them how proud I am of them and how smart they are for focusing on their job. I smile, pat them on the shoulder, and let them know they are special to me. When you're a well-behaved student at AIPCS, I will compliment, support, and pay you because that is what hardworking students deserve.

When students are lazy or disrespectful, they quickly face the consequences. I humiliate students in front of their peers. Some will cry, and I couldn't care less. My philosophy is I tried the niceness, and that didn't work, so let's try the other way. Do you understand embarrassment and harshness better? That's what it really comes down to. You know what I've noticed? When the first method doesn't work, the second one will in most cases. There are those people in life who follow the rules and who stay in line in order to reap the benefits of good behavior. There are others who seek to overturn the rules and test the system, and they get held in check through punishments. AIPCS represents this dichotomy and keeps students in line through rewards and punishments.

There is always a handful of students for whom nothing seems to work. They usually repeat their grade, leave the school, and continue to screw up at other schools. My philosophy differs from most educators. I don't believe you can save all students, especially those who act like barnyard animals. I am not an idealist. Educators waste too much time focusing on a small number of students who are just acting out and refusing to change their ways. The students who want to learn are held hostage by these clowns in the secondary public schools.

People talk about potential all the time, but what they fail to realize is that potential doesn't automatically turn into anything. It takes serious work and discipline to turn a student's potential into ability and talent. Latent potential is essentially useless if it never gets tapped. Sometimes you have to yell, threaten, and get all over students to pull that potential out, especially with ghetto kids. How many educators will admit this to the public? They say I'm being too hard on these students who are hardheaded and interfere with others' learning. Most principals in these ghetto urban schools are too easy on their students and teachers. They've got to send out a message that they don't put up with loafers.

I immediately ingrain in students my golden rule: If you act like a winner, you'll be treated like a winner. If you act like a fool, you'll be treated like a fool.

This story is one example. At the beginning of the 2005–2006 school year, the site administrator, Mr. Katz, brought to me two sixth-graders who looked like two wet tomcats who had been fished out of a ditch. One was the white boy Adam mentioned earlier, and the other was a small Mexican boy named Jose. Mr. Katz announced, "These two didn't do their homework for the second day in a row."

I fixed my gaze on the boys where they stood hemmed into the doorway. I gave them a loaded silent stare that made even the adults in the room uncomfortable, as they told me later.

I turned my attention to Jose, the small Mexican boy. "Where did you go to school at, boy?"

"Laurel."

"Do you want to go back there to repeat the fifth grade?"

"No," he mumbled.

"I'm serious now, boy. Do you want to pack up your shit right now and go back there?" I stood up and leaned over a chair a few feet from Jose and stared him straight in the eye.

"No," he said with his eyes watering and his arms stiff against his sides.

I let him stand uncomfortably for a moment while I shifted my attention to the larger of the two, Adam, and asked, "What grade were you in last year, fool?"

"Sixth," he replied in a voice too deep for a sixth-grader.

"What grade are you in now?"

"Sixth."

"Do you want to be in sixth grade 'til you're fifteen?"

"No."

"Why didn't you do your homework, then?"

"I didn't have enough time. My teacher made me work after school and I had to help my mom with the babies and—"

"Shut up."

"My teacher doesn't let me do my homework after school—"

"Shut up. *Shut up. Shut up.* I don't want to hear none of this nonsense. You ask your teacher next time if you may do your homework after school and help her clean, and she'll be glad to help you. All right?"

The boy nodded.

I turned back to Jose. "Where are your parents from?"

"Mexico."

"Where in Mexico are they from?"

"I don't know because they never told me," he said slowly.

"Why did they want to come here?"

"So I could get a better education." His "education" sounded more like the Spanish *educación*, the language of his parents.

"So you're basically saying, 'Fuck you, Mama. I don't care about an education.'"

He looked shocked. "No."

I continued, "Your parents worked hard to make things better for you. By not doing your homework, you're saying, 'Fuck you, Mama.' So which one is it going to be tomorrow: 'Fuck you, Mama,' or 'Thank you, Mama?' Are you going to do your homework or not?"

"I'm going to do it."

"Good."

I told Mr. Katz to have them go pick up trash, because that's the kind of work you end up doing when you don't have an education or you're lazy. I figure when students don't want to do the easy work (school work), then they can do the menial tasks that uneducated people usually have to do in life.

Adam made honor roll and qualified to take the SAT for the Johns Hopkins University Center for Talented Youth program. At the end of the year Jose's mama wanted to remove him from the school, which she did. When she realized he wasn't learning anything at Bret Harte Middle School, she wanted to bring him back to AIPCS, but I had already given his spot to someone else. One student leaves, and another fills his spot faster than you can say, "Dr. Chavis is crazy."

# chapter twenty-one

# A Method to the Madness

"When we remember we are all mad, the mysteries disappear, and life stands explained."

—*Written in the notebooks of Mark Twain, American author (1835–1910)*

"In the art of war there are no fixed rules."

—*Sun Tzu,*
*from* The Art of War, *circa sixth century BC*

I want people to think I'm crazy and ornery, so they won't bother me. It works. Ms. Sullivan tells me I'm crazy like a fox.

Though I have my share of confrontations, once I have cussed someone out or shown them my savage side, that person doesn't often return for a second round. My combative, ranting tactics keep idiots at bay in the ghettos of Oakland, California. There is a method to my madness.

I learned a strong lesson by contrasting my uncle Chambers Bell with my grandpa Calvin Chavis, who was a bootlegger, to show how kindness can kill you, but craziness can save you.

Uncle Chambers was a good man who always helped others. He'd give you the shirt off his back. He was always on the move, only stopping briefly to visit with you because he always had someone to go help. Uncle Chambers could never hold on to money. I used to look down on him because he was always broke. His house wasn't paid for, but he made good money in construction. When Uncle Chambers was murdered, it clicked. Since he was always going to help someone else and would always give away his last dollar, his kindness killed him.

One day when Uncle Chambers was in his late seventies, he collected his social security check from the mailbox and walked in the house. A young man knocked on the door later that evening. When Uncle Chambers opened the door, the white boy, named David Lester Suggs, hit him in the head with a hammer, took his money, and got high on drugs. Around three in the morning, Suggs felt the urge to confess to his crime. He went to the police station to say he had killed an old Indian man. The police could tell he was high on drugs, so they dismissed what he was saying as drug-induced nonsense. He then went to the sheriff's department to report what he had done. The first Indian sheriff in the area, Glenn Maynor, realized from Suggs's description that Uncle Chambers was the old man he had robbed and beaten. Sheriff Maynor sent one of his officers to go to the house to check it out. When the officer got there he found Uncle Chambers on the floor, his head swollen like a melon and bloody, but he was still alive. An ambulance rushed him to the hospital. He survived for several weeks on life support at Duke Medical Center before our family decided there was no use and pulled the plug from the life support system.

By contrast, my grandpa Calvin was considered a crazy old Indian man, and people did not mess with him. He would warn people not to step foot on his property; Grandpa would even shoot at those who went in his yard. As a bootlegger, he was involved in selling liquor, so he had to protect himself, but his philosophy was when people are afraid of you and think you're crazy, they won't mess with you. You see how it's passed on to me? When he was an old man, people would say, "Don't go over there to [Calvin's] place; he's crazy." He used to chew snuff and it would run down his lip and he'd say in a mean old man voice, "These niggers, Indians, and crackers around here ain't none of 'em worth a shit. If any of 'em come here and try to mess with me, I'll shoot 'em or cut 'em, and I want 'em to know it, too." Now that was Grandpa's attitude. Nobody meddled with him. Uncle Chambers gave everything away and was nice. When Suggs went to his house that night, he knew my uncle wasn't going to do a thing, and he killed him. Do you see how my view of the world has been shaped by experience?

While my hot-tempered ways can make me unpleasant to be around at times, they certainly have benefited me in life. When you're dealing with fools, you have to play the part, too, sometimes. A student named

Sidney Hawkins once told me I was like a mirror reflecting a person's behavior back to him. When a person approached me respectfully, I mirrored that respect. When a person acted like an idiot, I reflected the same right back. I thought that was a great insight for an eighth-grader.

When I ask students what teachers in hindsight they respect the most, they almost always mention the strictest teachers. When students can manipulate a staff member and get away with it, they lose respect. That's not to say you can't or shouldn't be nice to the students, but you can't let them get away with behaviors that both you and they know are wrong. When a student talks back to you, and you don't deal with it swiftly, then you can expect other students to start talking back to you, too. Once students feel they can disrespect you and you won't do anything about it, it's over. You've lost in their eyes, and in mine.

My personal straightforwardness and the strictness of the school are perfect for the student population at American Indian Public Charter School. These poor blacks, Mexicans, Indians, Asians, and whites are not going to heed a principal who lets them goof off and run around like barnyard animals. Most people want to say we're all the same, but it's a lie! We are not all the same. These kids need more structure and discipline because of the way they've been forced to grow up in Oakland. Sometimes they need to be chewed out to get them back in line and on that path to success.

People might say, "He's crazy," and they might not like me when I'm rough around the edges, but no one can argue with my students' test scores and attendance rates. This school is so good and has come so far—who else in the city has done what AIPCS has done other than the schools who use AIM-Ed: American Indian Public High School, American Indian Public Charter School II, Oakland Charter Academy, and Oakland Charter Academy High School?

I have a different way of handling misbehavior than most principals. I use unorthodox tactics to teach lessons and drive a point home. This story serves as an example.

I am a follower of the wisdom in *The Art of War* by Sun Tzu, which was written over two thousand years ago. *The Art of War* states, "Seize something he cherishes and he will conform to your desires." In Jeremy Shiu's case, who was mentioned earlier, it was hair. Hair that he cherished. And hair that he lost when he didn't live up to his side of an agreement.

I discovered Jeremy had developed a habit of stealing from his classmates when he was in the seventh grade. Since Jeremy valued his hair above everything else and I valued money, I decided hair and money would be the objects to put on the negotiating table. Jeremy agreed that if I caught him stealing I could cut off his hair. If he quit stealing and became a good student, I agreed to pay his college tuition for the first semester. That was the pact.

Well, about a year later, when he was in the eighth grade, I found out Jeremy had been caught stealing again at AIPCS. At the end of that school day, as he tried to walk out the door, I told Jeremy he was coming home with me. When he tried to get away and told me he wouldn't go, I made it clear he didn't have a choice. I had called his father and reminded him of the deal. Jeremy's father gave me permission to take Jeremy back to my house, which is something I do when kids act up at the school. At my house I do a combination of humiliate, intimidate, and motivate students. I try to turn them from losers into winners.

Jeremy said "no way" I was going to cut his hair. Mr. Jorge Lopez, the principal of Oakland Charter Academy, was over that evening. With his assistance, I took a pair of clippers and buzzed Jeremy's whole head clean. When I was done he looked like a scared lab rat.

When the staff heard what happened and saw Jeremy's head as proof the next day, there was a mix of shock, amusement, and disapproval, but mostly disapproval. I could tell Mr. Bates, a trust baby, felt bad for him. I said, "You know, I have one advantage over you. I know how to deal with darkies and whities and what works with them. I take action and follow through. I don't know what it is about liberal white people, but you all run around feeling guilty all the time and tell us that it's not our fault when we screw up." My attitude was I couldn't care less about the teachers who did not agree with my method of education. I laughed and had a great time embarrassing Mr. Bates and a few other staff. They almost broke their necks trying to get away from me as quickly as possible.

In our society when you're caught breaking laws, you lose privileges. Jail, for example, takes away a person's ability to live freely. Good behavior in prison can lead to an earlier release or to some privileges, but for the most part an inmate has no say in what he eats, when he gets exercise, what he wears, or where he lives. When you're found guilty of a crime, you usually lose something, and it usually happens abruptly. That's how I see the head shaving. Instead of going to jail or juvenile hall, Jeremy got a small dose of what it's like to lose something you value and to be made an example of to others.

Jeremy's head shaving became a publicly known incident when the *Oakland Tribune* ran a front-page article about the school on November 14, 2005. Other newspapers started picking up the story as well. It was even published in England—something about a headmaster shaving a lad's head. While you might imagine that shaving a student's head would create a negative reaction toward me and American Indian Public Charter School, the office phone rang off the hook that day with local family members inquiring about how to get their children into the school. You see, many minority families in Oakland want the structure and discipline that AIPCS provides. When I warn families who want to enroll their children that the school is strict, most of them say, Good, or, I know and that's what I want, or, I'm tired of my daughter being in a class where there's no control and it's not safe.

The head shaving got some attention; however, a few lost hairs from the head of a Chinese student weren't enough to offset the great test results our students achieve, which were highlighted in the *Oakland Tribune* article. When you're a good coach, you can get away with unorthodox antics. When your school is lousy, you can't get away with all the various acts I'm known to perform.

When the Oakland Unified School District was deciding whether to grant me permission to start American Indian Public High School, Jeremy's head shaving came up at the board meeting. This time the story was inaccurate, since it was alleged to have happened in public to an American Indian student. In actuality I shaved the boy's head at my house, and he is Chinese. The state administrator, Dr. Randolph Ward, heard all complaints at the meeting but decided to grant us the charter for the high school. On the night of that decision, January 25, 2006, board minutes were taken and condensed into a summary, which was posted on OUSD's Web site. Here is part of it:

> Tania Kappner, OEA [Oakland Education Association] Member, reiterated earlier speaker comments opposing the American Indian Public School charter on the basis of the completely outrageous punitive measures taken against students on campus and the clear unaccountability to disrespectful treatment of students, public shaving of student's head as to disrespect them in front of many. This is not quality education for Native American students.

Tania is a white liberal extremist who makes it a point to put her mouth in motion before putting her brain in gear. She is part of those far-to-the-left liberals who in my opinion are worse than the Ku Klux Klan. They pretend to be interested in minority students; however, they are only interested in their own personal agendas and pimp the students who are left in their care. Even when they know the facts, they adjust them to meet their goals of being leaders for us poor minorities. They love for minorities to have the illusion that we can make choices, but when families are given the chance to choose a public charter school, like AIPCS or AIPHS, for their children, these "saviors" always find a way to interfere. They have taken over the public school unions. They go into overdrive to prevent Indians, blacks, Hispanics, and Asians from deciding what's best for our children's public education. They keep us uneducated, and they make money in the process.

The board minutes continued with:

Margot Bohanon, indigenous California, and Chabot parent, said she met the Director of the American Indian Public Charter School. She cannot support the endorsement of a principal, who under different District standards, would no longer be principal of a school.

I am allowed to implement my educational methods because they work and the families love them. The school gets amazing academic and social results with our student population. No school in Oakland does as well academically as American Indian Public Charter School. I do not care about being fired. I am a man who believes in what we are doing with our students, not a coward who is afraid to lose his job. Oakland Unified School District does not set or control AIPCS's discipline policy because we are a charter school. I will rant, rave, shave, and pay as long as my students are succeeding in school. While corporal punishment in schools is forbidden by California law, as it should be, common sense is not. Embarrassment as a disciplinary practice is considered both inappropriate and ineffective by do-gooders in California education, but it is not outlawed. Some of those do-gooders are the same people running public secondary schools that fail our student population.

I received a letter dated March 15, 2006, about Jeremy's shaven head from the president of the California Teachers Association,

Barbara E. Kerr. In the letter, Ms. Kerr said she was writing on behalf of the California Teachers Association, a 335,000-member organization, "to express our concerns about your use of public humiliation to discipline students at your middle school." She claimed erroneously that I had "shaved the head of an American Indian student as a form of discipline." She called the head shaving "culturally offensive." She noted, "Public humiliation and shaming are unacceptable methods of dealing with students." Since charter schools are exempt from California's Education Code, Kerr admonished, "Exemption from the State Education Code must not result in the degrading punishment of children in charter schools." She said she had heard of my methods of discipline from the December 16, 2005, article published in the *San Francisco Chronicle.*

Is it a surprise that Ms. Kerr never visited AIPCS or sent anyone from her organization to see how the school actually operates? She got her information from the teachers union representing OUSD and from a newspaper article. How ironic that a white female opportunist representing California teachers writes that I am "culturally offensive" to Indians. I guess it is culturally offensive that a dumb old country Indian has created a method to educate inner-city students without wasting millions of dollars.

About six months later, a staff member interviewed Jeremy about the incident. I was not in the room when the interview occurred. Jeremy said at first he was "angry and pissed off," but about two weeks after having his head shaved he "realized Dr. Chavis was just trying to help me be successful. All Dr. Chavis wanted from me was to act better and get better grades." Jeremy summed up the incident's impact as, "I got over it." He also quit stealing from other students.

Jeremy laughed and said the head shaving was "okay for one time only," but he would not want it to happen again. Jeremy continued on to our American Indian Public High School, where he has been performing well academically and staying out of trouble for the most part.

Now, does it sound like Jeremy has been "traumatized" by having his head shaved? He sounds pretty normal to me. Doesn't it seem kind of funny that news agencies around the world were running a story on a Chinese boy having his head shaved by an Indian principal? Aren't there more newsworthy events to talk about?

When students like Jeremy act out, I see it as a teaching opportunity. I embrace the fools and use them as an example for what other students should not do. Every time his peers saw Jeremy's shaved head, they had a reminder of what stealing from each other would lead to. I have a statement on my office door that I'm quite fond of. It says: "You can never be a complete failure at American Indian Public Charter School. You can always serve as a bad example." That's what Jeremy stood for at the time. He has also served as a good example to his peers. Jeremy is a great young man whom I picture running a successful organization when he's older. He's got that kind of charismatic, risk-taking leadership potential.

Like Jeremy, I certainly served as both a bad and a good (though mostly bad) example to my peers as a schoolboy. Some folks who get involved in education were model students: straight As on their report cards, quiet, attentive, and well behaved. I had none of those attributes. My experiences as a student shaped and enabled me to relate to other hardheaded students. In particular, my first school experience reinforces this point.

# chapter twenty-two

# Ben Fumbles His Way Through Elementary School

---

*"A Lumbee Indian male is a child from one to twelve. He's a boy from thirteen to thirty-five and a man from thirty-six to sixty-five. Then after sixty-five some Lumbee males become boys again."*

—Lela Chavis (Ben's grandma) and Dr. Robert K. Thomas, a Cherokee elder

---

When I was growing up in Robeson County, we didn't have kindergarten, so I went to my first day of school at age six. I was enrolled in the first grade at Piney Grove Elementary School, an old wooden schoolhouse in the countryside. The school was for Indians only. It was several miles from where I lived, and I was going to take the school bus there for the first time in my life. The idea of riding a bus was thrilling! I got up early that morning and waited by the side of the road. Later I sat quietly on the bus seat watching the scenery pass by and wondering what school would be like.

When I got off the bus, the other students and I were led into the auditorium, where we were organized into classes. I was assigned to Ms. Hazel's first-grade class. She was a voluptuous Lumbee Indian woman with a freckled face who wore glasses. She smiled and brought us into the classroom and showed us where to sit. There were about thirty students in the class. A pretty girl named Shirley sat across from me at my table with about four others. The name Shirley stuck in my mind because that is my mama's name.

Ms. Hazel asked, "How many of you can write your name?" No

one said anything. She passed out large red pencils with no erasers and paper with big spaces between the lines. My grandparents Calvin and Lela had taught me how to write my name in the dirt with my finger, but I had never held a pencil before, never mind that enormous red pencil that was more like a tree. Ms. Hazel told us to write our names on the paper. With intense concentration I wrote a wobbly "Ben Chavis." Following Ms. Hazel's directions, I passed my paper to the end of the table, where she collected them. Ms. Hazel returned to her desk and started sorting through the papers while the class waited nervously in silence. She announced, "Two children got their names right: Shirley Jones and Ben Chavis. Come up to the front of the class."

Shirley and I took timid steps toward Ms. Hazel. I wasn't comfortable standing in front of the class, and I didn't get the gist of what she was trying to do, which was to congratulate us. All I knew was that we were getting a lot of attention all of a sudden, so I figured we must have done something wrong. I had heard about the paddlings students got in school in those days. I thought we were in trouble when Ms. Hazel, who was sitting behind her desk with her heavy legs sagging apart, summoned me over to her.

She said, "Come here, boy." I looked at her and stood still. Ms. Hazel repeated again, "Come here, boy." Expecting a good beating, I slowly walked over to her desk. All the eyes in the room watched. When I was a foot away, Ms. Hazel reached out and pulled me into her big bosom. I didn't realize she was giving me a hug because I wasn't used to that type of affection from strangers. My family didn't kiss and hug me. I couldn't breathe as Ms. Hazel held me against her chest. I felt suffocated and under attack, so I bit her breast. She screamed. Shirley started to cry, and everyone else started crying, and Ms. Hazel yelled out for Mr. Brewington, the principal, to come.

I ran out the door of the classroom and down the steps of the school. The schoolhouse was built up off the ground, so I ducked under the school and hid. Mr. Brewington peered in at me with his hawkish face and said, "I'm gonna get you, boy." Mr. Brewington sent Mr. Floyd, the janitor, who was about six feet eight, under the schoolhouse to grab me. As Mr. Floyd got close, I scurried out the south side and ran away as fast as I could. They didn't chase me. Now if I bit a teacher on the breast my first day of school, can you understand how no kind of student behavior surprises me?

When I got home from Piney Grove, Grandpa Calvin asked me

what happened. I told him the story, and of course his little grandson Ben was the victim. He asked if I wanted to go back to school, and I said no way. He didn't make me go back for some time.

Reflecting on it now, it was culturally inappropriate of Ms. Hazel to hug me. She was an Indian, too, but she had been to college, where she probably learned about positive reinforcement, which was not something that happened at our house with strangers.

A day or two after the incident, Mr. Oxendine from Piney Grove Elementary School came by my home and talked to Grandpa Calvin. He told Grandpa I was a mean boy who needed to be taught. He was right. I was sitting up in the crab apple tree with overalls and no shirt on, listening to the conversation from a distance. Before Mr. Oxendine left, he walked by the tree, looked me in the eye, and said, "Boy, we're gonna get you."

When he was gone, I clambered down from the tree and asked Grandpa Calvin, "Whatcha gonna do, Grandpa?"

He said, "Boy, you don't want to go back to school, do you?"

"No." What boy does at six years old who can fish, hunt, and hang out with his grandpa?

"Well, you can stay here with me then."

Other than maybe one more week, I never attended school for that entire year. In fact, I even missed the first couple of months of the next school year. My grandpa Calvin told Mama I was going to school. It took her a long time to find out we were deceiving her, because she was busy working in the fields and as a maid. My grandpa was supposed to be taking care of me during the day, so Mama just assumed he was taking me to school when he came by in the morning to get me. Instead, I would follow my grandpa into town, to people's houses, and to the Bottoms, a place where bootleggers and drinkers of all races got together. My mom eventually figured out I was skipping school that year, but she didn't force me to go back. In addition, I developed a kidney problem because of the accident with Pappy that required me to be hospitalized for a long time.

I know this sounds like a strange thing to say, but that year with Grandpa Calvin and repeating first grade saved me. I wasn't ready for school. As people so often say, timing is everything. I needed another year to explore before being in a school environment. That year I learned so much from watching my grandpa Calvin interact with others. It's incredibly valuable when people take their children and grandchildren around with them as they do business or visit with people. Children pick up and learn things from watching their family members in action. My experiences with my grandpa Calvin taught me how to interact with all kinds of people in all kinds of situations.

When I returned to school, it was in the first grade again. I enrolled a couple months late, but otherwise the school year passed without much incident. In the second grade, however, I started to get into more trouble. I missed at least thirty days of school that year. Most of the times I skipped school I went fishing in the Lumber River. The teacher would send notes home with me. I still couldn't read and didn't start to read until the beginning of the third grade, but I knew those notes weren't going to say Ben was a good boy, so I would tear them up. My mom couldn't read much, either, but I figured it was safer not to give her any reason to question what was going on with me at school. I was a boy who got in trouble and tried to get away with it, so as a principal I can figure out the troublemakers quickly, deal with them, and relate to them.

The one aspect that stands out in my mind about second grade was the weekly spanking. Every Friday my second-grade teacher, Ms. Locklear, gave us a spelling test. For every word you misspelled, you got a swat to the rear. The odd thing was that you could have someone else take your spanking if they volunteered. I figured out a way to beat her system and profit by it at the same time. I would take other students' swats for money. They paid me with their lunch money, marbles, or anything of value. I knew I was going to get spanked anyway because I was terrible at spelling, so why not make some money in the process? On Friday I would pad my pants by wearing long johns. The extra clothing made the swats less painful.

One Friday Ms. Locklear figured out my trick. She dragged me into the coat closet, pulled down my pants and long johns, and started whacking my bare butt with a wooden board. She said to me, "Ben, you think you're smart, don't you?" I deserved to be beaten for undermining her system, but I didn't agree with her logic of spanking kids for misspelling words and allowing other kids to take their swats. It didn't make sense to me.

But I responded better to negative consequences than positive reinforcement. It didn't especially bother me that the second-grade teacher beat me on the butt, but it certainly bothered me when the first-grade teacher tried to hug me. My family was not affectionate, and Mama would beat me with anything that was around when I was a little devil. If we had owned a lawn mower in those days and I acted a fool, she would have picked it up and hit me with it. My mama was a tough lady. She weighed ninety pounds, but she scared me to death. She kept me walking a straight line for the most part.

The Lumbees I was raised around are a lively, lusty, loud people. You can drive past churches in Robeson County with your windows rolled up and still hear Lumbees praising the Lord. My loudness is often misconstrued as aggression on the West Coast. When I'm loud, I'm just expressing myself. When Lumbees are truly mad they will either fight you or have nothing to do with you. When I was growing up, Lumbees weren't ones to talk about feelings or show affection. We are the most successful Indian tribe in America when it comes to business because we don't play. We work. We ain't ones to sit around and discuss your feelings, but today some are moving in that direction.

In my personal life, I'm not into affection. I call Marsha's family the kissing Latins because they want to kiss you every time you move. I don't go for all that, and I think it's from the way I was raised. I kiss my own children occasionally because eventually you start to cave in. Marsha criticizes my lack of affection. She tells me, "You think giving money is a sign of affection." I do indeed see giving money as a sign of affection! She's right. See, from my perspective, I was born poor and brought up to believe that a man should take care of his family, and a large part of that has to do with money. My use of money as a sign of care and my hard-knocks approach to discipline at the school stem from my background. So much of what I do relates to my childhood experiences in Robeson County.

For instance, from one of my sixth-grade teachers, Mrs. Ann Phillips, I learned the valuable educational practice of teaching students lessons beyond the school day. Educators can make an impact by taking a troublemaking child home with them for a day and making that child do his work. In today's lawsuit-worried climate, in lieu of taking a child home you can interact with him after school on campus. Again, the key is building relationships with students that reveal to them you are a caring human being who wants the best for them and that you are willing to go beyond the school day to show it. It really made a difference to me when Mrs. Ann Phillips took me home with her in sixth grade. Fed up with me not doing my work, she warned if I didn't have my homework the next day, I was going to have to go home with her to do my work.

When the next day came around, and I didn't have my homework, she made good on her threat. After school, she made me pack up my belongings and go with her. She put me in a quiet room at her home and helped me with my homework. After I cooperated and did my school lessons, she bought me a toy car. As a poor boy, that toy meant a lot to me. It was a great reward. From then on, I always did my work in Mrs. Phillips's class and had a new attitude toward her. To keep encouraging my good behavior, Mrs. Phillips would praise me in front of the class and tell me I was doing a good job. She was also quick to point out when I was out of control.

Like Mrs. Phillips, I often take a student or several students from American Indian Public Charter School home with me. It's always the troublemakers I take home, the students whom the teachers have had difficulty controlling and motivating. By the time I am through with them, they usually behave better in school. I take a military approach and break the student down, sometimes to tears, and then build the student back up.

One time I brought two seventh-graders home with me: Tony, a Chinese boy, and Bobby, a black boy. Tony was crying when he first got there. I was working in the backyard, and my friend Dr. Albert Wahrhaftig was watching over them as they did their schoolwork in the kitchen. Albert came outside and kidded, "The slaves in the galley are hungry, and they say they want to go home."

I chuckled and said, "I want them to starve. You know what Tony's mama said to me earlier? 'Hit him.' Tell them they can have some of the cornbread I made last night and water." Then I asked him to look over the algebra problems they were working on. By the time I went back in the house, the boys were working diligently. I started explaining that I knew they were smart and had great potential and that I believed in them, but they couldn't keep acting like fools in class. As I spent time with them and explained my views, the boys realized I was looking out for their best interests. They may have been embarrassed, angry, and ashamed at first, but once those emotions wore off, they started to understand the underlying message. From then on, when Tony and Bobby did something good in school, I made sure to praise them in front of their classmates.

My other sixth-grade teacher, Mrs. Mary Lamm, remembers me as a boy who lacked ambition and direction. One day she showed a movie about Jim Thorpe, the all-American athlete, whom she considered an inspirational figure for Indians. The movie made a big impression on me. Mrs. Lamm noticed how excited I was about the movie and how often I mentioned it in class, so she said to me, "Well, Ben, why don't you be the next Jim Thorpe?" I smiled. I liked that idea. From then on, I would run around the playground and in and out of the schoolhouse. Mrs. Lamm noticed I was fast, so she told me that when I got to high school, I needed to approach a friend of hers, the cross-country coach Francis "Boogie" Bass. I did indeed run for Mr. Bass, who helped me grow as an athlete and gain entrance to college. Mrs. Lamm continued to support me after the sixth grade. She cheered for me at cross-country and track meets and was there to congratulate me when I graduated from college and again when I finished graduate school.

Mrs. Lamm and Mrs. Phillips were able to break through my hard head and motivate me. Not all of my teachers saw what I could accomplish, and I had quite a bad reputation with some of them. When I was a grown man and working as a professor, I bumped into Ms. Clark, a former elementary school teacher of mine, at the Winn-Dixie grocery store in Robeson County. I said, "Hi, Ms. Clark. Do you remember me? I'm Ben Chavis. I was in your second-grade class for part of the year." (She was not the teacher who swatted me for misspellings, but I played hell in her class, too.) Ms. Clark looked at me skeptically and then said she remembered me. She asked what I was doing. I said proudly, "Well, I'm a professor now, and I actually just got asked to be a visiting scholar at UC Berkeley next semester."

She said, "Son, don't lie. I'm just glad you're not dead or in jail." I followed up by saying I was only joking about my job, although I was telling the truth, and told Ms. Clark it was good to see her again. She remembered the little devil in her second-grade class, and it was impossible for her to picture him teaching at a university. So when I tell you I've never met a worse student than myself, I'm not joking.

# chapter twenty-three

# Out from Under the Hype of Violence

"When people ask me where I'm from and I say Oakland, people respond, 'Oh, really? What are you doing in Oakland?' I guess they think I seem fragile. I'm used to riding the bus home at night, and it doesn't bother me at all. I'm always on my toes as far as being aware of my surroundings. Yes, it is a crime-filled city, and yes, we have negative stereotypes, but I don't think I'd want to grow up anywhere else. I love Oakland; I think I want to live in Oakland for the rest of my life."

—*Lyzanna Chairez,*
*former AIPCS student from 2001 to 2004, now attending UC Berkeley*

"It was great to be the only kid from Oakland in my AP Economics class [taken at the Academic Talent and Development Program at UC Berkeley, a summer program for academically advanced youths]. Most of the students came from the San Fernando Valley. I felt proud. I was also the only Mexican in the class. The students were mostly Chinese. I used to talk to the only white kid in the class. The minority. [He laughs.] I had to take a lot of jokes about Oakland and its violence from my classmates. 'People get killed there, right?' Like I care. I'm alive. I haven't been shot at. I've been robbed. I used to get that question a lot. 'Have you been robbed? How many of them were there?' They'd look at me wide-eyed, the skinny kid with glasses being tough. Not too hard to imagine, right?"

—*Edgar Cervantes, a senior in AIPHS's first graduating class of 2008–2009*

Like American Indian Public Charter School students who are seen as living in a violent, crazy place named Oakland, there is also much hype surrounding the land I call home.

When I flew back to Lumberton to visit my family a few years ago, I was dressed in a suit and seemed to the people seated around me to be quite professional, so when I informed a lady I was going to Robeson County, she said, "You had better be very careful down there. Those Indians are crazy." It was out of concern for me that she made that comment. How could anyone with common sense be offended? Our other seatmates agreed with her assessment. I enjoyed hearing their perspective and was glad they felt the way they did. At least I knew they wouldn't come around and bother my people like ole Catfish Cole and the KKK. Outsiders, like the passengers on the plane, have a similar view of Oakland. Heck, sometimes when you just tell people you live in Oakland they think you're a gangster, because they only know what they see in the paper or on TV.

When you read the *Robeson Journal*, a popular newspaper among Lumbee Indians, you begin to see why outsiders form the opinions they do about Robeson County. The front page is covered with articles about murders, rapes, robberies, shootings, and other violent crimes, often with a bizarre or macabre twist. One article in 2005 talked about a young Indian man recently released from jail who beat and raped his grandmother and stole her money to buy drugs.

In addition to being a transportation hub for agricultural and industrial goods, Interstate 95 provides a major drug corridor through Robeson County. The combination of drugs, poverty (the 2002 per capita personal income was $18,328 in Robeson County, compared to $30,906 nationwide), and lack of education leads to a high incidence of crime; however, business provides my people with a choice they did not have in the past.

I'm not pleased with the violence and drug abuse in my county, but I am proud of many of our ways of life. It's as though Robeson County has two faces: a down-home country peacefulness and a dark underbelly of crime and violence. Oakland has a similar duality.

Robeson County isn't a generally well-known area of the country, but one event in 1993 put it briefly in the nation's limelight: the murder of the basketball star Michael Jordan's father, Mr. James Jordan. When news of the murder was first announced and there were not yet any suspects, the Reverend Jesse Jackson said it was racism against the black man. He said the black man wasn't safe in the South. Then he found out two darkies (a black and an Indian) killed Mr. James Jordan, and ole Jesse fled like a fly in a rainstorm.

The murderers, Daniel Green and Larry Martin Demery, ages eighteen and seventeen, respectively, snuck up on Mr. James Jordan, who was asleep in his red Lexus, a gift from Michael, in a makeshift rest area where he had stopped to sleep after returning from the funeral of a friend. Mr. James Jordan was parked off I-95 near Lumberton. The two young men, who did not know who he was, shot and killed him and stole his car. They rode around in the Lexus for four days after the murder and made several calls from Mr. Jordan's cell phone, which led the police straight to them. Mr. James Jordan's body was found in a swamp dangling over a tree limb about two weeks after he was murdered.

This news might have dismayed some Americans, but this type of armed robbery would not be considered peculiar in Robeson County. The only difference was the victim was famous, so the media swarmed the area. Green and Demery, though only eighteen and seventeen at the time of the murder, were already career criminals. Prior to killing Mr. Jordan, Green had spent two years in jail for fracturing his friend's skull with an ax, and Demery had been charged less than a year before with assaulting an elderly woman with a cinder block.

One of the murderers was Lumbee Indian, and the other was black. This prompted the sheriff at the time, Hubert Stone, to claim something along the lines of, "If you see an Indian, white, and a black together, you know a crime is being committed." In Robeson County many Indians over fifty don't trust blacks or whites and don't socialize with them. Their perspective is when you see an Indian man hanging around with a black or white man, you'd better keep an eye out because they're up to no good. Sheriff Stone was speaking the truth as he saw it, but some people outside of Robeson County said he was racist, and the boys didn't stand a fair chance in the courtroom. The sheriff was merely reflecting the views held by many of the county's residents.

Demery's mom stopped by my family's old antique shop and said her son was innocent. She said, "You know these people around here are racist, and that man was a queer." She claimed Mr. James Jordan tried to lure Demery and Green into his car for sexual reasons. Since Mr. Jordan was dead and couldn't defend himself against her accusation, that was the excuse she gave for her son's actions, an excuse commonly used in Robeson County, because many of its residents have no use for gays.

I like to say I received my BA in social science from the University of Arizona and a Ph.D. in politics from Robeson County. Living in Robeson County taught me how to keep on the lookout to survive as a youngster. If you can survive Robeson County, you can survive anywhere in the United States.

Tragedy struck when I was in second grade, but at the time I didn't view it as such. I had a friend named George Brooks, who was in the third grade. The two of us found a nickel—just enough to buy candy from a local store.

After school, we took off running across a cow pasture to see who could make it to the store first. I was the faster runner, and I stopped at the edge of the cow pasture to see how far behind George was. George must have thought the race was supposed to last all the way to the store because he kept running full speed past the edge of the cow pasture and into West Fifth Street.

I watched as a car slammed into George. I stared at the ripped-up body on the road and thought not about George but about the trouble I would get into. I wasn't supposed to be there, and I thought I was going to get killed for running the road like a swamp rabbit.

A few days later, I went to the Brookses' home for the funeral. The women bawled their eyes out while I sat there speechless. There was an open casket in the living room with little George tucked inside. I looked down into the casket and thought, "Damn, George. You messed up." I was hardened to George's death then, but thinking about it now always chokes me up and brings me to tears.

I was completely desensitized to death. That same year my uncle, a bootlegger named Carl Walter Bell, drowned while fishing dead drunk in a boat in the middle of a pond. Another time I saw two white guys shot right in front of me at the school bus stop. Their brains fell to the sidewalk. It reminded me of the mashed potatoes mixed with ketchup I had eaten that day at school, and I threw up. But you know, I just grew up around death and became accustomed to it.

Growing up in Robeson County also hardened me to what I would consider petty crimes, such as theft. I don't think you're a serious criminal until you kill somebody, and you had better not incite anger in people who can do you harm unless you can give it back to them. My classmate Benny Oxendine got part of his face and arm blown off with a shotgun. I stood there in the yard trying to get him to lie on the ground with his eye hanging out of his skull and I thought, "You idiot, you got what you deserve." He had threatened his older uncle, who balanced out the age difference with a gun.

In my youth, Robeson County was a kill-or-be-killed kind of place. You were just trying to keep from getting hurt.

In part because of all the violence and murder in Robeson County, people who live there seem at ease around death. They don't fear it. Death is seen as God's decision in my neck of the woods, and it touched our home. In a small community like the one I grew up in, we encountered death every week because relationships there are intergenerational. At age six, I would know someone who was ninety-nine. I was always going to a funeral because someone was always dying. Every time I go home to Robeson County, I have a funeral to attend. You may not know the person who died but you know a relative, so you pay your respects. In Oakland, I rarely go to funerals, but it's different where I grew up. Death was always at your door, but you moved right on and accepted it as a way of life.

People in Robeson County talk openly about death and take pictures of the dead. I've been at funerals where my relatives have tried to jump into the casket with the deceased. None of my family members where I come from choose cremation. They want to see the body, and they'll say how pretty the dead look. Just look at a photo album my folks have; there are all kinds of pictures of my grandma, grandpa, uncles, aunts, cousins, and friends lying in open caskets with their bodies covered in their best outfits. I had never seen many of the men in a suit before they passed on.

Every time I'm back in Robeson County, I go to the graveyards to pay respect to my ancestors. The sacred places for Lumbees are the churches, graveyards, and the Lumber River. In the Lumbee Indian community of Prospect behind the largest Indian Methodist church in the United States is a cemetery where many of my relatives lie. The graves of Lela Chavis (my grandmother), Margaret MacLaughlin Locklear (my great-great-grandmother), and John Archie Locklear (my great-great-grandfather) are all there. The grounds of the cemetery are always meticulous, and most of the graves have flowers or other items placed on them that bear witness to a recent visit. It is a peaceful, clean place where we can visit with our ancestors. I know about family members from the 1700s whose stories have been passed on to me by visiting their graveyards and talking with family. Lumbees are obsessed with the dead. We love 'em!

I don't think folks in Oakland are as comfortable with death as the folks in Robeson County, but they see a similar amount of crime and murder. Likewise, both areas have low high school graduation rates, high poverty rates, and drug problems. Oakland Unified School District's graduation rate for the 2003–2004 school year (as reported by America's Promise Alliance) was 45.6 percent, which placed it in the bottom ten of large city districts across the nation. (According to the California Department of Education Web site, however, OUSD's reported graduation rate for that same year was 60.2 percent.)

From looking at census statistics, Oakland's population is about 400,000, while Robeson County's is about 130,000. About 65 percent of people (age twenty-five and older) in Robeson County are high school graduates, while about 48 percent of Oakland's population has completed high school. Only about 11 percent of the population in Robeson County has a bachelor's degree or higher. In Oakland, it's about 31 percent, which goes to show that Oakland does have a solid population of college-educated people, who are mostly white and who moved in from other places.

In Oakland in 2006, there were 148 homicides, the vast majority of which were street shootings. Some people love to make Oakland sound like a hotbed of random violence, yet if you look at the murder statistics, there is consistency. According to a *San Francisco Chronicle* article ("Most Oakland Homicides in 2006 Were Shootings") by Jim Herron Zamora, most shootings took place on street corners in particular neighborhoods in East Oakland and most occurred between the hours of eight p.m. and four a.m. Most of the victims were males, 67 percent of whom were black, while 23 percent were Latino. All of the identified suspects except one were males, 66 percent of whom were black, while 28 percent were Latino. Most of the homicides that were solved were gang- or drug-related. Seems like there's a pattern to this gangster lifestyle, doesn't it?

I tell our students, when you're in the library studying you don't have to worry about getting shot. When you're standing around on a street corner at midnight on gang turf in East Oakland, then you're a fool who's inviting trouble. Fights, robberies, and carjackings are common in Oakland. It's hard for students and their families to shield themselves from those crimes, but what about the homicides? I'd say most people in Oakland avoid certain areas of the city after dark.

During the day, Oakland has its share of crime and trouble, but again I think the image of Oakland as a hard-nosed, gangbanging place is often overhyped. Normal people don't have to fear for their lives as they walk down the street. It's mostly gang members killing other rival gang members late at night. We had some below-the-snuff gang members who would loiter around the gate at the end of the school day and try to mingle with the students. Ms. Sullivan got pissed at them one day, cussed them out, and told them to get away from the gate. We didn't know at the time that they were associated with the Acorn Gang, one of the three major gangs in Oakland; the other two gangs are called Ghost Town and Lower Bottoms. (Can you believe it? I came all the way across the country to the big city, and they have a gang called the Lower Bottoms?)

These gang members could be seen hot-boxing (smoking pot) in an old beat-up car in front of the apartment complex next to AIPCS. It's possible they were also the ones who broke into the high school one night, smashing glass, breaking the door, and stealing an office computer and other valuables. To Ms. Sullivan and me, the boys were a nuisance and a bad influence on the students if unwatched. In the newspaper, these guys and their dealings seemed more daunting. They were part of the Acorn Gang, which got its name from its main drug-dealing turf, the Acorn Housing Project. Over four hundred law-enforcement personnel conducted a raid on the gang in June 2008, making over fifty arrests, seizing firearms, coke, pot, and thousands of dollars in cash. The apartment complex next door to where these lowlifes hung around was part of the bust, which was called Operation Nutcracker. I assure you there are plenty of "nuts" in our city, as in other parts of the country. The Oakland police attribute numerous homicides to the Acorn Gang, as well as carjackings, robberies, and drugs and weapon trafficking. As you can see, these fellows kept pretty busy.

To give you an idea of the degree of nepotism in Oakland, Deborah Edgerly, the Oakland city administrator making $254,000 a year to oversee the police department (among other duties), allegedly tipped off her nephew about the Acorn Gang bust because he was affiliated with the gang. She denied the charge but was fired by Mayor Dellums during the police investigations. Ms. Edgerly has since come under investigation by the FBI for payroll abuses, including allegations that her children received pay as summer interns even though they didn't work for a month of their internship. Well, that's the same thing you see in the Oakland public schools: favoritism, nepotism, poor job performance, and misspent taxpayer money. Do you see the consistency in wasting tax dollars in Oakland?

One statistic I'm really proud of is that since I've been principal no student has been killed while attending American Indian Public Charter School. Prior to my time as principal, several AIPCS students were killed outside of school. I think the difference is the structure, discipline, and guidance our students receive at the school, which they have learned to carry over into other parts of their lives. I know that when some students walk out our gates, they have to transform their image to survive in the rough neighborhoods they live in. That's their reality. But they can take with them the common sense and the discipline they've learned at American Indian Public Charter School to avoid getting involved with the wrong crowd or situation.

Two American Indian brothers who attended AIPCS met a bitter end when they got caught up in the hustle of the street. One day in the late fall of 2002, a young man recently released from jail walked into the school and started heading down the hallway. I came out of the office and asked him what he was there for. He said he was there to see his brother, Andrew Moppin. I told him he needed to sign in at the office. He said, "I'm not going to sign in to no fucking office. I'm gonna see my brother." I said, "Yes, you are. You need to come in here and check in." Well, he didn't like that, so he started cussing at me, and I transformed into a first-rate fool. I don't mind when someone calls me a red savage because I am one when there's a need to be. He told me let's take it outside, so we did. We walked out to the corner of Thirty-fifth and Kansas and then he jumped me. I went to grab his legs to try to upend him, but I couldn't pick him up. A parent leaned out an apartment window nearby and yelled, "Get him, Dr. Chavis! Get him!" Well, he mostly got me. He punched me in the ribs, which I found out later caused a fracture. I pulled my belt off and popped him on the hands with the buckle, which caused him to back off at light speed. He retreated, cussing me out, saying he and his friends would get me some other time. I told him to bring whoever in the hell he wanted to and to make sure he told them how an old man put his ass on the run. Then I went back to work.

Later that day, his mom came by the school all blown up like a bullfrog and said she was going to pull her son Andrew, a ninth-grader, out of the school. I told her Andrew was a smart boy with strong potential and that if she removed him, he'd end up in jail just like his stupid brother. Well, she didn't want to hear that and was pissed and said her son was not finished with me.

My ribs looked the color of a bluetick coonhound for a couple of weeks, and I did not follow any more jailbirds to Thirty-fifth Avenue. I made it a point to have a staff member call the Oakland police and let them deal with the street deadwood from that incident on.

Andrew never returned to AIPCS after that day. It was a shame. He was a good boy, a good-looking kid, and a good student who had started attending school on a regular basis.

As far as I know, Andrew never reenrolled in school, because I never got a transcript request. His mom in the meantime tried to get me fired before the school board, but that didn't lead anywhere. Andrew started hanging out on the street and taking up with idiots. He had the gangbanger look with the sagging pants and got arrested for selling pot. His brother, my street wrestling partner, got killed in 2006 near Thirty-fifth Avenue and International Boulevard. He was shot dead, and the police never figured out who did it.

One year later, on December 31, 2007, Andrew, then twenty years old, was driving down International Boulevard, the same street where his older brother was shot dead, when police pulled him over for a traffic violation. Andrew got out of the car and started running toward Fullers Funeral Home, a place owned by a former AIPCS student's family. The story goes that he reached down to pull up his baggy pants while he ran. When he did so, the police thought he was reaching for a gun, so they shot him. He died at age twenty on the streets of Oakland when he could have been a sophomore in college, like his former classmate Edward Moreno, who now goes to Dartmouth. Andrew left behind a mother with no sons and a girlfriend pregnant with his child. Andrew's girlfriend was the sister of Dean Vargas, whom I mentioned earlier.

Andrew Moppin and his brother needed structure and discipline. Without it, they became more young, wasted blood to be mopped up on the streets. I make the students wear their pants up to their waists while they're in school. The gangbanger image of the sagging pants is what resulted in Andrew getting killed. It's hard to run when your pants are falling down your thighs. When Andrew reached for his rear waistband, the police figured he was reaching for a gun, and they made a split-second decision. How can you blame them? I make it a point to share Andrew's story with our students because they can learn from it.

Some educators will say their goal is to get students out of Oakland. I have a more pragmatic approach. I want our students to run Oakland when they get older and have completed their higher education. I love Oakland and know many of the students feel the same way. They could have a major impact on the city in the future because they understand it and can rise above the negativity to provide perspective and change.

Despite its reputation as a gritty, violent place, Oakland has gorgeous neighborhoods and homes. I love walking around Lake Merritt and enjoy views of the San Francisco Bay from my house. There are redwoods, hiking trails in the hills, lakes, parks, great food of all kinds, and interesting people. Oakland's temperate climate provides nice weather all year round.

People tend to be attached to the place they grew up, so our students have a real fondness for Oakland. It is home for them. They have family, friends, and positive memories of the city. It is the same for me with Robeson County. Instead of wanting to leave the area and put it all behind me, I still keep my Southern roots and own a farm and home in Saddletree, Robeson County. It is a single-story Victorian that I loved as a kid because the Wellingtons owned it, a family I considered rich in those days. It was a dream come true for me as an Indian to buy a former "plantation home," as I perceived it. I keep horses, cows, goats, chickens, geese, ducks, and various crops. My friends and relatives sway in the rockers on the porch and watch the children play on the farm. I get back eight to ten times a year. I can look past the violence and drug use and see the other side of Robeson County, just as I can look past Oakland's violence and drug use to its positive attributes.

Both Oakland and Robeson County have their share of problems, but they also have many merits. Most people living in either location try to ignore the trouble and go about their daily lives in the place they call home.

# chapter twenty-four

# Up from the Bottoms: Bootlegging and Preaching: How I Learned the Gift of Gab and a Love of Free Market Capitalism

"You can't have four hands putting in and twenty-eight hands taking out."

—*What Ben Chavis's dad, Buck Bell,
says when asked how he supported his family of fourteen members*

"Boy, a man that's got money in his pocket can do things. If you want to be able to do things, you gotta have money."

—*What Ben Chavis remembers Mr. Cutler Moore saying to him as a child*

You can learn so much from the people around you, especially when you are a keen observer of human behavior. When I was growing up, my two grandfathers had an enormous impact on me. Grandpa Calvin was a bootlegger, and Grandpa Charlie was a preacher. As you can imagine, they didn't like each other very much; however, they contributed to each other's business. Grandpa Calvin's clients put up the cash to party and get drunk all week in a place called the Bottoms. Then on Sunday those same clients would "save their souls" at Grandpa

Charlie's church. As Grandpa Calvin, the bootlegger, would say to me, "I take their money during the week, and he takes it on Sunday."

I used to watch both of my grandfathers at work using their special gifts, and I loved it! From observing Grandpa Calvin's bootlegging transactions, I learned that money is color-blind, a lesson that has made me a free market capitalist to the core. By tagging along with both Grandpa Calvin and Grandpa Charlie, I also started to recognize how priceless the gift of gab is.

You see, in order to build a successful organization, whether it is a real estate company or a school, you need to create strong relationships with people. For many Asians, blacks, Indians, Hispanics, and whites that means you'd better have the gift of gab. You'd better be able to talk and get people to trust you, or at least remember you. My philosophy is that the more people you talk to, the more people will be talking about you, and the more visible your organization will be in the community. I'm always talking about American Indian Public Charter School—the students, the staff, and our accomplishments—because I want people to remember us, to think of us, and to tell other people about us. Word spreads, and when you have the results, such as our test scores, to back up what you're saying, people pay attention. If you cut to the quick and get right down to business with poor minorities who drop by the school's office, you risk being perceived as rude or just another administrator in their eyes. They feel more comfortable if the conversation is casual. Principals in the inner city can come off as unfriendly when they interact formally with people who aren't used to formal interactions.

The staff gets frustrated with me sometimes because I'm often chatting away with someone when they come in the office wanting a question answered or some kind of work done. But I'm the PR man. I believe in using productive human relations when I'm the face of the school. I know my constant talking can be grating to the people I work with day to day because they've heard my spiel, they know what I'm going to say, and they have a lot of work to do; however, they must be aware that other people's first impressions and lasting impressions matter to me. For example, when the site administrator comes to me with a report that needs to be reviewed, she might have to wait longer than she deems necessary in order for me to wrap up my conversation. Reports will come and go, and believe me, the district and the state will give you

many a report to fill out and sign and fill out and sign and it's madden-
ing—but a good relationship can last a lifetime.

I enjoy staying in touch with people and families who have come
through the school. One mother, Priscilla Wilson, shared, "One thing I
like about American Indian is the teachers follow up and Dr. Chavis
continues to ask me about Aaron—how he's doing in basketball, how
he's doing in school—and about Roshea. He's still concerned. So they
still follow them after they leave AIPCS. They just don't say they're gone
and that's it. Ms. Simmons [a former teacher] still calls Roshea. They
still keep in contact. And all the kids visit American Indian. They're like
a family." Relationships are key. The extended family we create at
American Indian Public Charter School is crucial to the school's success and impact on the community. One way in which these relationships are built is through frequent interaction and conversation—in
short, from talking to people. I learned the valuable gift of gab from my
grandfathers.

My grandpa Calvin, the bootlegger, was a real talker. He'd get his
mules, Nell and Bell, and he'd say to my grandma Lela, "Well, Lela,
you want to go to town?" She'd say, "Naw, I'm gonna stay around
here." She was a hard worker. He was more of a bullshitter, like a lot
of us men. He'd say, "I've got some business in town." That would
mean he'd go talk. My grandpa Calvin couldn't make it to town without stopping to talk to someone. You could track his progress to Lumberton by the piles of mule dung along the side of the road. He knew
everybody. If he went to town six days a week—and he usually took me
with him when I was a young boy—he might get there twice. My
grandpa stopped along the way to talk to everyone he crossed paths
with. I'm like that, too. Walking through Oakland, I'll talk to people
whether I know them or not. On the days Grandpa Calvin actually
made it into town, he'd tie the mules up to a post next to the court-
house and talk to the people passing by or gathered there under an
old water oak tree. In order to generate his bootlegging clientele, he
had to network with people in the only way his country self could—by
talking.

It was illegal to buy or sell alcohol in Robeson County, so there was
a need for booze that sharecroppers, like Grandpa Calvin, filled. He
didn't dare make moonshine at home because my grandma Lela was
very religious. She didn't go for any of that stump-hole business. He

had to go into the woods to make it. He made his moonshine from corn, and I helped carry mason jars full of strong-smelling liquor with him down to the Bottoms, the place where drinkers and bootleggers in Robeson County came together at night until their money or credit ran out. It was called the Bottoms because it was very low land located a quarter mile south of downtown Lumberton across the railroad tracks. To get there, we passed by the town's jailhouse, separated from the river by a narrow road, where inmates would wave or holler at us and ask about their family. We'd say hi and chat back. Again, you had to talk to everyone.

Because the Bottoms was located in the floodplain of the Lumber River, when the Lumber River overflowed its banks in the spring, its dark, muddy waters would pour into the party. I assure you it would take a lot more than the rising water to stop a drunk headed for his favorite bootlegger in the interracial Bottoms, where all were equal in pursuit of a drink and good time. Once the rising water reached the first floor, the bootleggers would move business up to the second floor, and prices tended to rise with the water. For a dime, I would wade out to some drunk's car in the yard to roll up the windows or retrieve a fishing pole from the trunk. The men would drink and fish out of the second-story window as though they were on a yacht with Hemingway in Cuba. The drunks always tipped first-rate for the services they were provided by the bootleggers, by women of the night, or by a young Lumbee Indian boy who enjoyed the whole affair and had money jingling in his pocket.

My grandpa Calvin brought moonshine to sell to other bootleggers, usually good-sized minority women who were tough as rawhide. Some bootleggers traveled outside the county, especially to South Carolina, where it was legal to buy alcohol, and they'd purchase cans of Schlitz and Budweiser to resell later. The bootleggers were their own circuit, connected and tight.

It wasn't uncommon to see male kids like myself at the Bottoms. In some cases I think women sent their sons along to keep an eye on their dads' behavior, but neither my mom nor my grandma would have approved of me going there. It was a place of ill repute, if you catch my drift, some of it paid for in cash, some of it earned with enough booze and sweet-talking.

Drunks are entertaining when you're a little kid because they're gambling, dancing, fighting, and telling stories and you're there to witness it all! It's not a great environment for a kid, but it was fun at times. The drunks, bootleggers, and ladies of the night down in the Bottoms knew more about culture than anyone else I spent time with. They didn't have regular jobs, so they just sat around telling jokes and stories at all hours of the night. They'd talk about events that took place in the 1800s. I would learn about people who had been dead for almost a hundred years before I was even born. They were great at passing on oral histories. Lumbees are a talking culture. I've been able to use that ability to talk with people and relate to them as a way of forging both personal and professional relationships.

The Bottoms also taught me a lot about human nature. Let me tell you something about deviants' behavior. It doesn't matter what color they are when it gets dark. The whites, blacks, Indians, Asians, Hispanics, and any other group in the world are all welcome; once they get to drinking or doing drugs, they're all buddies. Think about it. Look at drug addicts on the street; they don't care what color you are; when you've got drugs, you're their buddy. Who is more accepting of race than them?

From my experience, drunks and bootleggers were the first ones to integrate in Lumberton, North Carolina. The drunks who congregated in the Bottoms crossed racial lines before politicians, schools, churches, and restaurants did. The bootleggers were free market capitalists to the bone. They didn't let segregation and race interfere with making a dollar. The Bottoms was an integrated establishment because all races were welcome as long as they paid their way. This was not the case during the daytime. I met my close friends, twins named Mick and Rick Stoker, when we were young boys down at the Bottoms. Since Mick and Rick are white, they went to a different elementary school than me, but because Mick and Rick's father was a bootlegger and a good boozer who spent his weekends in the Bottoms, we met.

Mick says, "Lumberton was triracial if you will. Pretty much thirty-three and a third across the middle: white, Indian, and black. Everybody had their own neighborhoods. The Indians were in West Lumberton, the blacks were in South Lumberton, and the whites were in East Lumberton and North Lumberton. There were a few blacks over there in East Lumberton, but not many, and they had a small neighborhood they called 'New Town.' But it wasn't segregated at the Bottoms on Friday and Saturday nights when our daddy would get together with the other bootleggers, and they'd all pass out drunk, and their little white, black, and Indian children would run wild."

I capitalized on the drunks' laziness—Indian, black, white, whatever—
and I learned at an early age not to discriminate, either. Like any service
provider, I accomodated their needs. They'd be gambling or something—
ain't no drunk or gambler wants to get up when they think they have a
chance at winning something. Woozie or numerous others would say,
"Hey, boy, go get me a Schlitz." There were only two beers available at
the Bottoms: Schlitz and Budweiser. I'd run to the back to get them a beer,
and they'd tip me a penny or a nickel. To me, that was a lot of money.

I never wanted to be like the drug dealers, drug addicts, or alcoholics I knew because I found some of the drunken behavior at the Bottoms disgusting. The men would piss on themselves as snuff ran down
their chins. Nasty. I saw firsthand what drinking could do to a person,
and I've steered clear of such a destructive lifestyle. My grandpa Calvin
became an alcoholic after my grandma Lela died, and our visits to the
Bottoms became more and more frequent. Drinking was how he dealt
with her death. In his later years, he found God and mended his ways.
He became a great Christian and drew on his experience as a front-row
sinner to discourage others from taking the same crooked roads he had
traveled. Grandpa had an inspiring story that surely encouraged many,
including myself, to heed his swamp logic, which was surely influenced
by his experiences at the Bottoms.

The Bottoms was one of the many places I learned to be money-
minded from a young age. I teach our students to be young free market
capitalists as well. I tell the students, "There ain't nothing like having
some money in your pocket." I remember a guy named Mr. Cutler
Moore from when I was a little boy. I don't know if he ever had a full-
time job in his life, but to me he was rich and a political wizard in
North Carolina. He'd stand on the corner with a big cigar and he'd
address my grandpa Calvin when he was passing by, "Mr. Chavis, how
are you doing today? You got your grandson there with you, I see." He
wouldn't give you anything for free. He'd ask, "You working, boy?"
When I got him a newspaper, he'd give me a penny. He always had
money. Mr. Moore had a fancy pocket watch, and he was always
dressed up. He was the first guy I remember seeing dressed nicely all the
time. Mr. Moore would shake the change in his pockets, and he'd say,
"Boy, a man that's got money in his pocket can do things. If you want
to be able to do things, you gotta have money." I looked at him with
his expensive clothes and air of importance and thought, "Hell, yeah."
Mr. Moore's statement about having money in your pockets has stuck

with me ever since; I've always worked to have money and to do what I enjoy in life.

One summer when I was ten, I hired myself out as a farmhand for six dollars a day. I traveled to Bladen County, which is east of Robeson County, and spent the summer away from my family. I loved it. It was all boys. We stayed in shacks and worked from six in the morning till six in the evening. We made fifty cents an hour, which was great money in my eyes. It was my first dose of travel and independence. I loved meeting the other Indian boys, seeing a new place, and getting paid. To this day I am still friends with Gerald Goldsby, now a Lumbee tribal council member, who also worked on the farm that summer. All the Indian boys I met then are successful now. They knew what it took to succeed in life and were willing to put forth the sweat and sacrifice to make it happen.

Though marbles aren't money, to me as a young boy they were their own form of special currency and an indicator of social status. It's like with our students today who might be impressed by someone's sneakers or cell phone. Ricky Stoker said to me recently, "If you were a good marble player in our day, you were a bad dude." It's true!

We collected marbles called cat's-eyes, beach balls, and lollies, which were big marbles. They'd come in all kinds of sizes and colors. Whatever marble I didn't have, I wanted. If you were successful, you walked around with a lot of marbles bulging out of your pockets. You'd have the glass shaking in your pockets like they were coins, and you'd be strutting all over the schoolyard and community.

The object of the game was to win the other players' marbles, which was the equivalent of legally winning their money, an endeavor I enjoy to this day. My friends and I would draw a circle in the dirt and place our marbles (usually five each) inside. We'd stand outside the circle and take turns shooting. You would try to knock the marbles outside of the circle because then they became yours.

Now, I was never very good at playing marbles. I was what you would call a middle-of-the-pack marble player. There was this one girl, Sandra Lucas, a Lumbee from Pembroke. She was the best marble player in the whole county. She went to the state championship. She'd whoop us all, but I always had the most marbles. Now how did I get the most marbles when I couldn't play that well?

I had a goat named Bandit, and he was part of my team. Bandit would eat anything. You could throw him a tin can, and he'd start gnawing the paper off it. So one day I threw a marble near him. He picked it up with his mouth and ate it. Two days later I saw it lying there on the ground. Cha-ching. There was a moneymaker.

Bandit became the star of my countrified spectacle. When I told other kids my goat ate marbles, they didn't believe me and insisted on seeing for themselves. I'd build the suspense as I led them over to my backyard, talking a good game about the amazing, glass-eating goat. They'd toss their marbles near Bandit and, sure enough, he'd eat them quicker than you could blink. The audience was usually speechless at first. Then my friends would start laughing as they threw their marbles in Bandit's direction. It was first-rate entertainment that lasted as long as the marbles were thrown near enough for him to gobble them up. They slid down Bandit's throat like coins in a slot machine. The marble-less kids would eventually leave, and over the next day or two, Bandit would digest the winnings. I'd pick my hard-earned currency out of the droppings and wash it off.

My unwitting business partner, Bandit the goat, and my ability to sell intrigue filled my pockets with marbles and elevated my status. I still sell intrigue. As the principal of American Indian Public Charter School, I capture visitors' interest by shocking and impressing them. I say things like, "Yeah, we may have a school full of poor darkies, but we're one of the top middle schools in the state!" My eyes widen as visitors look at me suspiciously. "Come here," I say, "look at these test scores."

I'll open a binder, point to statistics, and say, "See: one hundred percent of my eighth-graders scored proficient or advanced in math! Now, none of these other sorry middle schools in Oakland can say the same." I continue my banter, alternating between playfulness and straightforwardness, and then ask visitors if they want to see for themselves the number-one middle school in Oakland. I'm more excited than I was as a young boy leading my friends to Bandit the goat.

The marbles were a status symbol to me as a child, just as the school is a status symbol to me as an adult. I profited from outthinking my fellow marble players and from finding opportunity where there didn't appear to be any. I pride myself in outthinking other principals, entertaining myself and others, and running a great school that will give students the same opportunities I had in life.

My grandpa Charlie Bell was a preacher who also had a strong impact on me as a child and influenced the way I run American Indian

Public Charter School. Though I wasn't related biologically to him (he was Buck's father), I considered him my grandfather. I spent time with my grandpa Charlie (known as Reverend Bell or Mr. Bell to others) when he was an old man and no longer ran his own churches. He died at age ninety-two in 1975. In the later years of his life, my grandpa Charlie would take me with him to local church services. He was a religious leader among our Lumbee people. The ministers always approached and asked him to say some encouraging or uplifting words to the congregation. Grandpa Charlie would stand up and talk about how the Lord changed his life. He described times when the Lord spoke to him, and how he listened and became a better man. The congregation would jump up, holler, cry, smile, clap, and sing in response. It was always mystifying to me at these moments how some folks who were seized by the spirit would run up the aisles with their eyes closed but somehow never smash into the door. It was as though St. Peter spared them the headache and embarrassment of colliding with the wood by turning them around and sending them running off in the other direction.

When Grandpa Charlie was a guest of honor or special reverend at a local church, I got to sit in the front pew with him. People gathered around hugging him, introducing themselves, and slipping small amounts of money into his hands.

I was a little boy in those days, and the attention was great! My grandfather was like a celebrity; everybody seemed to know and love Grandpa Charlie, and they all wanted to be around him. I thought, "I get in trouble all the time, but I get to sit in the front row with my famous grandpa, and I get to eat first, too!"

People love their preachers down south, boy. They're like gods! I loved the prestige my grandpa Charlie carried. I noticed he could say things, be they controversial or blunt, and get away with them. I liked that about Grandpa Charlie and have emulated his way of talking to people. Because I run a successful school in the inner city, I earn certain credibility among minorities and other citizens. I have worked hard, paid my dues, and proven that my education methods work. That provides me a forum for sharing my views, condemning philosophies I disagree with, and urging people to follow the right path, just like my grandpa the preacher did in my childhood.

Dr. Albert Wahrhaftig, an anthropologist and personal friend of mine, says I remind him of a preacher when I stand at the school doors at the end of the day and say good-bye to the students or tell them to say hi to their mama for me or to remember what I told them about coming late to class. Many blacks, Indians, Asians, and Hispanics have close relationships with their preachers. Preachers have power and influence in the inner city. They get people to do things that improve their lives. They'll use shaming; they'll use embarrassment; they'll come down hard. I know minorities respect their preachers and their preachers' tough approach to teaching, so I use that style because it comes naturally to me and it works.

I don't consider myself a religious man, but I go to church and recognize how important an institution it is in Oakland and in many other communities. In order to be tightly connected with people in the inner city it's vital to understand the lessons they're receiving and to know the preachers teaching those lessons.

In Grandpa Charlie's day (prior to the 1960s) the two best jobs Lumbee Indians could get were teaching and preaching. Lumbees weren't allowed access to government jobs. They couldn't be mailmen, policemen, city or county workers. The Lumbee Indians who were teachers or preachers were considered the top echelon of Lumbee society. Many people, like my grandpa Calvin, participated in bootlegging. They had few other choices because they were not allowed to participate in the legal free market system in North Carolina.

Because Lumbees were excluded from government jobs, the church became and still remains their most important institution. Lumbees were not allowed to attend public schools until 1887, so the churches educated us. As Grandpa Charlie would say, "God has always been here for our Indian people." The church was there when the government was not. For that reason, many Lumbee Indians don't believe in separating church and state. Religion finds its way into education in Robeson County even though the law says it can't.

Everything influential in Lumbee communities springs from the churches; they are the training grounds for Lumbee teachers, businessmen, and politicians. You better have a foothold in the church if you're running for any kind of office in Robeson County.

Preachers there still hold the respect of the people more than anyone else, but luckily the restrictions placed on Lumbees have been lifted, and there are job opportunities outside the church. But all that came later. In Grandpa Charlie's time, he worked as a sharecropper, farmer, carpenter, brick mason—you name it, he would do it. On top of that, he founded several churches, such as New Point on Highway 41, where I almost got killed as a child, and worked actively as a preacher in the area. Grandpa Charlie hired a plowboy to help him farm while also using his own thirteen children for that purpose, which freed some of his time and allowed him to expand his businesses and trades.

Up until the 1920s, Lumbee Indians, like the plowboy Grandpa Charlie hired named Joe, indentured themselves. Joe lived with my grandpa's family for about fourteen years. He would do all the plowing using either a mule or an ox, and while he'd be doing that, Grandpa Charlie would build things for people out of brick or lumber, or he would train horses and sell them.

There was a basic framework to what Grandpa Charlie did and to what I do at American Indian Public Charter School. He saw the importance of getting people (his plowboy and his thirteen kids) to help him. He taught me that your words have to mean something, and you have to put out a good product. My product is our students. Our schools look better every year. It's the same with the rentals I own and manage. I'm always thinking, "How can I make my businesses better?" (I think of our schools as businesses.) I learned the important lessons of hiring good people to help me, making my words mean something, and putting out a good product from my grandpa Charlie.

Growing up, I wasn't allowed to sit around and be lazy at home. I always had to work. My dad, Buck, was a brick mason, farmer, and antique seller, among other things, just like his father (Grandpa Charlie). I labored beside Buck in the fields and sold produce during summer. We grew and sold watermelons, peas, peaches, beans, and almost anything else people wanted to eat. Buck, my stepbrother Wayne, and I would set up under a tree on the side of the road. Buck would either carry the produce in the wheelbarrow, or he'd drive the dark green 1948 International truck over. He never did have a license. I did that type of work ever since I was a little boy. I remember wearing a carpenter's belt because we kept the money in it. Sometimes my cousins would pick me up, and I would sit in the back of the old truck as we drove through the black part of town calling out, "Watermelon. Honey sweet." You'd say it all slow and easy like a summer day, and people would come running.

When people ask Buck how he managed to raise such a large family, he responds, "You can't have four hands putting in and twenty-eight hands taking out." In other words, if he and my mama had to provide for the whole family by themselves, it just wouldn't happen. This is a lesson he learned from Grandpa Charlie. The key was getting the children to work, which was something I always remember doing. We use the same mentality at American Indian Public Charter School, where all the students are expected to do their part to help the school run well. One student will be in charge of collecting homework, for example, while another one will have to sweep the classroom. Everyone is expected to contribute.

I also learned from Grandpa Charlie and most of my Lumbee relatives the importance of God and religion to my people and others. If a religious relative of one of the students comes to see me, I can quote scripture from the Bible to support my points. I can show them I'm on their side by referencing the "good book" and knowing the duties of the God-fearing, God-loving Christian with the best of them. I respect and acknowledge that religion provides a structure and belief system for many people who need it. I'm a big believer in structure, and it doesn't matter to me how people give themselves structure as long as it's there and it works for them. I can make it work for me as well.

In order to prevent theft and to appeal to the religious morals of the Latinos, blacks, and other Christians in the community, I put a cross that represents the four directions on the front of the school building. When I first took over American Indian Public Charter School, theft was a problem. Once I put that cross up, the problem ceased. Ain't no minority going to rob a church if they think God's looking.

Similarly, before the 2005 school year kicked off, I inserted groups of green tiles into the stucco wall lining the walkway to the school entrance. Each group consisted of four tiles touching corner to corner with a square space in the center. The pattern resembles both a Christian cross and the four directions (north, south, east, and west), a popular symbol in American Indian religion and a very important symbol for me personally. You could say I see the idea of the four directions as representing balance and order. I'm superstitious about the four directions. In all my buildings I make sure the four directions are represented in some way, such as having four doors, one on each side of the building, or inserting the symbol into the wall or floor. I get obsessive about it. To me, there are four races. Everything comes down to four. Each direction has significance. I always sleep to the east, but I don't know why. When Lumbees die, their bodies are often buried in the eastward direction.

A former teacher, Ms. Sullivan, asked me one time about the symbol inserted on the school's walkway. She said, "Is that a cross or the four directions?" I gave her my characteristic sideways glance and joked, "It's a cross when I'm dealing with the Latinos and blacks; it's the four directions when Indians or anyone from the state asks me about it."

Ms. Sullivan always gets a kick out of my tendency to morph into different roles like the trickster in American Indian folklore. I pretended once to be her lawyer to help her recover the deposit from a landlord who was trying to cheat her. Anyone who's worked for me has seen me in different modes: talking like a hick on the phone to some good ole boy in North Carolina, being charming and polite to an elderly lady who has come to visit the school, or using Ebonics with teenagers out in front of the school.

Ms. Sullivan used to say to me that I had two dress modes: suit or rags. It's true! She said something like, "You either walk into the office dressed all dapper in a full suit and tie, or you wear old workout clothes that probably should have been burned ten years ago. Your nylon running pants swish as you bustle all over the office trying to do a million things at once." One Halloween during the school-wide party in the gym, Ms. Clementine, the ninth-grade teacher, asked me where my costume was. I was in workout clothes. I said, "I'm wearing it. I'm dressed as an old fool." I wasn't exactly kidding. I do look pretty raggedy in my old running pants and T-shirts.

When Ms. Sullivan started teaching at AIPCS, I took her out to lunch near the school, which is my custom with new teachers. I was wearing beat-up workout gear, which was quite possibly the same outfit mentioned above. Two genteel old ladies were seated next to us, so I, in my typical way, struck up a conversation with them. When the subject of American Indian Public Charter School came up, they asked what I did there. I said, "I just try to clean up and keep things neat." I gave them the impression I was the janitor. They just nodded and smiled, finding me nice and probably unimpressive. Ms. Sullivan shared with me later that she was surprised to hear me introduce myself that way. Can you understand why I would do that?

# chapter twenty-five

# Cleanliness: A Chore and a Mentality

"Let everyone sweep in front of his own door, and the whole world will be clean."

—*Johann Wolfgang von Goethe,*
*German writer (1749–1832)*

American Indian Public Charter School is clean, bright, and safe. When visitors come through the gate on Magee Avenue, they find flowers and trimmed grass along the well-swept walkway. Going up the outside staircase, they pass lively students scrambling to P.E. Once through the front door, on the right-hand side visitors notice our Wall of Fame board honoring the students who have been accepted into the Johns Hopkins University Center for Talented Youth program. Their smiling faces stand out proudly against the blue background. On the left in the office, the administrative assistant is seen talking to a family interested in enrolling their child, while a teacher makes copies and checks her box. Once they're signed in, I take guests past photos of the staff and of Governor Arnold Schwarzenegger from his first visit to the school. I pause in front of the bar graph showing our yearly test score improvements.

Turning to the left where the corridor forms the long part of an "L," light from the skylight brings a soft glow into the building. I point to hand-drawn numbers pinned to a red bulletin board and explain how Ms. Albright's class has achieved eighty-seven consecutive days of perfect attendance so far. The floor is clear and polished and few if any students can be seen in the corridor. One visitor asks to use the restroom; when she comes back out she asks why there are no mirrors in the bathroom. I tell her I want students focusing on their minds while they're here, not wasting time fussing over what they look like.

Sometimes when the hallway is so quiet and no students are in sight, visitors ask me where the students are. They're surprised to find out a class is in session behind the wall three feet from where we stand.

When we walk in, children wearing white collared shirts and khaki pants sit in straight rows of desks looking forward at the teacher, who is writing a math problem on the board. Students know not to turn toward the door when it opens. Our motto is we are "A School at Work." I tell them, "People come here to see you work; you are the celebrities they want to see." And that is generally what guests do see when they walk into any of the classes: heads bent over desks and the sound of pencils writing on paper, a school literally at work.

The gym downstairs, which serves as both the lunchroom and physical education area, maintains the same sense of tidiness seen upstairs. This is a pleasant school, a place where learning is happening among order and control. Visitors tell me they're impressed, that it's not what they expected from an Oakland middle school. They remark how clean the campus is.

Clean and simple is the way we keep American Indian Public Charter School. Some teachers have found this out the hard way when they've walked into the office and discovered that something of theirs had been thrown away. "Where's my lunch?" they'd ask. Or, "What happened to my box of tissues?" When you leave something on my table, it ends up in the trash. Don't expect an apology, either. It wasn't an accident. Don't leave your property in my office, and I won't leave mine in your classroom. Some teachers in the past have found my minimalism ridiculous, but that's okay with me. I've never been in a nasty school that was successful.

I joke about a "religion" I've named Chavism. I told a man named Peace on the subway in Chicago about it one time. He was trying to convert me to his new-age belief system, so I decided to give him more gobbledygook to ponder. I explained that the chief tenet of Chavism is cleanliness. The man was so gullible and impressed that he asked me to send him pamphlets. I bet he's still checking his mailbox. In September 2004, I passed out a memo to all the teachers about Chavism that read as follows:

We have very small classrooms and an even smaller Dumpster
for trash. The key belief in the religion of "Chavism" is
cleanliness.

I recommend each of you appoint a group of "Deacons" in
your class. They can get rid of the sudden growth of newspapers,
boxes, and other collectibles that are creating an eyesore and
firetrap at American Indian Public Charter School.

The Gods are always pleased by the clean souls!! I know
many of you do not consider yourselves religious. It appears
some of you are being converted to the religion of "Pack Rats."

In addition, please do not accept any donations of any sort
to our school.

The memo was a spin on my firm belief in cleanliness. When you
keep a place clean you take responsibility for it, which gives you a sense
of ownership. I want the students to see the school as their own, make
it nice, and take pride in themselves and their surroundings. It's similar
to the way some home owners feel. They want their friends to come
over to their place and look around and think, "This is a nice place."
The home doesn't have to be luxurious for people to feel that way. It
just has to feel like some care has gone into its appearance. It is the
same thing at a school. Students who go to an orderly, clean school feel
better about being there than when the school is covered in trash and
graffiti. When a school is covered in trash and graffiti and surrounded
by large chain-link fences, like many schools in the inner city, students
will not take ownership of it. They won't feel pride. As a result, some
of them will disrespect the place and make it look even worse.

Because I want the students to feel pride in their school and contribute to its upkeep, cleaning is a fundamental part of every school
day. Students are all assigned jobs, and they clean their respective classrooms at the end of the day. One student will clean the white board, for
instance, while another sweeps the floor. A group of students is in
charge of hauling the Dumpster to the street on collection day, while
another group of students is responsible for setting the tables up before
lunch and putting them away after lunch. Every student has a chore for
which he or she is responsible, and these chores often switch over time
from one student to another. What doesn't change is the fact that the
kids are expected to take care of the school and maintain its orderly
appearance.

Having the students pitch in to keep the classrooms, gym, and campus clean keeps the operations of the school streamlined. We don't have to hire staff to operate the lunchroom or to do daily cleanings. Our janitors come twice a week for the intensive cleaning of the bathrooms and waxing of the floors, but we don't expect them to clear the floor of paper and debris, because our own students do that. We instill personal responsibility and respect for one's school and community in the students. I don't want them to ever think that someone will clean up after them, because that is not what happens at AIPCS or in life. It bothers me when I visit another school and see that students have dropped their trash on the ground or written on the bathroom stalls, because it shows disrespect. Like most lessons with young people, you have to explicitly teach them what to do, how to do it, and why you do it. The value of cleanliness through personal contributions is one of the many lessons we instill in our students.

They enjoy doing their chores because it gives them a sense of ownership and makes them feel like part of our family. Maintaining the classroom and keeping it clean are extra responsibilities the students can assume and demonstrate they are capable of handling. The school is their own, and they like having a role in it and working together to make the school run smoothly.

When Christhian Cortes, a twelfth-grade student at American Indian Public High School, was asked why the students have to do chores, he responded, "The chores make us responsible. It feels like I'm in my house because I do the same thing." The chores give students that home/family feel and they reinforce responsibility. Our students have a lot of rules to follow, a strict dress code to adhere to, high academic expectations to meet, and a role to play in the positive image of the school. All of this leads to the structure that many students like Christhian need. Many of the students Christhian knows who attend other high schools in Oakland are involved in gangs, doing drugs, and are not taking their education seriously. When asked why he thought they were behaving that way, Christhian said, "Nobody is strict with them. No one is telling them what to do or how to behave like they do in this school. They just give them freedom and don't care. The teachers probably don't care if they go to school or turn in their homework. The staff cares more about the students at this school."

Christhian, like most of his classmates, expects to be told what to do, to be provided with structure, and to walk the line or expect consequences for it. I'll ask Christhian to do such things as carry boxes or move desks. It's like the military, where soldiers are expected to make their beds, shine their shoes, and do whatever a higher-up asks of them. Like the military, we don't tolerate insubordination, either. Everyone is expected to help out. It's what leads to a family feeling, a sense of equality, and order.

Christhian is a typical young man in the sense that he doesn't always do what he's told to do in the way he's told to do it. I remember one time in detention a teacher asked him to move textbooks to another classroom and stack them neatly on the shelf. When he finished sooner than she expected, she checked on what he'd done and saw that the books were sloppily strewn on the shelf. She told him to go back in there and do it correctly. It's constant oversight with our students. When they take a shortcut, we make them go back and do it the right way.

They may not always like it, but students such as Christhian thrive in the structured environment of American Indian Public High School, which includes cleaning and chores. Christhian says if he went to one of the larger Oakland public high schools, "I'd probably be all messed up, not doing my work, cutting school every day, and on drugs because that's basically what students there do." According to Christhian, the drugs they take are heroin, coke, and marijuana. His friends make fun of him for going to AIPHS. "They think I'm a geek because I go to this school, but I know I'm smarter than they are. They can say whatever, but I'm trying to get a better education and trying to be something in life. I want to keep on going, not drop out like a lot of people I know."

Christhian is also trying to make his dad, who passed away a few years ago, proud of him. "My dad always wanted me to be the first to really make something of my life, make myself something big, not be a screwup. So, yeah, I think he's proud of me. My mom is happy I'm at this school because it's strict. We get in trouble for anything, but it's going to help us get a great education."

In the last year of his life, Christhian's father was really sick and knew he was going to die. He spoke to Mr. Jorge Lopez, Christhian's principal at the time at Oakland Charter Academy, and told him he was really worried about his son. He didn't want him to go down the wrong path and thought he needed oversight and guidance. Mr. Lopez assured Christhian's father that after he died he would look after Christhian as if he were his own son. After a year of being sick and suffering,

Christhian's father passed away, and the funeral took place on a Friday. That was the only school day Christhian missed all year. He made up for his absence the very next day by attending Saturday school. Christhian was already proving to his father that he could be something in life. Mr. Lopez continues to keep his promise by watching over Christhian like a son.

As Christhian explained earlier, he thinks it's important for youth to be told how to behave. He knows that discipline is part of that equation and that he's expected to do what he's told at AIPHS, whether it be his homework or cleaning the windows. No one in Christhian's family has had a higher education; he strives to be the first one and will be. Part of the process of preparing Christhian for college and providing him with life skills is giving him personal responsibilities and teaching him how to meet them.

My high standards of cleanliness have brought me into conflict with some of the staff. One year Mr. Hannibal, the P.E. teacher, got upset several times after I got on him about the dirty bathrooms in the gym. I tried to tell him when I'm loud it doesn't mean I don't like you or I want to fight; that's just the way Lumbee Indians are in my family. When I walked into the gym, I'd say loudly, "Damn, this gym is nasty. You gotta keep these bathrooms clean." He focused on projects he didn't have to do and neglected part of his job. He suggested the students were deprived. Mr. Hannibal wanted to offer them sports, his idea of nutrition, and slide shows. I wanted them to get in good physical shape and to learn how to clean the gym by themselves. What is wrong with that? Did he think these mixed breeds had a maid at home? I think not.

Mr. Hannibal thought it wasn't fair for the kids to have their P.E. class cut short a few minutes by having to clean. He believed they had enough responsibilities already. I disagreed. These students have responsibilities at home and at school. Those responsibilities give them structure and make them aware of the larger context: their family, school, community, and society. A household, a classroom, and a democracy all function on the idea of people pitching in and doing their part to make a positive whole. After Mr. Hannibal was replaced by Mr. Eng, the gym was clean, and the students' physical fitness improved. Today, they are in the top 1 percent in academic and physical fitness in California. They've also demonstrated their ability to take responsibility and ownership for the upkeep of the school.

A seventh-grader, Peter Choy, has to wash the dishes, cook breakfast, and take out the trash at his home. His father is a cook and his mom sells food off a cart in Chinatown. Sometimes Peter helps his mom cook the food she'll be selling that day. Peter's family members put pressure on him to get an education. He shared, "My grandma told me that my two brothers didn't finish school and neither did my mom, but my dad was a teacher in China in math. I really want to finish school so I can earn some money." In addition to his homework and class work, Peter is also responsible for doing desk and binder checks for his class, which he enjoys.

A lesson I want to instill in students is being poor is no excuse to be nasty. That's the way I grew up. Most Lumbees take good care of their property. When we were driving through my community of Saddletree, North Carolina, I pointed out to Marsha how neat people's yards were. Surrounding the prefab homes were trimmed grass, bright flowers, pecan trees, and azalea bushes. The Lumbees believe poverty is no excuse for living in filth.

Oakland, on the other hand, is a place where poverty and nastiness often go hand in hand. Every day our students pick up trash before and after school, because every day people just drop their trash on the streets and sidewalks. It gets blown and thrown onto our campuses. Every day you'll see glass liquor bottles, Cheetos packages, plastic bags, fast-food wrappers, and gum. And every day, you'll see our students in their white-collared shirts and khaki pants picking it up. The staff also pitch in. Mr. Dennis Wong used to pick up any litter he saw on his way to P.E. class with his ninth-grade students. He instilled in our students that in order to keep our schools an oasis of cleanliness off Macarthur Boulevard and Thirty-fifth Avenue, we all need to contribute to their upkeep.

We want students to know that they are different. They don't do the stupid things people expect of teenagers in the inner city. We want to set an example. One time when Ms. Sullivan picked up trash on Thirty-fifth Avenue alongside the high school students serving their after-school detentions, the families who came to pick up their middle school students started to join in. Pretty soon there was a big group of people—students, staff, and families—bent over, cleaning up the area. It created a sense of what we're all about. We respect ourselves and our property, and we act accordingly. We take care of what is ours and serve as an example to the community. By doing so, we also maintain good relationships with the businesses nearby. The real estate employees love how our students clean in front of their office every day. If our students ever get loud or act out in front of their windows, they come to tell us, and we take care of it. It's more of the old way in which the schools, businesses, and community members worked together to educate young people.

Ms. Sullivan shared with me that seeing our students go about their daily chores reminded her of the monks she saw sweeping and tidying up a temple in Japan. Like the monks, it is part of the students' daily routine and duty to clean their space. She saw the student chores as a daily cleansing ritual, like the one she witnessed in Japan.

Perhaps the monks' cleaning is a part of their spiritual path. The students' cleaning is preparation for mental productivity. When you're in a clean school, you're ready to work!

# chapter twenty-six

# Mental Work or Physical Labor: You Make the Choice

"Some say it is unfair to hold disadvantaged children to rigorous standards. I say it is discrimination to require anything less—the soft bigotry of low expectations. Some say that schools can't be expected to teach, because there are too many broken families, too many immigrants, too much diversity. I say that pigment and poverty need not determine performance. That myth is disproved by good schools every day. Excuse-making must end before learning can begin."

*—George W. Bush, in a speech on September 2, 1999, to the Latin Business Association Luncheon in Los Angeles, California; the speechwriter Michael Gerson is credited with the now-famous phrase "the soft bigotry of low expectations"*

Cleaning is used at American Indian Public Charter School to promote a sense of respect and responsibility for one's self and one's surroundings. But cleaning duties can also be assigned as an alternative method of education when a student continues to get in trouble or be disruptive. For example, if a student refuses to do his homework or to follow a teacher's directions, and detention, Saturday school, and embarrassment aren't changing the student's behavior, I think, "What we tried didn't work, so let's try something else." It's a process. It's obvious the student didn't like the mental work of the classroom, so we try physical work. I sometimes say to misbehaving students when I pull them out of the classroom and have them pick up cigarette butts, sweep the yard, or scrape gum off the sidewalk, "At least you'll be trained to be a good janitor."

I'm providing students with a choice: You can do this work or that work. You can focus on your academics or you can do physical labor or both. Most students in the end will choose academics, but it will be their choice. They can have labor-intensive jobs if they want, but we give them the opportunity to get an academic education so they have options. That way they can make career decisions for themselves and not have those decisions made for them because they are uneducated.

The teachers will hand students who are screwing off in class gloves and cleaning supplies and tell them to get busy scrubbing, while their peers remain in the classroom learning. Many of our students' families came to this country, either legally or illegally, so their children could have better opportunities and not have to clean homes, pick crops, or dig ditches. We reinforce this reality to our students. When they choose to not do their homework or follow the teacher's directions, we give them a taste of their alternatives in life. I show them firsthand the type of work their families have to do, the type of work their families wouldn't be forced to do if they had the same educational opportunities our students have at American Indian Public Charter School.

Compared to digging ditches, studying math is easy. Compared to scrubbing toilets, listening to the teacher is easy. Don't get me wrong: I don't look down on physical labor—I respect it. I love construction and working with my hands. In college, I worked in the evenings as a janitor, and I found it very satisfying because it was the only time I could look around and instantly see the progress I had made. That progress took the form of glistening floors and disinfected sinks. I could see the product of my work, which appealed to me. I continue to do physical labor and enjoy it, but I have an education that allows me to do mental work as well.

What options do students in Oakland have without an education? When they aren't academically prepared or given vocational training to be janitors, construction workers, or mechanics, they enter the workforce with no skills. There is such a demand for illegal immigrants to perform labor-intensive work in the United States because our own uneducated people lack the training or willingness to do the work themselves.

I figure our students are going to learn one way or another. When they don't want to do the work of the classroom, I'll show them how to clean, build things, garden, whatever. I'll ask their families to drop them off at my place on a Saturday, and I'll put them to work. Most of them find they don't like doing physical labor. They realize it's better to behave themselves and do their lessons in school so they can stay in the classroom and not have their free time taken up.

Our students' families work hard to support them. It is because of that hard work and sacrifice that I want the students to honor their families by being diligent in school and getting the kind of education their parents never had. A tenth-grader, Ana Bahena, explains, "My parents say they want me to have better jobs than they have because they don't want me to have to work as hard as they do." Ana's dad is a truck driver and her mom is a housecleaner. In Mexico, where they were raised, Ana's parents didn't get far in school because they had to start working at an early age in order to financially support their families. Ana says, "Right now I'm having the opportunity not to work and to go to school to learn. What motivates me is I want to go to college, and I want to impress my parents with what I can do."

Many immigrants living in the United States who are originally from Mexico have only an elementary school education. Part of the reason they came to the United States was to give their children better educational and career opportunities than they ever had in Mexico. Karely Ordaz, a high-strung, intelligent, good-looking, and impatient twelfth-grader at American Indian Public High School, knows she is lucky compared to her mom, though she sometimes needs to be reminded of that fact. Because there was no middle school in the small village of La Palma, Mexico, her mom started working as soon as she finished sixth grade. Karely can tell her mom would have been a conscientious student; she just never had the opportunity. After sixth grade, the time for classroom learning was gone for Karely's mom. She worked in the fields picking chili peppers.

Karely's mom's life in Mexico was like my mom's life in rural North Carolina. My mama never received more than an elementary school education. As a young girl, she picked cotton beside the other sharecroppers, which exposed her to hard labor and hazardous chemicals. When the Lumbee women picked cotton they wore skirts, which left their calves and ankles exposed. The cotton bolls would scratch against their skin and sometimes cut it open, so when the morning dew mixed with the poison on the crops and seeped into the cuts, the sharecroppers could get serious infections. Mama almost lost her left leg from such an infection when she was a young girl. She couldn't afford to see a doctor, but luckily my grandma Lela knew to bandage her leg with salve and Epsom salt. Mama cried in pain through the night, and in the morning the bandage was completely green. She still has white splotches of scar tissue on her left leg. It's hard to say whether my grandma Lela died from the same kind of exposure, but a life spent in the cotton and tobacco fields among poisonous chemicals had to have taken its toll. Whatever caused Grandma Lela's death, it took her at the young age of forty-nine.

My grandma and mama had a much harder life than I did, just like many of our students' parents had much harder lives than they have had in Oakland. People talk about walking in somebody else's shoes. I couldn't walk in my mama's shoes, I'll tell you that much. And our students probably couldn't walk in their parents' shoes. Their families don't want them to pick chili peppers like they did, clean houses like they do, or take bilingual and multiculturalism courses. These are things most people from Mexico already know. The families want their children to learn mathematics, English, science, and history to further their education and opportunities in the United States.

Karely's life is not easy in Oakland. It is, however, an improvement over the life her family had in Mexico because she has more financial and educational opportunities. Karely lives with her mom, dad, and sister in the bottom of a duplex in the Fruitvale district of Oakland. Two Mexican families share the top. There's a trailer in the back where other tenants live and a taco truck that the landlord, who owns a restaurant, keeps in the yard. About once a month, someone jumps the fence and breaks into Karely's place. Hobos get in the yard and squat in the taco truck. She often sees a strange white man on the bus who wears gloves and black clothes who broke into her house one day and stole her dad's tools. He came in the house while her mom was cooking in the kitchen with the door open. Karely heard her mom scream. Her dad chased him, but he was too fast and got away. In Karely's neighborhood it's common to see prostitutes strolling the sidewalks and young men burning rubber in the streets. Her block is full of body shops, so it's loud and gritty.

Karely's family moved from Mexico twelve years ago. From the village of La Palma in the state of Michoacán, where Karely was born, the family moved to Tijuana in search of more work. But after living there eight months without making enough money, they decided to see if they could make it to the United States. Karely arrived in Oakland at age four and started kindergarten at Hawthorne Elementary School without knowing any English. By third grade, she was fluent. Karely has a 4.0 GPA at American Indian Public High School. Karely's family is happy they're in the United States because they're much better off financially than they would be in Mexico. Karely says that even though the Oakland neighborhood they live in isn't safe, it's the best they can do, so it's good for now.

One day in tenth grade, Karely, Nena Pulido, and Jose Pena were all absent in the morning. Ms. Sullivan wondered why they hadn't shown up yet. Just as she was about to make the first phone call, Nena called her in a panic and said the police had her block cordoned off and weren't letting anyone leave. Her neighbor in the apartment complex had a gun and refused to hand it over. Nena assured Ms. Sullivan that she, Karely, and Jose would get to school as soon as possible. They walk together to AIPHS in the morning, so they all got caught up in the incident. True to her word, Nena arrived with Karely and Jose an hour later just in time to catch the end of English class. At lunch, Nena explained that the brother of a woman who lived in the complex had called the police after the woman's husband had beaten her up. The husband has mental problems and had already pulled stunts like this before. He had a gun, the wife was crying and didn't want him to go to jail, and he wouldn't hand the gun over or let the police in, so the police busted in, shot him in the leg, and took away his rifle. Apparently he still lives with his wife in the same apartment. Like Karely, Nena's place is often broken into.

Edgar Cervantes, a twelfth-grader in Karely, Nena, and Jose's class, says his parents have pushed him to get a college education ever since he was in kindergarten. Edgar says of his father, who works in construction, "He tells me, 'I want you to go to college so you won't be like me—*para que no trabajes como un burro* [so you don't have to work like a donkey]. Look at me. Look how dirty I am.' My dad didn't have a chance to get an education. It was work, work since he was a child." Edgar, on the other hand, has the opportunity to take summer courses with the UC Berkeley Academic Talent Development Program and the Johns Hopkins University Center for Talented Youth program. He has the options and knowledge his father has dreamed of for him. With excellent teachers like Ms. Shelley Kahn who push students to their utmost potential, Edgar has been provided with the tools he needs to pursue higher education.

It would break my heart to see students like Edgar disappoint their families. That's why we make them acknowledge the sacrifices their families have made and the opportunities their families have fought to give them. I won't let students blow off their education without first trying alternative methods. Edgar has seen firsthand those methods being used on some of his peers and he makes sure to avoid them. He says with a chuckle, "I wouldn't do anything bad enough to make you tell me to clean the toilet. I keep that in mind."

I got mad at Edgar and Karely because they were complaining and hanging out with dumbies who had the intelligence of a woodchuck that was raised on skunkweed. I made it a point to break through their hard heads one day. I said, "You know what, you guys think you're equal to everyone else, don't you? Well, you're not. Neither of you are citizens, so your asses could be deported any minute. You're getting a free education, yet you're whining about having too much homework and you're hanging around American-born losers. Think of the sacrifices your families made for you to be here. Do you think you have what it takes to walk across the desert late at night just so your children can go to school and have opportunities? You guys have it made compared to your families.

"What will make you more equal to other Americans is a great education. You two are smart! Get a degree in math or science. Do you know women from the Philippines were recently allowed into this country because they were nurses and there was a shortage here? This country needs smart, hardworking people. We should send some of our own American-born losers over the border in exchange for their hardworking people. I would love to send a boatload of lazy people to Castro in Cuba. There are several people in my family and numerous welfare communists from the Bay Area who could be squeezed into the boat." I made it clear I had high expectations for them and let my lecture sink in.

Edgar and Karely don't want to have the kind of menial jobs their families have. At Edgar's age, I knew when I got older I didn't want to continue working in the fields or pushing a wheelbarrow. Unlike Edgar, however, sports provided my way out, not academics. Running track was a way to avoid the grueling farmwork required of me at home, where I always had a chore to do. One chore I especially hated was feeding the hogs. Buck and I would take slop from the restaurants, bring it home, boil it to kill the bacteria, and then feed it to the hogs. I would get up at four a.m. to feed them, go to school, and then come home after school and feed them again. One thing I quickly figured out about sports is when you have practice, you don't have to head home after school, and I got to hang out with my buddies Marvin Butler, Carson Lowery, Dennis Oxendine, Willie Chavis, and Randall Hammonds. Buck really gave me a hard time about running. He said to me, "You're lazy. You just don't want to work. That's why you're into sports." He saw right through me, but he didn't see that sports were a way out for me. Buck had farmwork, bricklaying, and an antique business to run. He didn't have time or tolerance for a son who wanted to run. It seemed like loafing to him.

My friend Gene Locklear, also a Lumbee Indian from Robeson County who was an athlete, had similar confrontations with his father about baseball. I didn't know Gene when we were boys. We met as adults and realized we had a lot in common.

Gene became the first Lumbee Indian professional athlete. He played major league baseball for the Cincinnati Reds, the New York Yankees, and the San Diego Padres. But when Gene was growing up in Robeson County, there was no one in the Lumbee community for him to point to and say, I want to be a professional athlete like him. Gene had to set the example for Lumbees; there was no example set for him. In our Lumbee Indian community in the Jim Crow South, it didn't make sense for an Indian to play sports. Only white people played sports, so what would a Lumbee Indian gain from athletics other than putting off work? That was the mentality in my house and Gene's.

The woman rules the roost in the Lumbee household, so for both Gene and me it was our moms who intervened and allowed us to play sports, even though our fathers saw it as a waste of time. Gene remembers when his dad told him he couldn't play baseball anymore. There was too much work to be done on the farm. Gene was so upset that he ran out of the house crying. He picked up a stick in the yard and started tossing dirt clods into the air and swinging furiously at them. Whack! Whack! Whack! He continued in a fury until he heard his mom call his name. Gene knew from the tone of her voice that she had stuck up for him, and he would be allowed to play baseball.

My dad, Buck, griped and muttered about how I was just lazy and that's why I wanted to run, but my mama supported me and allowed me to stay on the track team. At an awards banquet held at the end of my sophomore year at Magnolia High School, I was named the most dedicated athlete in the school and the most valuable player in track. Buck, who was sitting at my table, laughed. He said, "Dedicated? It takes him an hour to do what I say. Buddy's so lazy, I could outrun him." My mom cut the criticism short. She told him, "Shut your mouth. This is Buddy's night. Don't ruin it for him." Buck took the cue from my mom and shut up quickly.

Gene and I can now look back on our lives and understand our fathers' perspectives. Gene grew up in Robeson County in the '50s and '60s with no car or television. His family made about $3,000 a year, which was enough to buy sugar, bread, clothes, and other basic supplies. Gene's family grew corn, tobacco, cotton, and vegetables, and they also owned some woodland. His dad brought in additional cash by using his excess corn to make and sell moonshine. Gene was an only child. At any one time as a boy, he owned two pairs of slacks and one pair of shoes. Gene realizes why his dad didn't want him to play baseball: he was a much-needed laborer in a family stretched tight.

After playing professional baseball, Gene became a professional artist. His paintings hang in the White House! Gene, in speaking of farming, baseball, and art, says, "What is work, and what is work? I want to work—do my art—to keep from really working, like on a farm or in an office." He remembers spring-training sessions in which players would be vomiting and complaining about the grueling workouts. Gene reflected on his days spent cropping tobacco and thought he'd much rather be running wind sprints than bending over cropping tobacco leaves in hundred-degree heat.

I know what Gene means about working in the fields. At twelve, I got a summer job cropping tobacco and found out how grueling it was. I worked from six in the morning until six in the evening. In those days, the tobacco was cropped by hand. Since the plant matures from the bottom up, the first leaves ready for cropping are down at the base of the plant. We would walk along the rows, bent over, grabbing the leaves from down near the soil. I worked fast. In addition to cropping the tobacco, I had to haul it, unload it, and set it up to dry in barns. We had to climb up the rafters of the barn and hang the tobacco leaves off wooden sticks placed between the rafters for it to dry. That part of the job was scary. If you lost your footing, you had a long way to fall.

I believe growing up as poor Indians in Robeson County gave Gene and me an advantage over many other people because of the work ethic that was instilled in both of us. Gene is not like other artists I've met. When I commission Gene to do an art project, he gets it done on time and as requested. Other artists I've hired kept pushing back the deadline and making excuses. The difference is our background and how we were taught to work hard and smart.

My cross-country and track experiences laid the foundation for the way things are run at American Indian Public Charter School. I've got the Johns Hopkins Wall of Fame, the class attendance records, and the individual attendance competition. When students work hard, they are rewarded with money, attention, and praise. When we require students to repeat the year because they are not at grade level, it is like redshirting them. My whole educational philosophy is based on a sports mentality. There's no affirmative action in sports. Everything is based on hard work and competition. Everyone lines up on the same starting line at a track meet no matter what their color or income. The value of hard work was instilled in me through my family upbringing and through sports. Hard work is what I heard and lived. By making American Indian Public Charter School "A School at Work," I'm just doing what comes naturally to me.

When asked why, if sports had such an impact on me, I don't promote athletics more at AIPCS, I tell people that we are using sports as a theoretical framework for academics. When it comes to minorities, many secondary schools overemphasize sports and downplay academics. If you think about it, there are many more university scholarships in academics than there are in sports. I was an athlete and got a college education through sports, but I wasn't good enough to get too far with running. When I was a young guy I thought running would lead me somewhere. In the grand scheme of things, I wasn't that good of a runner, and I don't fool myself to think I was. When you come from a small town, people think you're an all-star. Some folks in Robeson County still see me as I was many decades ago. "Didn't you make the Olympics?" they ask. No. What prepared me for life in a global society was getting an education, not just running my red hide around a track. Running reinforced discipline and hard work, which prepared me to accept the challenges of education and life.

My education provided me with the option to work with my head, my hands, or both. I tell our students it is always better to have choices than to be pigeonholed into a path in life due to a lack of preparedness. We put all our students on the same starting line, teach them how to run the race, and give them plenty of first-class training, motivation, and strategy. I assure you our students will be leading the race to excellence in Oakland and other parts of the world in the near future. They are preparing for the opportunity every day in class at American Indian Public Charter School.

# chapter twenty-seven

# Big Bad Bossman

[*Describing her initial interview at AIPCS.*] "I get here—and at the time Rebecca was still working here—and she had made some kind of mistake and was distracted. She hadn't been doing what she was supposed to be doing. So my first impression of Dr. Chavis is—I still don't know who this man is—but I see him come out in a T-shirt and his little track pants and he's yelling at her—you know the way that he does. 'Honey, you need to do your job correctly. If you don't want to do your job, you can just leave and never come back,' etc., etc., etc. And I'm thinking, 'I don't even know if I want to do this interview.' By my first impression, I don't want to work here. I don't want to work for a man who does this. But I stay and I go into my interview and he comes out to meet me of course with a totally different attitude. 'Oh, hi, how are you doing? So nice to meet you.' So we talk and he hires me on the spot. . . . I thought Dr. Chavis was an interesting guy. He used language I wasn't expecting him to use in an interview, but I could see that underneath he had a really good purpose and really good goals, so I thought this was a person that I would want to work for, but I realized there were aspects of his personality that could be abrasive and expected maybe there would be times that we wouldn't agree on everything. My dad was very much a disciplinarian and always expected us to do well in school, and there was nothing less. I think I identify with Dr. Chavis's point of view in that sense, his no-nonsense attitude, because my dad had the same kind of attitude about things. . . . I'm applying to law school now. Working here and for Dr. Chavis has made me a much tougher person. I don't take things as personally as I used to; I'm more direct, and I think that

I fight more for what I want. I think I've gained a lot of confidence
working here, so I believe that will play into practicing law."

—Ms. Susan Albright,
a sixth-grade teacher at AIPCS, November 2007

I see my staff members as a family, and one thing that every family
needs is loyalty. I ask all the teachers what they want to do after three
years of teaching at American Indian Public Charter School, because
my philosophy is that if you work hard for me, I want to support you.
Students and families know the teachers who are doing a good job have
my backing. Otherwise, the system would break down.

When the heat comes down on a teacher, I deal with it because I
want the teachers focused on teaching. That's not to say I won't fire a
teacher for not doing his or her job, because I've fired plenty of teachers, but when you work hard and are loyal to me, I will be loyal and
work hard for you. By loyalty, I mean a commitment to the school's
model and mission. I expect my staff to show dedication to what we're
trying to do. While families have their skirmishes, especially in my tribe,
in the end you take care of each other, and that's how I regard the
AIPCS family.

For the most part, I've had good relationships with my staff. Some
of them might not see eye to eye with me, but when they uphold the
school's philosophy and succeed, I make sure to acknowledge and reward them with bonuses and praise. I have a top-down, paternalistic
approach to running a school, which doesn't work well with everyone
because it's sometimes different from how they were brought up or
taught.

Most teachers adjust to my system, but the 2005–2006 school year
was the staff year from *Alice in Wonderland*. I learned a lot about so-
called tolerance that year from a group of young people who thought
of themselves as progressive, yet they only accepted the ideas and practices that fit neatly into their agenda. I had great relationships with
several staff members that year, but some of the teachers couldn't stand

me. After a while that feeling became mutual as they persisted in trying to run things according to their white-guilt values.

Before the 2005–2006 school year even officially began, clashing beliefs between some of the teachers and me were already an issue. Some of the teachers had taught at American Indian Public Charter School before, and some were new. I had concerns about several of the returning teachers. Part of the problem was that half of the full-time teachers were friends before they started working at AIPCS, so they became a clique who ended up feeding off each other's complaints and victimization of minorities.

I'm sure it drove those teachers crazy to be raised in middle- and upper-class families and to have attended some of the best private schools in the United States, only to find themselves in the left-leaning Bay Area working for a country Indian from the South, who was a sharecropper with uneducated parents, who paid his way through college and sent his family money each semester, and who graduated from a state university yet didn't see himself or AIPCS students as victims. It was against everything they had been taught in their religion of left-wing liberalism.

During summer school, we had a staff meeting in June that set the tone for the rest of the year. It became clear that some of the teachers felt sorry for the students. They wanted to provide more extracurricular activities for them. Some of the teachers weren't doing the work they were hired to do, and that was a concern to me.

Several teachers complained at the meeting when they heard they were going to have yard duty. Yard duty entails watching the students get picked up at the end of the school day. I assigned teachers different days to monitor the pickup point on Thirty-fifth Avenue. Some teachers felt yard duty, coupled with their detention duty, was asking too much. I was born working in the tobacco fields, and they were born bitching to their parents about having to clean their rooms. Hell, I guess it was a shock that they were asked to pitch in and look out for our students' safety.

I said teachers at other schools had to do yard duty. When a teacher responded that other schools had longer lunches, I got pissed and said, "Well, we're one of the only schools in Oakland where teachers have a prep period every day. But, shit, if you think you got it bad here, I'll send you to another school for the day. You can sub there and see what it's like to follow their schedule." I ripped a couple of lined yellow sheets off a Post-it pad and put it in front of one teacher. "Here, you go first." She didn't do anything.

I paused, looked around, and said, "You all like to talk too much, if you ask me. I know it's 'cause you're young, but I'm old, and I get irritated easily."

Then I addressed another issue that had been bothering me. The teachers were planning play activities for the students instead of teaching core academics, which is the whole point of summer school. American Indian Public Charter School's summer school is not a camp. It never was designed to be fun. Summer school prepares students for the upcoming school year. I said, "I'm not going to have any of this two afternoons in a row for special activities nonsense. Academics come first. We need to remember our focus: hard work and academics. I've been helping out at other schools that want to adopt our model, and they've been hearing from you about these fun afternoons you're planning this summer, and now they want to do it, and I'm, like, what is this? I pay for summer school out of my own pocket because I believe it gives our students an academic edge.

"Some of you need to read the mission statement and credo. We make sure the kids know it, but do you? Our slogan says we're 'A School at Work,' not play. People want to visit us because we're successful and different. 20/20 is coming here for that reason, but you want us to be the same as everyone else. Our model works; theirs doesn't.

"You know what the problem is: you're all middle and upper class and you want to give these kids the opportunities you had. Well, you can't do it. You can't give them all the basketball camps, piano lessons, and art classes you attended. But you know what you can give them? Your academics. They need your academics. They don't need your love, your touching, or your pity." My cell phone buzzed on the table and thrashed around. I let it continue as the silence in the room deepened.

I said, "You guys think you're sensitive. I know you do. But I don't think you're sensitive. I don't think a sensitive person would take half of the ninth-graders to the Oakland A's game and leave the other half behind because they didn't come to our school last year. I felt bad for those kids. We're all supposed to be a family here. What kind of fucking welcome to the family is that?" Once again, no one responded. Some of the teachers liked to gossip to each other but not to my face. That's the cowardly left-leaning culture of the Bay Area.

After other logistics were covered, I squirmed in my chair, raised one eyebrow, and said, "Okay, guys, I've got something for you." I sprang up from the table and came back with a stack of white envelopes with their bonuses inside. I had asked the board for larger-than-normal bonuses because I was confident we would score exceptionally well on the STAR tests. The promised amount was $500 for improved scores, but I gave each of them $1,500 instead. I also released the checks in June rather than waiting until August, when the scores would be officially reported. The teachers who had perfect attendance that year received an additional $500 for their dedication.

The room got quieter as they all looked inside the envelopes at the blue checks. "What do you think, Mr. Bates?" I joked, "Yours was fifteen dollars, right?" I thought the money would make the teachers appreciate their jobs and get them back to thinking about the reason we were all there: to teach these kids and give them a future. I'm not sure that plan worked with all of the teachers, though I know some of them really appreciated it.

A couple months later at the teachers' retreat in Portland, Oregon, I lit into Ms. Figlio, a new teacher, over what I considered middle-class jaw jacking. We had flown out early that morning from Oakland and had just sat through a long talk about the previous school year and plans for the following school year. We moved to the patio area under a cloudy Portland sky at the Kennedy School bed-and-breakfast, which was a former schoolhouse, to continue our discussion. The retreats were a reward to the staff. I paid for everyone to fly to Portland, stay in the hotel, and receive two free meals a day. The retreats are supposed to be a time of planning and staff bonding, but I got the feeling that some of the staff didn't want to be there. The momentum of that day's meeting was starting to wind down, as was my patience.

When Ms. Figlio said she had been giving students detention during summer school when they didn't bring a lunch to school, I, who was not aware of this, cut her off. I said, "What a bunch of nonsense. I'm not about to tell no poor people what they can and cannot eat. You're into tolerance, yet you're putting your values on poor people?" Ms. Figlio argued the students needed food and proper nutrition to focus. Those who didn't eat lunch wouldn't pay attention or do productive work in the afternoon. Other teachers agreed.

I stood up from the table and raised my voice to make sure they got my point. "Go to Lighthouse [an Oakland charter school] then. They feed their students three meals a day; however, they are letting them starve academically and die from ignorance. I wish all of 'em wouldn't eat. They need to be on a diet. Minorities have high blood pressure, they're diabetic, obese, and you want to make them eat some more. We are here to feed their brains, not their guts."

The teachers know I will raise hell in a heartbeat. They waited for me to finish. The fastest way to defuse a conflict with me is either to admit you're wrong or stop talking. I will go on and enjoy every second of it otherwise. I explained that AIPCS qualifies for the Free and Reduced-Price Lunch Program, but I choose not to provide it to students. I'm focused on feeding their minds.

Mr. Hannibal said that research shows proper nutrition leads to higher achievement in school. I said, "Let me tell you something about research." I used my hands to put quotation marks around the word "research." "I did research for years and believe me, you can find research out there that supports anything you want it to." When some people's funding relies on the results of their research, they will bend the truth in order to generate the findings they had hoped to discover.

I knew I'd be leaving American Indian Public Charter School's day-to-day operations that year in the hands of the site administrator, Mr. Katz, so any time something disagreeable came up in my presence, I jumped on it quickly. That's just the way I am. My friends Rick and Mick Stoker say my bark is stronger than my bite. My bite can be strong, too, but it only comes after several series of barks. Teachers who abide by the school's policies generally have smooth and friendly interactions with me, and I give teachers several chances to come around. In fact, I respect the ones who challenge me when they have good points to make. I'm not always right. When teachers have ideas about academics, I'm all ears, and most of my ideas have come from smart people.

After the retreat and early into the school year in September 2005, I informed the staff we would be switching to a health plan that would cost them a little more money than the previous plan. We had more employees that year and needed to minimize cost, so when I found a better deal through Kaiser, I dropped the policy with Health Net.

I apologized for the changes in our health care plan, which resulted in higher copays (from $10 to $40) and higher rates for emergency care, but I also reminded the teachers they were fortunate to have their entire health insurance plan paid for. If they worked for most other schools in Oakland, they would be paying at least half of the health insurance premiums. After some grumbling went on around the table, I said that health care costs had risen, that we could not afford our current plan, and that I, too, would be switching plans with the rest of the staff. I found out later that some staff members said I was lying and short-changing them. Shortly thereafter, I received a letter signed by most of the teachers asking me to reconsider my decision.

It asked that a meeting be held to further discuss the health insurance issue and requested that I compromise by, according to their claim, spending "approximately $10 more per person per month" in order to have a better health plan for the employees. Where did they pull that number from?

I took a black marker to the letter. In the margin next to the statement ". . . we are frustrated to learn that we are now losing those benefits and would like to suggest a compromise," I wrote "bullshit." I underlined the sentence "We fully understand we do not always get what we want or what we deserve." I circled the word "deserve" and drew an arrow to my note: "I think some of you deserve to be sent to see a quack," and I also wrote, "99.9 percent of the time you do," meaning they almost always get what they deserve.

To the suggestion that the school "consider using one of the many grants we are offered in order to subsidize health care," I circled "grants" and wrote, "Are you guys crazy? Hell, I know some of you must be crazy!" Next to Mr. Bates's name, who had a health insurance plan with his family instead of the school, I drew four sloppy question marks to say why are you involved in all this when it doesn't even concern your health care?

Those teachers should have noticed how I respond to complaint letters from families and learned accordingly. It was an insult to the teachers from the beginning when I didn't write a typewritten letter in response and instead just wrote messily all over their letter using different pens and styles. I refused to schedule a meeting with them about the health insurance policy as they requested, because meetings with them were usually gripe sessions and a waste of time.

After getting that letter, I was motivated to teach each of them a good lesson. I had been paying for the teachers' portions of their health care premiums out of my own pocket, a fact unknown to the staff. I had treated the teachers like family, only to be treated in return with scorn and greed by some of them.

I tried to do things for the staff that other employers didn't do, so the staff could brag and feel good about their jobs. Our teachers could say they got bonuses, higher salaries, independence in their classrooms, half days on Fridays, out-of-town retreats, and complete health insurance benefits. The fully paid health insurance was another thing I did for loyalty, but some of them didn't appreciate anything. Did the whiners read their contract? It said the employee will pay a portion of his/her health care. I made sure the contract explicitly said that in case the staff ever had to pay part of their health care. Kaiser gave us a better deal for the school. What was I supposed to do: neglect the financial interests of the school?

The biggest insult of all is that the teachers would accuse me of cheating them out of money after everything I had done for them. I tried to put money in every one of their pockets. When I saved the school money and made wise spending decisions, I could approach the board about merit pay for the teachers. I didn't tell the staff I was going to give them $1,500 bonuses. Do you think I was in the mood to give $1,500 bonuses at the end of that year? Their mentality was just like what you see in many public schools. Those teachers didn't see me as a human being. To them, I was a bureaucratic administrator who was just trying to screw them over.

I think that's where the class difference comes in. Those teachers had been taught that you always have to watch the administrators in a hierarchy. They wouldn't think to go take their employment contract and read it. When the teachers whined at me, I gave them a quick introduction to Ebonics. So I had issues from their perspective. I was honest. I told the teachers what I thought, and I was blunt about it, so they'd say about me, "He's a psychopath."

I'm always looking down the road and thinking of how I will manage the school's money as the school grows and changes. I handle the school's money as if it were my own. My mama didn't think about herself when she was starving; she thought about her children. Do you think those teachers are ever going to understand my family values? They went to private schools, and their parents sent them money whenever they needed it. When I went to college, I used to send my mama money. So we *are* different in many ways from my perspective. I don't lie to myself or anyone else and say that we are equal, because that is not reality. I disliked their selfish attitude that they were owed something. Their attitude was let's go have a meeting, let's demand our rights, let's have a Marxist revolution. Their meetings were all talk and no action, like most social-justice exploiters of the poor and un-educated.

The students were more appreciative than the teachers that year. The kids were always respectful and did their work. Mr. Hannibal said they were just afraid of me, but what would you expect him to say? I could have gotten away with paying the teachers a lot less. I could have said the school had no money, and in order to help these poor kids we'd have to cut back on teacher salaries. But I've never done that. I've never poor-mouthed the staff, asked them to raise money, or work for free.

I said to Mr. Bates, who had already told me before the health care letter was written that he planned to leave AIPCS at the end of the school year, "You can leave as you stated; I don't care. You called me a liar, so you can get on down the road and do whatever you please. The rest of this year, you do your job, and that's it. At the end of the year, good luck to you." I had previously told Mr. Bates I would help him start his own school, but I was not going to help someone who talked behind my back. He was speechless. He called me later that day whim-pering, said he handled it all wrong, and couldn't sleep. What did he expect me to do—prescribe him sleeping medication?

I'm consistent to a fault; when people who are supposed to be my friends or family attack me, there's no forgiving them. In the old days, people would say Indians are savages. The tolerance quacks today say we're not. We are! My family and I will turn into savages in a heartbeat when you screw with us. Do you think these people who want to fight for everyone's human rights will accept me for who I am? They are sup-posedly into acceptance; however, they have no tolerance for anyone who has a different philosophy or way of doing things from them. I think most ghetto secondary schools need at least one savage to deal with those brain-dead fools who have been dumbed down by the social-ist ideologies of universities.

That group of teachers would never hire a person like me. If they were running a school, do you think they would employ a fiscally con-servative darkie who produced a herd of mixed-breed children that makes President Obama look like a purebred white man? I hired them: a diverse team, not in color, but their perspectives and lifestyles were very different from mine. I could look past their views and alternative lifestyles as long as they were doing a good job teaching our students.

There was a good side to the situation. I saved money, and they learned a lesson for life: to think. Before you go into battle, what does *The Art of War* say? Figure out your strategies and know who your enemy is and what you are fighting for. Is the battle worth fighting? These are all lessons I tried to teach them. I'm a teacher, too, and I had a good time doing my job of educating this particular group of low-level hardheads.

I can get offended and take things personally when it comes to educating our students. I have worked with some students who have been through hell in their families. I reflect on my early childhood and the suffering I went through with my old man. I have seen the students cry, and I have cried; however, I stick to the goal of education, which changed my life for the better and will do the same for our students. For me, it's part of the circle of life that I can share with these students. I can improve their lives through academics.

When it came down to it, I didn't give any of the teachers who signed the letter a Christmas bonus. All of those who signed except one either quit or were fired at the end of that year. The one who returned, Mr. Berniker, was new to our system and was just going with things when he signed that letter. I'm sure he learned from that pack of hyenas to think before you join a pack that is about to run over a cliff.

The health insurance disagreement had long-lasting repercussions that year. It divided the staff early between those who chafed against the American Indian Model of Education and those who did not. That and other incidents made me wary of bringing into the family again teachers who couldn't get past their ideology. From that point on, I started to screen candidates more selectively.

The job posting on our Web site states:

AIPCS is always in search of teachers and staff who are smart, ambitious, and motivated to teach inner-city youth. We are looking for hardworking people who believe in free market capitalism to join our family at AIPCS.

AIPCS believes in setting a high standard for ALL students regardless of race, ethnicity, language, economic standing, etc.

Multicultural specialists, ultraliberal zealots, and college-tainted oppression liberators need not apply.

·If you believe "hard work" is the key to academic success for minority students, poor students, and all other students, we encourage you to submit the following documents by fax or e-mail:

1. Cover letter
2. Resume
3. Official or unofficial transcripts (undergraduate, graduate, etc.)

Prior teaching experience is not required. You must be willing to enroll in a credential program if you do not currently hold a teaching· credential. Candidates must also pass the CBEST and CSET examinations.

Through this job application process, employees know up front what we will *not* tolerate at American Indian Public Charter School.

# chapter twenty-eight

# Sophath: One Among Us

"My first day everyone basically scared me by saying if you don't give detentions, you're getting fired. So I said, okay, I'm going to give a lot of detentions. It ended up being fine because on the first day there were a couple kids who weren't in uniform, a couple kids came in late, a couple kids didn't do their summer homework, so I ended up having a good amount of detentions, so I knew I was okay. [Laughing.] . . . I definitely notice that my kids now really know what to expect from me. They understand what behavior I'm not going to accept, and they don't test anymore. They used to test. What can we get away with? What can we do? Now, they say, Okay. She's not going to let this fly; we're not going to do it. . . . If you notice, the people who haven't been successful here tend to have an outlook of, 'Oh, let the kids decide.' Although that may work some places, it doesn't go with our model, and I think the first step to being a good teacher here is understanding that rules are important and you have to believe that. I don't think you can enforce something you don't believe. . . . I really have fallen in love with teaching. The problem is now I'm so spoiled working here because they pay us really well, they treat us really well, and the kids are really well behaved. So I'm used to that and don't know if I could ever teach anywhere else. [Laughing.] . . . When people talk about teaching to the test, when don't you teach to a test? There's no job in this world where you don't have to be ready in some way for some kind of standardized test. If you're a doctor, you have to take MCATs and then you have to take your boards. If you're a lawyer, you have to take the bar. So I think it's preparing kids to understand that you need to be ready to prove your knowledge in a testing format because no one's going to sit down with you and say, 'Well, you failed your boards but you can really explain it well to me, so you can be a doctor.' I feel like that's just life. . . . I think the press in general is always going to try to find something wrong and especially the way Dr. Chavis handles things I can see how it could be considered non-P.C. We're in an age where you don't call anyone anything but the proper name. I understand that, but at the same time is that really working? I don't think so. There are a lot of kids leaving high school still unable to read. . . . I think one of the most important things that Dr. Chavis does is he says don't hide behind your race. By saying, 'I'm not smart because I'm black or because I'm Asian or my parents don't speak English' is just completely untrue because you are just as smart as those rich people sitting on the hill. You just have to work hard. I think it's really important not to let students have an excuse to not succeed."

—Ms. Liana Tallerico,
*a seventh-grade teacher at AIPCS in 2006–2007*

I always like to hire smart people at American Indian Public Charter School. It doesn't matter to me what color or class they are as long as they're intelligent and dedicated. Every once in a while hires come around who have a similar background to the students, which is great because they don't see the students as victims, and they realize structure and discipline are important. One such woman is Sophath Mey, a young, dynamic Cambodian who graduated from UC Berkeley, grew up in East Oakland, and still lives with her extended family.

Sophath interviewed for the administrative assistant position, and as I normally do in interviews I asked about her family and upbringing. See, by the time interviewees have stepped through the school's door, I've reviewed their cover letters, resumes, and college transcripts, so I don't need to ask typical interview questions. Ms. Liana Tallerico was shocked how I only asked about her boyfriend and family before offering her the job. She thought we were just small-talking, but that was the interview. Liana had been reviewing potential interview questions and responses with her college counselor to prepare, so I caught her way off guard. We both laugh about it to this day.

I'm already serious about hiring people based on what I've seen in their cover letters, transcripts, and resumes. Cover letters tell me whether candidates can write and what their attitudes are toward education. College transcripts show grades and give me insight into the depth of their education in math, English, science, and history. Candidates' resumes let me know what kind of work and experiences they've had in the past. With that information already at hand, I can find out what kind of people they are.

When Sophath Mey came in for an interview, I realized we had a lot in common. We both grew up in a way that most people would consider disadvantaged. In a way, growing up poor gives you an actual advantage over others because it instills values, lessons, and toughness in you that you wouldn't get in easier circumstances. Sophath grew up in a rough neighborhood on Eighty-third Avenue in East Oakland. She still lives there. People continue to get shot near her house; she still hears helicopters, sirens, and gunshots, but she's used to it. It doesn't scare her because she's learned to survive in the ghetto.

Sophath's parents came to the United States as Cambodian refugees. She was two years old when they stepped foot on American soil. Sophath shared with me a haunting story about her mom's experiences as a young woman. In the late 1970s, Sophath's mom, who had been separated from her family because of the war, was forced to line up in a field in Cambodia with hundreds of other people. The Khmer Rouge started killing each person one by one. Instead of shooting them, the soldiers used the butt ends of their guns to whack the people in the skull until they died. Her mom still remembers the awful sound of the guns crashing against bone. The Khmer Rouge killed so many people in the field that day that they got tired and it got dark, so they let the rest of them go. Sophath's mom was one of the survivors.

After being in the communist camps, refugee camps, and the Philippines for a health checkpoint, Sophath's parents arrived in the United States in their midtwenties with no education, with no knowledge of English, and with what Sophath considers post-traumatic stress disorder. Sophath's parents received public assistance through her childhood. Her dad would sometimes get really depressed. Her parents have always been very grateful to the United States and see the country as a savior.

Sophath's mom is strict. She's old-school—very traditional. She protected Sophath and Sophath's younger siblings. They were only allowed to play inside the gate of their home. Sophath would ask, Can I walk to the corner store? No. Can I walk to the park? No. Everything was a no. Sophath's mom protected her children, so they didn't see much of what was really going on in the community. For example, when people walking by asked Sophath for bleach, she thought they were just too poor to buy their own cleaning supplies. It wasn't until she was much older that she realized they were junkies trying to clean their drug syringes.

Because they were so poor, Sophath's family never got an education. In Cambodia it was assumed that when you went to school you were going to learn and be appreciative. Teachers were treated like religious figures who deserved praise. Sophath's mom instilled respect for educators into Sophath as she navigated her way through the Oakland public school system.

Sophath attended Castlemont High School, which she described as chaotic with no discipline and no structure. There were some very dedicated teachers who did everything possible to help students succeed, but it was strikingly different from American Indian Public Charter School. A student got stabbed once, and there were race riots—usually blacks against Mexicans and vice versa. The academics did not prepare students for college.

Sophath ranked number five in her graduating class at Castlemont, but looking back on it she thinks she was probably writing below middle school level in high school. She didn't realize she had an educational disadvantage until she got to college and saw how well other students were writing and how they were able to read effectively and take notes in class. She had to teach herself how to take notes and had to play an intense game of academic catch-up.

In high school she took Advanced Placement (AP) classes, but they didn't have AP books or AP rigor. Her principal said that due to safety concerns they had to put funding toward building a large black gate around the school, so they didn't have money for AP textbooks. The students kept fighting it and eventually got AP U.S. history books a few weeks before the AP exam. Sophath knows she and her classmates weren't doing AP-level work because she didn't pass any of the AP tests she took. Do you see why the College Board started making schools apply for official AP status for their courses?

Despite not passing her AP exams, Sophath looked good on her high school transcript because she had a high GPA, lots of extracurricular activities, and core academic courses. She got accepted to UC Berkeley and her mentor sat her down and said, "I don't care what you say. You're going to Berkeley." She didn't know at the time that it was a high-ranking university. When she enrolled she thought she was smart and ready for the challenges of higher education, but Sophath had a harsh reality check when she realized how far behind she was compared to her classmates and how ill prepared Castlemont High School had graduated her.

She was determined to succeed nonetheless. In her first semester she did well because she tried so hard and put so much effort in. As time went on Sophath started feeling really insecure and thought maybe she was going to be one of those kids who got out of Oakland but never made it through college, that she would be another inner-city dropout.

Sophath withdrew from UC Berkeley her second year for one semester because she was struggling academically, in debt, and trying to hold down a steady job. She felt insecure and broke, but she decided to do whatever it took to graduate. She took out more loans, reenrolled, and kept working hard. I am really proud of Sophath for persevering and graduating from college. Many other people in her situation would have given up and dropped out.

Sophath agrees with the educational philosophy of AIPCS and the way we do things here because it reminds her of how she was raised at home. Even though she went to a chaotic high school where people were acting stupid and not taking their education seriously, when she went home it was different. She had responsibilities and structure.

American Indian Public Charter School reminds me of the one-room schoolhouses of the past. It reminds Sophath of a school outside the United States, where even if you went to the poorest countryside in Asia or Mexico, when you walked into a classroom, you would find proud people. You wouldn't see students throwing papers and acting out. You'd see them sitting there wanting to learn in structured classrooms with discipline. They wouldn't have anything fancy—just chalkboard, chalk, and seats. We endorse the same mentality at American Indian Public Charter School and are conservative with our spending. When we can get used items such as desks and fix them up, we utilize them; however, we make sure our students have the best textbooks that are aligned with California and national standards.

Sophath thinks it's ridiculous how Oakland Unified mandates that mailings be sent home to families in their native language. Many immigrants can't read or write in their own language and those who can almost certainly can't read the formal, legalistic language that the memos are written in by public school educators. When Castlemont High School sent memos to Sophath's home, her mom couldn't read or write in Cambodian, so it was, like, great, you translated it for us, but we can't understand it, so why not send it in English, because then I can explain to my mom what it says?

At our schools we write all of our memos in very simple English. I laughed when a new teacher handed me a letter she'd written to families asking for permission to attend a field trip. (All memos have to be approved by the office before being sent home; I don't like surprises.) It was a long, dense letter with some five-dollar words thrown in. There was no way most of the families would understand it. I knew she'd spent a lot of time on it, but I told her to reduce it to three sentences of basic English. She was a good sport and saw it as a fun challenge to write Ernest Hemingway–style memos from then on.

Like me, when Sophath went to college, she felt free. She was outside of the East Oakland death triangle, as they call it, and was able to see new places. In college she got her first experience going snowboarding and visiting Las Vegas.

A lot of people don't realize how little inner-city kids see of their surroundings. The first time Sophath saw the famous San Francisco tourist sites of Fisherman's Wharf and Alcatraz she was a sophomore in college and was doing an outreach program for high school students called REACH. (Oakland is just across the bay from San Francisco.) Many of our ninth-graders who went to Pier 39 on a field trip had never been before. A former AIPCS teacher was shocked when almost none of her students had ever been on the Golden Gate Bridge. One student was confused and asked, "Is that the expensive bridge?" Indeed it is.

Sophath values structure and discipline and wishes she had had the same experience and academic foundation in middle and high school as our student body. We give our students so many tools, such as the SAT, PSAT, and AP courses, and we pay all costs for these tests because we want them to succeed. We teach our students about being responsible and taking care of themselves, and we also keep our kids safe. Our schools are places of calm amid the chaos of Oakland. Sophath sees how frequently people come by American Indian Public Charter School to ask about getting their child in the school because they want the most for them and know we can provide it.

I helped Sophath get her little brother into a better elementary school called Laurel when she realized he wasn't being taught much at his other school. He wasn't happy about it, but I told her, "He'll hate you now, but he'll thank you later."

I am a true believer in hard work and loyalty. Sophath works hard and is great at what she does. We support each other and have plenty of laughs along the way. I could see her making an excellent principal because Sophath knows what it takes to succeed and could impart knowledge and experience to the next generation.

# Conclusion: Creating Educational Excellence Through Replication

"These students' parents came to this country to give them better opportunities, but what do we do instead? We ruin the second generation of immigrant students. We put them in screwed-up schools with so-called progressive educational philosophies, and they start learning the gimme attitude. 'I want a free lunch. You gotta give me something.' The parents learn the dialogue, too, and it starts being a culture of mediocrity. The parents and kids develop excuses, and then that generation is lost. I try to put the hunger back into education."

—*Jorge Lopez, whose schools, Oakland Charter Academy and Oakland Charter High School, are thriving under AIM-Ed and his leadership*

"Hopefully Canada will recognize a great program and adopt it even if America does not."

—*Michael Coteau,*
*trustee and vice chair of the Toronto School Board*

The American Indian Model of Education (AIM-Ed) will continue to replicate in Oakland, California, and beyond because it works for students, and organizations such as the Koret Foundation are interested in helping schools succeed.

It is an interesting story of how I came into contact with the Koret

Foundation. I am an old-school country Indian who is leery of the good intentions of most people. It was decided after my first year at AIPCS that we would not pursue grants to support the school because it could compromise our educational model. I have seen too many schools accept money from foundations and get pulled off their mission in an attempt to please their funders. I have met and turned down some wonderful people who were interested in giving money to our school. Ms. Debra England, the educational program officer with the Koret Foundation, was the most persistent.

In 2004, she contacted me and said, "I have reviewed the academic results of your school and would be interested in talking with you, Dr. Chavis, about our foundation possibly working with AIPCS." I barked into the telephone and said, "I don't want your money! We don't take grants at AIPCS." She was speechless for a second and said, "Fine, would it be possible for me to visit your school?" I thought, "Who is this crazy white lady?" It was agreed for her to come the next day, which was Saturday School. She was at our school from 8:30 a.m. to 1:00 p.m. asking what seemed like a million questions.

Two years later, in 2006, we accepted funding from the Koret Foundation to create American Indian Public High School. Today, AIPHS is the fourth-highest-performing high school in California. Every senior in the school is taking Advanced Placement (AP) calculus and AP literature and has been recruited or accepted by the top universities in the United States. Thank God for the call from Ms. Debra England, a hardworking Jewish woman who persisted in building a relationship with a crazy Indian to help fund the eventual creation of two high schools (AIPHS and OCHS), another middle school (AIPCS II), Pre-Advanced Placement courses in all three of our middle schools (AIPCS, AIPCS II, and OCA), and Advanced Placement courses for all the eleventh- and twelfth-graders in the two high schools.

These schools all use the American Indian Model of Education. To recap, AIM to Educate consists of self-contained classrooms with students who remain with the same teacher for three years from sixth through eighth grade, excellent attendance brought about through rewards and consequences, intelligent and dedicated teachers capable of teaching multiple subjects, an emphasis on core academics and particularly on language arts and mathematics, the adoption of current standards-based textbooks and curriculum, an extended-year calendar, strict structure, and discipline.

AIM-Ed provides thousands of students with the structure, discipline, academic and social skills needed to be productive members in a free market capitalistic society. I am blessed that the creator, God, Buddha, Muhammad, or whatever one chooses to call their savior, led me down a path of life that is more wonderful than I could have ever planned in a thousand lifetimes.

In July 2007, I retired as principal of American Indian Public Charter School after seven years. It was time for a new adventure that focused on expanding AIM-Ed. I am the chief executive of replication. I train school districts in various parts of North America that are interested in implementing AIM to Educate (www.americanindianmodel.org), and I've been sharing our students' academic successes in order to generate interest in education reform. I spend as much time as their schedule will allow with my children (Celeste, Lela, Ben Henry, Margaret, and Elizabeth), and grandchildren (Armondo and JJ). My children, grandchildren, and the students at AIPCS are much better academically in school than I was as a youngster.

My daughter Margaret attempted several times to run away from school, like her dad once did. She was caught three times before reaching the gate and once just beyond the gate; luckily the security system is much better now than during my public school days. The ability to run from school was passed down through my DNA to the children. Their academic achievements, music, and art ability are the result of the hard work in school that each of them puts forth, as well as their mom's intelligence and commitment to our children having numerous educational opportunities in life. I expect our great-grandchildren and their descendants to continue a tradition of pursuing an education that will allow them to fulfill their dreams.

It's a treat to visit AIPCS and see the excellent job administrators, teachers, staff, students, and families are doing at the school. They are preparing students with the academic and social skills for a wonderful life in our society. Some people have asked me how I could step away from my position as principal. I truly believe a great organization will continue to perform at the highest level when the leader has mentored or prepared successors with the skills to continue the process after he or she is gone. This is the stamp of a true leader. I am proud to say that the teachers who did their administrative internship with me are exceeding the academic standards achieved during my time as principal at the school.

In 2008, AIPCS continued to improve, scoring 967 on the API. This made American Indian Public Charter School the fifth-highest-scoring middle school in California out of about thirteen hundred middle schools in the state. AIPCS was also the top-performing charter school in California. The students continue to take part in the Johns Hopkins University Center for Talented Youth (CTY) program in the summer. AIPCS has the highest participation rate in CTY of any school in the United States because we really promote CTY and push our students to qualify and participate in it.

Before I retired as principal, we instituted another summer program for AIPCS students called SAIL, which stands for the Stanford Academic Institute of Learning. SAIL takes place on a college campus. For six and half hours a day for three weeks, students engage in rigorous mathematics, writing, science, economics, or other advanced courses, as well as physical fitness training. In the SAIL college program, all of our seventh-graders enrolled in algebra the summer before their eighth-grade year. This contributed to 100 percent of AIPCS students testing proficient or advanced in algebra in 2008. The school has come a long way over the years from its low point in 2000, and it will continue to improve in the future.

The following are a few unique individuals I have come to know as a result of working at American Indian Public Charter School who are replicating the American Indian Model in other schools:

1.  Mr. Jorge Lopez completed his educational internship with me at American Indian Public Charter School; afterward he ran at light speed with the American Indian Model at Oakland Charter Academy (OCA), a middle school in the Hispanic community of the Fruitvale district in Oakland. When Mr. Lopez took over OCA in 2004, about 10 out of 160 students were proficient in math and language arts. The school's test scores were terrible overall, and OCA was placed on a school improvement plan by the California Department of Education. The school's focus had been on bilingualism, multiculturalism, and diversity. The former directors and staff had no idea language arts, mathematics, history, and science were the true "diversity" the students needed in order to succeed.

    Mr. Lopez is a go-getter; he replaced most of the staff and substituted the culture of nonsense with the American Indian

Model at OCA, where 98 percent of the students are Hispanic and over 95 percent of them qualify for the Free and Reduced-Price Lunch Program. As a result of his hard work and adherence to the model, OCA's Academic Performance Index score surged 207 points in two years, from 650 to 857. In 2008, Oakland Charter Academy was the third-highest-performing middle school in Oakland (behind AIPCS and AIPCS II), with a score of 902 on the Academic Performance Index. After three years at OCA, every eighth-grader in 2008 scored proficient or advanced in language arts and algebra. The majority of those students had entered OCA in the sixth grade below grade level. What a success story and proof that the American Indian Model works when a great leader is willing to work hard and stick to it. Oakland Charter Academy is only the second public school in Oakland to receive the National Blue Ribbon Award from the United States Department of Education. Mr. Lopez has also trained Mrs. Evelia Villa and Mrs. Sandra Reyes to be effective school administrators.

2.  On January 25, 2006, Dr. Randolph Ward, the state administrator of Oakland Unified School District, approved our new high school, American Indian Public High School (AIPHS). Based on AIM-Ed, it opened in June of 2006. Carey Blakely, who had taught at AIPCS, was hired as the new site administrator to lead AIPHS. Ms. Blakely understood the model and was the first to implement it at the high school level in the country. The school opened with ninth- and tenth-graders, who were all required to enroll in honors courses. In addition, they had to take a minimum of one college course each semester in Mandarin, science, geography, or economics. The expectations were and are very high for those AIPHS students.

    During AIPHS's first two years in operation, 100 percent of the tenth-grade students passed both parts of the California High School Exit Exam (CAHSEE) on their first attempt. (In Oakland Unified School District in 2006–2007, 40 percent of the tenth-graders failed the English portion of the exam, while 39 percent failed the math portion.) At the end of its first year in operation, with an API of 940, AIPHS ranked as the fifth-highest-scoring high school in California out of about twelve hundred high schools. This was a result of the staff and students' hard work.

In the summer of 2007, when Ms. Blakely moved to Southern California, Mrs. Janet Roberts, also a former AIPCS teacher, took over leadership of AIPHS. Under Mrs. Roberts's excellent leadership, the school achieved a score of 958 on the API, making it the fourth-highest-scoring high school in California. Every senior in AIPHS's first graduating class is enrolled in AP calculus and AP literature, and all of them will take the AP exams for those courses. One hundred percent of the seniors have already exceeded the A-G requirements (the minimum course requirements needed to be eligible for admission into the University of California system) and will meet the California State Department of Education requirements to graduate a semester early from high school. The students have enough Advanced Placement and community college credits to enroll as juniors in the University of California system after graduation. In the summer of 2008, Mrs. Roberts was appointed executive director of all the American Indian Public Charter Schools. She has set a blistering pace to ensure the students are prepared with the academic skills to compete with other students from around the world. The drive and passion Mrs. Roberts has as a school administrator make her a joy to be around.

3.  After receiving charter approval from the state administrator of Oakland Unified, Dr. Kimberly Statham, we opened a new middle school called American Indian Public Charter School II. AIPCS II opened its doors downtown to sixth- and seventh-graders on June 21, 2007. At the end of the first year, thanks to the dedicated staff and students, AIPCS II scored a 917 on the API. Mr. John Glover, a former AIPHS teacher, now runs AIPCS II in its second year as the site administrator. The school is headed off to a bright future because Mr. Glover loves his work and is committed to ensuring the success of the students through the model. Students and families in Oakland are fortunate to have Mr. Glover, Mrs. Roberts, Mr. Lopez, and Ms. Sophath Mey, who are smart young people who have chosen public education as a career.

4.  In 2007, Jorge Lopez created the second high school, Oakland Charter High School (OCHS), based on the American Indian Model. At the end of its first year in operation, OCHS scored a 939 on the API. Both OCHS and AIPCS II are located together in a building on Twelfth Street downtown on what we call the Milton and Rose Friedman Campus. Dr. Milton Friedman won the Nobel Prize for Economics in 1976. He is best known for advocating the concept of a free market protected against intrusive government regulation. He was a friend and leader for those of us interested in providing all students and families a choice in public education.

Milton Friedman passed away on November 16, 2006, at the age of ninety-four. He is survived by his wonderful wife and colleague, Rose. Rose Friedman wrote to me in a letter dated July 9, 2007, "I remember my husband saying that if any charter school would succeed, it would be yours." I was honored to receive such a compliment from wonderful human beings who worked throughout their professional careers to make our country a better place for all people.

In the same year Oakland Charter High School and American Indian Public Charter School II were granted approval, Dr. Statham also approved plans for Cole Middle School, a failing public school in Oakland, to reopen based on the American Indian Model. Their plan was to put the new sixth-graders in one school and the seventh- and eighth-graders in the other. The sixth-grade students would be in self-contained classrooms that looped. After three years, the schools would merge back into one.

I decided to see how their implementation was going in their first year. When I swung by Cole Middle School, I was extremely disappointed. There was nothing that resembled our model but the self-contained classrooms. Upon entering the school's front office, I met the security guard—who was the only person with any idea about the American Indian Model—then a curriculum person, secretary, and principal. They had one full-time sixth-grade teacher, one long-term sixth-grade substitute teacher, and a full-time P.E. teacher. There was not an opportunity to meet the janitor, cafeteria staff, or personal coaches for the teachers and principal as assigned by the Oakland Unified School District. What logical person would hire all these employees to work in a middle school serving fewer than sixty sixth-grade students? The principal said she needed more assistance. Unfortunately for them, they had grant money that was targeted to create "small schools" in the district that sustained their social experiment in top-heaviness in nonteaching positions.

They should have hired two full-time classroom teachers, one full-time administrator, a part-time P.E. teacher, and a part-time tutor/ resource specialist. The focus should have been on the classrooms, not the office. One key to successfully implementing the American Indian Model of Education is to avoid being top-heavy. That's the tendency of many public schools, but it's not the way of American Indian Public Charter School and its sister schools.

The American Indian Model should be replicated because it works and can change children's lives. I'm not keen on the idea of partial replication or employing too many administrators, consultants, and classified staff. When schools say they're going to use one or two aspects of AIM-Ed in combination with other educational models, I think, "Oh, boy." If you're already running a successful school, that would be one thing. When your school is failing students, it's time to throw out the model you've been using, not salvage tidbits of it for personal flair or enjoyment.

Excluding Cole Middle School, because they did not adhere to the model, the five schools using the American Indian Model in Oakland are all part of the 900 club in California public school rankings. AIPCS, OCA, AIPHS, AIPCS II, and OCHS all have Academic Performance Index scores in the 900s. That puts them in the top 1 percent of schools in the state. No other secondary school system in California has produced such high academic results. Three of our schools are ranked among the top ten academic performing public schools in California.

I expect to continue replicating new schools in California and expanding the American Indian Model into other areas. I figure if you can create good schools with AIM-Ed in Oakland, you can make it work anywhere.

The American Indian Model of Education we have created at AIPCS and replicated will change the lives of students, educators, and the community over time. Change is possible in secondary education for poor, minority, and white students when educators are committed to implementing family culture, accountability/structure, high expectations, and free market capitalism. I'm always open to teaching people how to use AIM-Ed, so don't hesitate to get in touch if you're interested! Go to aipcs.org for our contact information.

Outside of Oakland there has been interest in and use of the model. After hearing me speak in April 2006 at the American Indian Exemplary Institute, founded and directed by Dr. Dean Chavers in Albuquerque, New Mexico, the superintendent of Box Elder Schools, Bob Heppner, and the principal, Dave Nelson, discussed our students' academic and social achievements at AIPCS on their flight back to Montana. They said I was "either nuts or just that good." They decided to adopt AIM-Ed at their middle school in the fall of 2006. The Box Elder Schools are located on Rocky Boy Reservation, where 98 percent of the student body are Indians of the Chippewa and Cree tribes.

Like me, Principal Dave Nelson loves analyzing student data; he enjoys telling people that in the 2002–2003 school year, Box Elder had twelve hundred write-ups for disciplinary problems and about a one-third student-body turnover rate. By 2006–2007, the discipline reports were reduced to about a fourth, and the student turnover rate was reduced by half. In reading scores for 2007, 89.5 percent of third-graders tested proficient. That was one of the highest rates in Montana for third-grade reading achievement. Box Elder Elementary won a National Title I Distinguished School Award in January 2007.

Mr. Nelson is white; however, I do not believe it's the color of an educator's skin that makes him or her successful in working with any race of students. Could it be an educator's game plan, dedication, and commitment to preparing students with the academic tools needed to succeed in school is what counts? Our children need and deserve smart, dedicated people who are willing to challenge them at a high academic level. Mr. Nelson is that kind of person. Mr. Lopez is Hispanic; Ms. Blakely is white; Mrs. Roberts is part white and part Asian; Mr. Glover is white; I'm American Indian. What we have in common is that we have all succeeded in achieving outstanding academic results among American Indian, Asian, black, Hispanic, white, and poor students because we don't treat them as victims but as individuals with untapped talent we know we can cultivate.

Michael Coteau, trustee and vice chair of the Toronto School Board, was so impressed during his visit to AIPCS in 2008 that he is preparing a proposal for his board to adopt the American Indian Model as a pilot project in one to three public schools in Toronto, Canada. Mr. Coteau saw what we were doing as back to basics, which ironically makes our model revolutionary today. AIPCS reminded him of *Little House on the Prairie*. Mr. Coteau thinks AIM-Ed holds the key to providing students with what they need most: a core education in an ever-changing world. He pointed out the problems the Toronto School District faces, such as a high dropout rate among black students, First Nations students, and Portuguese students, and he believes the American Indian Model should be explored as a solution to those problems. Mr. Coteau is arranging for me to give a presentation on the model to the Toronto School Board, which represents a school district of 550 schools, 265,000 students, and a $2.3 billion budget.

In recent developments, Mr. Jerry Smith, director of Laguna Development, and Mr. Richard Luarkie, lieutenant governor of the Laguna Pueblo Indian Tribe of New Mexico, have spearheaded the effort to implement the American Indian Model in their tribal school system on the reservation. At their request, I made a presentation to the Laguna Pueblo Tribal Council trying to convince them of the merits of AIM-Ed.

Joel Klein, the chancellor of New York City public schools responsible for overseeing more than 1.1 million students, and Reverend Al Sharpton, the renowned civil rights leader, will be cosponsoring an upcoming convention in New York City on closing the achievement gap. The convention will be a joint effort of the Education Equality Project and the National Action Network. I have been asked to serve on a panel representing schools that work. New York City mayor Michael Bloomberg, Los Angeles mayor Antonio Villaraigoso, U.S. education secretary Arne Duncan, and other major leaders will attend the convention. I look forward to the opportunity and am honored by the invitation.

Oakland Unified School District has never asked me to address their entire board. They say you have to be a prophet outside your own land. I assure you I'm no prophet, just a country Indian boy who went off to the big city and got a good education through college and life's adventures. I'm certainly all about financial profit in my real estate business and the success that life offers each of us! I believe that the American Indian Model will help students in Canada and the United States have the opportunity for a better academic education. The biggest compliment to our work at American Indian Public Charter School is when other schools adopt our model.

The amount of attention and press that American Indian Public Charter School and its sister schools have received is truly flattering. It was an honor when California governor Arnold Schwarzenegger visited us not just once but twice! In his first visit in 2006, Governor Schwarzenegger said in a speech that what had occurred within the walls of American Indian Public Charter School was "an education miracle." What a privilege to have Governor Schwarzenegger recognize the mighty achievements of our small school in the inner city and shake the hands of our students and staff. Mr. Schwarzenegger is a smart, wonderful human being and very thankful for the opportunities he was given as an immigrant to the United States. He chose to give back to California by serving as governor and donating his salary to the state. The governor is a true original American success story who related instantly with our students.

It was also incredibly exciting when ABC's *20/20* included American Indian Public Charter School in a special one-hour report on education in 2006. The ABC crew spent several days at our school and flew me out to New York City to interview with John Stossel in his studio. Mr. Stossel is a funny, captivating person who is passionate about education reform. The *20/20* special report was called "Stupid in America" and looked at what's gone wrong in our nation's public schools. It featured American Indian Public Charter School as an exemplary school and a beacon of hope in public education. It was such a proud moment for the students, families, staff, and community members associated with AIPCS to watch the school be praised on national television.

We have worked hard, succeeded, and raised some eyebrows, which has gotten AIPCS plenty of media attention in other outlets as well. The major Bay Area newspapers both did front-page articles on our school—the *Oakland Tribune* in 2005 and 2007 and the *San Francisco Chronicle* in 2006. We also had airtime on National Public Radio and on local and national television networks. In one program by the Christian Broadcasting Network (CBN) in 2007, Pat Robertson said to his coanchor at the end of a newscast on AIPCS, "I congratulate that principal. Isn't that [story of the school] terrific?"

Numerous books and magazines, including *Free to Learn: Lessons from Model Charter Schools* in 2005 by Lance T. Izumi and Xiaochin Claire Yan (I have known Mr. Izumi for two decades; he was a national leader at the beginning of the charter school movement and continues to be an advocate for quality schools); *Sweating the Small Stuff: Inner-*

*City Schools and the New Paternalism* in 2008 by David Whitman, who has supreme insight into the issues facing education; and *Government Technology* in 2006, have also discussed what we're doing at our schools. In what I consider a really funny line by the author Jack Cashill in *What's the Matter with California?*, Mr. Cashill referred to me as "the all-around coolest guy I met in California." This statement, made about a dim-witted country Indian from the South who has gone to the not-so-big city, confirms California is in real trouble. It was a pleasure giving Mr. Cashill a tour of Oakland and our school on a perfect Saturday afternoon.

Mr. George F. Will, the Pulitzer Prize–winning journalist and columnist for the *Washington Post* and *Newsweek*, interviewed me and visited AIPCS in the summer of 2008. It was an honor that Mr. Will was interested in learning about our work. He shared his insights into education, politics, and the presidential election over a Chinese lunch. His dry sense of humor and great deal of common sense are refreshing qualities. Mr. Will said I could make more politically incorrect statements in one sentence than anyone he had ever heard before. I informed him it didn't take any effort in California to be politically incorrect. A few weeks later, in August 2008, Mr. Will published in his syndicated column a great article about our school that ran in newspapers throughout the United States.

Ms. Lyanne Melendez, a reporter with ABC 7 News in San Francisco, has done several special reports on public education, noting the high academic achievement of our student population and awards the school has received at the state and national level.

Mr. Steven Maggi of the Evergreen Freedom Foundation and producer of the documentary *Flunked* featured our school in his award-winning film that addresses the problems in public education and shows examples of schools that are proving remarkable achievement is possible and happening in American education.

Mr. Mitchell Landsberg, the Pulitzer Prize–winning reporter of the *Los Angeles Times*, recently contacted me about AIPCS's high academic success with economically disadvantaged students, and he plans to write about our schools after he spent time in Oakland with our students and staff.

For me it has been an honor as an educator to meet so many unique individuals committed to enhancing their knowledge of public education who have come to meet our students and observe how the American

Indian Model works. These visitors witnessed firsthand our students, staff, and families' glorious triumph against the odds in Oakland, California, and shared their stories with other people around the world.

Grandma Lela was indeed right: I have been "blessed" with the greatest opportunity that life could offer, which allowed me to spend time working with students each day. I loved every second shared together with the students, teachers, staff, and families at our school. It was never a job to me, just the chance of a lifetime to do what I loved doing. What more could a person ask for?

It was a pleasure sharing a bit about my life and the American Indian Public Charter School story with you. When will you come to visit our schools and students? I promise they will inspire and impress you. If there isn't a flood in Oakland, you may get a glimpse of this crazy, blessed Indian walking the halls of AIPCS with the grin of a fox that has entered the henhouse.

# Appendix

## Common Sense & Useful Learning at AIPCS
### by Dr. Ben Chavis

1.  The school facility is open daily from 8:30 a.m. until 4:00 p.m., except Saturdays, Sundays, and all holidays known to mankind.
2.  The staff of AIPCS does not preach or subscribe to the demaguery of tolerance. Adults not willing to follow our rules will be sent packing with their rags and bags!
3.  Squawkers, multicultural specialists, self-esteem experts, panhandlers, drug dealers, and those snapping turtles who refuse to put forth their best effort will be booted out.
4.  Bootlicking or self-promoting is not allowed by any politician who enters our classrooms. Politicians should beware: teachers are on duty!
5.  We do not believe standardized tests discriminate against students because of their color. Could it be many of them have not been adequately prepared to take those tests?
6.  The staff does not allow students to wear hats, gold chains, or ear-bobs in the building. Adults are not allowed to use cell phones, beepers, and other gadgets in our school.

7. Dr. Chavis does provide psychological evaluations to quacks and Kultur specialists on a sliding scale. See him immediately for such rates.

8. All solicitors should note the nearest exit upon entering this institution of learning. We view such alley cats with a fishy eye.

9. No more than one psychologist or school administrator is allowed in our school at a time. This rule is part of our commitment to high academic standards.

10. Photographs of the director or staff are on sale at the front office. Payment must be made in advance. *Cash only!* The photographs will be sent to you by Pony Express.

11. The staff of AIPCS is of the first rank. We request that you do not flirt with them. They will accept your cash donations!

12. Visitors are welcome daily. Due to the time it takes to reeducate university visitors, we are limiting their number to a maximum of four individuals a week.

13. It will be difficult for our staff to meet with those educational experts who "know it all." We are willing to meet with such tomcats on Halloween night.

14. How does anyone convince a billy goat or taxpayer that school administrators possess above-average intelligence? How will we address this educational dilemma?

15. Our staff does not subscribe to the back swamp logic of minority students as victims. We will plow through such cornfield philosophy with common sense and hard work!

16. If you wish to share any suggestions regarding this list, our commonsense committee accepts suggestions from 8:30 a.m. to 8:31 a.m. each holiday.

# The American Indian Model of Education
# (AIM to Educate/AIM-Ed)

## Family Culture

1.  Families are guaranteed if they follow and support our model, their children will be prepared to graduate from college.
2.  We create an extended family with administration, teachers, staff, students, family, and selected community. Students and staff are expected to clean and take care of the school property.
3.  Teachers spend three years with their students in sixth through eighth grade teaching all core academic subjects, which creates an environment of strong academics and family culture.
4.  When a sixth-grade student is acting up in class, he or she will be sent to sit on the floor in a seventh- or eighth-grade class. A seventh- or eighth-grade student who acts up may be sent to sit on the floor in a sixth-grade class.
5.  All students are provided free tutoring in any subject before school, after school, or on Saturday. Students are employed as tutors to work with other students who need academic support in core academic subjects.
6.  Former AIPCS students enrolled in college are hired to work with our current students.
7.  No student has been expelled since the American Indian Model was implemented in 2000.

## Accountability/Structure

1.  Teachers provide students with ninety instructional minutes in language arts and ninety instructional minutes in mathematics each day. Teachers assign a minimum of two hours of homework each night.
2.  We hire smart administrators and teachers based on their high academic achievement and ability to follow the American Indian Model. We fire administrators and teachers who do not meet those expectations. We reward all employees who adhere to the model.
3.  We analyze all test results in order to group students by ability

in mathematics and competitive sports. A student's state and national test results are used to gauge the accuracy of achievement in the classroom.

4.  State testing is held one week after staff and students return from Easter break. There are no field trips until after California Standards testing. Only students who have worked hard and followed the rules may attend field trips.
5.  Progress reports are sent home every three weeks for students who are failing. A C– is a failing grade. Report cards are distributed every nine weeks. Administrators must sign off on all student progress reports and report cards before they are sent home.
6.  We retain those students not willing to work toward improving their academic or social skills to advance to the next grade level.
7.  Students are informed of their academic progress and the school's academic progress continuously. Students are expected to set academic goals and work toward them.

## High Expectations

1.  We demand hard work and high academic expectations from all students and staff.
2.  We implement professional development where administrators and teachers train their colleagues, while students train incoming students on the culture and expectations of the American Indian Model.
3.  We set forth a rigorous academic program aligned with standards-based textbooks and a uniform grading scale that all administrators and teachers must follow.
4.  After-school detention and Saturday school serve as consequences for students who break school rules.
5.  We celebrate Christopher Columbus Day, Martin Luther King, Jr., Day, and other various holidays **by attending school**. This attendance policy was created by students and staff.
6.  We follow an extended school year with an average of two hundred instructional school days with mandatory summer programs that include: AIM summer school, Stanford Academic Institute of Learning (SAIL), Johns Hopkins University Center

for Talented Youth (CTY), and University of California at
Berkeley's Academic Talent Development Program (ATDP).

7. Teachers finish core academic curriculum textbooks by April 5
   each year. After state testing, teachers begin the next grade
   level's core curriculum of mathematics and language arts.

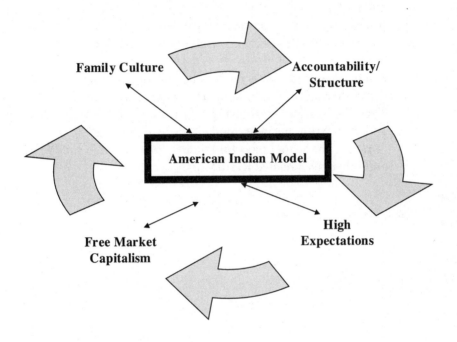

## Free Market Capitalism

1. We encourage classes to compete with each other and instill in
   students the values of a free market capitalistic society.
2. There are clear, consistent, and high expectations in the student
   contract that are enforced by all employees. Student consequences (detention, Saturday School, embarrassment, cleaning,
   among other punishments) are given for not following school
   rules.
3. Families choose to enroll their children in an American Indian
   modeled public school. State and federal funding follows the

. student to the family's school of choice. This is the same funding model of vocational schools, community colleges, and universities in the United States.

4. We focus on excellent student attendance (99.5 percent). Students and staff are given cash awards for perfect attendance, hard work, and for reinforcing the school's mission statement and credo.

5. Job descriptions are posted that cause administrator or teacher applicants to self-select out from applying for a job with our school.

6. , Financial rewards are given to all employees for increased student achievement on the California Standards Tests.

7. The administrative leadership focuses on fiscal responsibility and a superior business model. There is no fund-raising by families. The school pays for student trips, the SAT, the PSAT, and other costs related to students.

# American Indian Public Charter School Academic Performance Index (API)
## 2001-2008

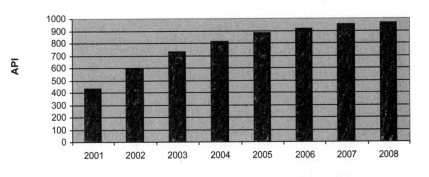

| Year | API Score | Met Growth Target/NCLB |
|------|-----------|------------------------|
| 2000–2001 | 436 | Yes |
| 2001–2002 | 596 | Yes |
| 2002–2003 | 732 | Yes |
| 2003–2004 | 813 | Yes |
| 2004–2005 | 880 | Yes |
| 2005–2006 | 909 | Yes |
| 2006–2007 | 950 | Yes |
| 2007–2008 | 967 | Yes |

The American Indian Public Charter School (grades six through eight) has the highest API score of any school in Oakland. AIPCS received the National Blue Ribbon Award, given to the top two hundred schools in the nation. The students exceeded the standards set by the No Child Left Behind Act each year. Note that 97 percent of the students qualify for free and reduced-price lunch; 98 percent of the students are minorities; and more than 74 percent of the students speak English as a second language.

## American Indian Model (AIM) Students' Ten Commandments
### by Dr. Ben Chavis

1. Thou shalt remember that laziness is the quickest path to failure. Thou shalt accept that family culture, accountability/structure, high expectations, and free market capitalism will lead to success in school and life.

2. Thou shalt accept full responsibility for thy failure or success in school and life. Blaming thy family, friends, or circumstance will not lead to success. Blame is an excuse for failure, laziness, and leads to being a victim.

3. Thou shalt covet the studying of ninety minutes of English-language arts and ninety minutes of mathematics each school day, with a minimum of forty-five minutes for each class of science, social studies, physical fitness, and two hours of homework to build a sound educational foundation for *all* students.

4. Thou shalt be aware that affirmative action and diversity specialists have made a professional career based on people's color and sex. These individuals are committed to human inequality to ensure they are employed.

5. Thou shalt be aware that "affirmative action" for minorities is the most blatant form of racism in the United States. Why dost thou think Africa, China, or the Navajo Indian Nation does not have affirmative action programs for white people?

6. Thou shalt choose common sense over left-wing liberal ideology. Thou shalt also choose common sense over right-wing ideology. Thou shalt avoid ideologists as though they are the plague.

7. Thou shalt be aware of quacks who believe in communism. Thou hast the quickest route to freedom through free market capitalism and private property ownership. Hast thou ever heard of illegal immigrants risking their lives to enter Cuba?

8. Thou shalt pursue higher education and free market capitalism. As Frederick Douglass stated, "It means light and liberty. It means the uplifting of the soul of man into the glorious light of truth, the light by which men can only be made free."

9. Thou shalt remember that standardized tests are not aware of anyone's skin color or sex. Thou shalt put forth thy best ef-

forts; hold thyself to the highest academic and social standards that enhance all students' ability to compete in a free market capitalist society.

10. Thou shalt always be part of our AIM to Educate family. Thou hast been prepared for success through family culture, accountability/structure, high expectations, and free market capitalism. Thou shalt embrace the challenges of life and turn them into a productive educational experience.

## California's Highest-Scoring Middle Schools
## 2007–2008

| Middle School | District | Academic Performance Index (API) Score |
|---|---|---|
| 1. Hopkins Junior High | Fremont Unified | 987 |
| 2. Joaquin Miller Middle | Cupertino Union | 976 |
| 3. Elkhorn | Lodi Unified | 975 |
| 4. Kennedy Middle | Cupertino Union | 971 |
| 5. American Indian Public Charter School | Oakland Unified | 967 |

*Source: San Jose Mercury News*, September 5, 2008

AIPCS ranks fifth in California and first in Oakland Unified School District, according to 2007–2008 Academic Performance Index (API) scores. AIPCS continues to improve each year. AIPCS's API goal is to achieve a score of 1,000.

# California's Highest-Scoring High Schools
## 2007–2008

| Middle School | District | Academic Performance Index (API) Score |
|---|---|---|
| 1 Gretchen Whitney | ABC Unified | 985 |
| 2. Oxford Academy | Anaheim Union | 983 |
| 3. California Academy of Math and Science | Long Beach Unified | 962 |
| 4. **American Indian Public High School** | Oakland Unified | 958 |
| 5. Lowell | San Francisco Unified | 950 |

Source: *San Jose Mercury News*, September 5, 2008

AIPHS ranks fourth in California and first in Northern California, according to 2007–2008 Academic Performance Index (API) scores. AIPHS continues to improve each year. AIPHS's API goal is to achieve a score of 1,000.